Daughters
of the Earth

also by Carolyn Niethammer

AMERICAN INDIAN FOOD AND LORE

DAUGHTERS
The Lives and Legends

OF THE EARTH

of American Indian Women

by CAROLYN NIETHAMMER

COLLIER BOOKS

Macmillan Publishing Company

NEW YORK

COLLIER MACMILLAN PUBLISHERS

LONDON

To My Sisters

Who, in seeking answers for today and
    tomorrow
Might pause, and look at yesterday

Macmillan Publishing Company
866 Third Avenue, New York, N.Y. 10022
Collier Macmillan Canada, Inc.

Library of Congress Cataloging in Publication Data

Niethammer, Carolyn
    Daughters of the earth.

    Bibliography: p.
    1. Indians of North America—Women.
2. Indians of North America—Social life and
customs. I. Title.
E98.W8N53   970″.004′97   76-56103

ISBN 0-02-096150-2 pbk.

FIRST COLLIER BOOKS EDITION 1977

20 19 18 17

Macmillan books are available at special discounts for
bulk purchases for sales promotions, premiums, fund-
raising, or educational use. For details, contact:

    Special Sales Director
    Macmillan Publishing Company
    866 Third Avenue
    New York, N.Y. 10022

Printed in the United States of America

Contents

Acknowledgments

Although most of the information for this book was gathered from historical records, several modern Indian women were kind enough to share with me some of their life experiences so that I could gain a deeper feeling for just what it means to be a Native American. I would like to thank Veronica Orr (Colville), Annette Wilson (San Ildefonso), Dorothy George (Hopi), Marian Hufford (Navajo), Edna Baldwin (Kiowa), Pauline Good Morning (Taos), and Roberta Hazel Begay (Navajo).

I am also indebted to Constance Schrader, who suggested the idea for the book and encouraged me by her continuing belief in the worth of the project; Daphne Scott, librarian at the Arizona State Museum, who provided valuable research assistance; and Kate Cloud and Julie Szekely, who read the manuscript and made many helpful criticisms.

I would especially like to acknowledge the help of the late Dr. Thomas Hinton, who suggested source materials, freely offered his encouragement and knowledge, and checked the manuscript for anthropological accuracy. His friendship and his help will be missed.

"Gathering Buffalo Berries"—one of a series of photographs
taken of Plains Indians by Rodman Wanamaker in the nineteenth
century. *(Courtesy of the American Museum of Natural History)*

Introduction

To the typical American or European the term "Indian"—referring to the native inhabitants of North America—generally brings to mind a handsome brave resplendent in feather headdress and mounted on a fine steed; a scantily clad red man in face paint, dancing and whooping around a fire; or perhaps, for the more sophisticated, the weathered swarthy face of an aged medicine man whose deepset eyes reveal a knowledge of the mystic secrets of the universe.

The rare person who considers the word *Indian* to include women no doubt pictures either a regal Pocahontas or a downtrodden, burden-bearing, hunched-over wretch trudging behind—always behind—her warrior husband.

The truth is that although there were beautiful and powerful Indian princesses like Pocahontas as well as some drudges in tribes in which women were treated poorly, the lives of the vast majority of Native American women fell midway between these two extremes. The women raised the children, gathered food and cooked meals, built houses, nursed the sick, had sex with their husbands (and sometimes men not their husbands), prayed to their gods, and mourned the dead. The amazing thing is that they acted out these commonplace life tableaux in such a variety of ways.

During the two years I have been researching and writing this book, the most frequent question-comments I've received from friends to casual cocktail conversation partners are, "Isn't it true that Indian women were terribly subservient to their men?" and conversely, "Weren't most Indian tribes matriarchies where the women controlled the households?" The answer to both questions is that conditions varied greatly from tribe to tribe and Native American women as individuals and groups often had a great deal of power and authority over their lives. Men and women worked in partnership to most effectively exploit their environment—there were men's tasks and there were women's tasks, and both were valued and necessary for survival.

Of course in this age of heightened consciousness of the importance of women's roles, those feminists among us would like to believe in the previous existence of a matriarchy. But anthropologists, even those who consider themselves feminists, discount whatever meager evidence there is to support theories of historical matriarchies. There are tribes which can be considered matrifocal (where the mother role is culturally elaborated, valued, and structurally central), matrilineal (line of descent is reckoned through one's mother), and matrilocal (daughter takes husband to live at her mother's home). As yet, however, there are no well-documented reports of any societies in which women have *publicly recognized* power and authority *surpassing* that of men.[1]

Dr. Michelle Zimbalist Rosaldo, in her contribution to the feminist-oriented *Women, Culture and Society* (which she also co-edited), writes: "Women may be important, powerful and influential, but it seems that, relative to men of their age and social status, women everywhere lack generally recognized and culturally valued authority."[2] She is backed up by Dr. Sherry B. Ortner, who, in the same volume, boldly states: "The secondary status of women in society is one of the true universals, a pan-cultural fact." Ortner continues, "Yet within that universal fact, the specific cultural conceptions and symbolizations of women are extraordinarily diverse and even mutually contradictory. Further, the actual treatment of women and their relative power and contributions vary enormously from culture to culture and over different periods in the history of particular cultural traditions. Both of these points—the universal fact and the cultural variation—constitute problems to be explained."[3]

The facts stand up. Even in those Native American tribes in which women had a great deal of power and prestige, controlled the economic goods of the family, and held sacred ceremonial offices, the line was always drawn at some point: The sacred bundle could not be handled by a woman (who might be menstruating and thus defile it), certain offerings to very special supernaturals could only be made by men, or particular offices could be filled only by men, though women might choose the personnel for the positions and impeach them if they proved unworthy.

But how did the position of a Native American woman compare with that of the ordinary white woman of that time? Actually, the Indian woman's life appeared very much like that of our pioneer great-grandmothers. Both of them spent most of their time, both at work and play, with children and other women. Even at mixed gatherings, men and women tended to congregate separately. Yet, although their daily lives were the same in many ways, the Indian woman generally enjoyed a good deal more independence and security than the white woman.

Anthropologist Nancy Lurie writes: "Whether the cosseted darling of the upper class or the toil-worn pioneer farm wife, the white woman was pitifully dependent through life on the whims and fortunes of one male, first a father and then a husband. Bereft of virtually any political rights, she also lacked the security of a tribe who would be committed to care for her if she were orphaned or widowed. Traditionally the white poor woman was left with the denigrating embarrassment of accepting charity."[4]

Certainly the best information on what it was like to be an Indian woman in early America would be that obtained from Native American women themselves. Unfortunately the very early Americans left no written histories. The earliest accounts we have of the Native Americans were reports made by European missionaries and explorers. Being almost exclusively male, these writers concentrated on the male roles in Native American society. They probably didn't consciously censor out information on women; they merely looked at these strange societies through the eyes of their own culture, a culture in which at that time male activities were the only happenings of note.

Modern anthropologists—again, mostly male—have continued this tendency to consider women's activities as uninteresting and irrelevant in comparison with the heady stuff of male politics and public life. Additionally, much of the information that was gathered on women's activities came from male informants; in other words, Native American men were reporting—as truthfully as they could, no doubt—how they *thought* Native American women perceived and felt. Occasionally male anthropologists spoke with women, but we must assume that the situation of a typically shy Indian woman talking to a white male tended to color her story somewhat, perhaps in ways she did not even realize.

Introduction

There are a few notable cases where women investigators have worked with women informants (Landes, Underhill, Lurie, Bunzel, Bailey, Reichard, and others), and better yet, a few cases where modern but traditional Indian women have told their own stories (Qoyawayma, Sekaquaptewa, Shaw) and I have tried to emphasize these reports.

It would be impossible, of course, to tell the story of Native American women without referring to Native American men. Young Indian children received similar care and training whether they were boys or girls. As the youngsters matured into young men and women they formed marital, economic, and sexual partnerships.

Although I have not deemphasized the role men played in women's lives as I traced the experiences of Native American women from birth through courtship, young adulthood, and maturity and finally to death, I have always tried to stress the female point of view.

In an attempt at accuracy, I have also tried to present the customs of each tribe or society as they were when they were first "discovered" by white men and before extensive contact with Europeans altered traditional ways of life. Because of this the time frame is not the same for all of the groups. By the time the buffalo culture was flourishing on the Great Plains in the 1800s many of the East Coast tribes had been pushed out of their traditional territories by land-hungry settlers, and their cultures were beginning to disintegrate.

It is not always easy to separate even the earliest Native American cultures from white influence. Actually, the buffalo culture was a product of European settlement on the American continent. Many of the tribes that were a part of that brief but glorious expression were former woodland Indians who had been pushed out of their lands in what we now call Michigan and Illinois and Indiana by the constant westward migration of the Europeans. Furthermore, the groups that moved out onto the Great Plains would never have been able to exploit the buffalo to the extent they did without the horse, which was introduced by the Spanish. Native Americans did hunt buffalo before the arrival of horses, but the number of animals that can be killed by a hunter on foot in no way compares to the number of beasts that can be slain in a community effort of mounted hunters.

By the same token, the Navajos, whose culture has become so intertwined with sheepherding, were primarily hunter-gatherers who had wandered down from Canada over many years. They did a little farming until the Spanish arrived in the Southwest, bringing sheep and goats. The livestock were intended to furnish the food needs of the Spanish themselves, but a few head found their way into the hands of the Navajos.

Although customs affecting the lives of early Native American women varied greatly from tribe to tribe, the variations did not occur entirely at random. Neighboring tribes often had similar habits, owing to the fact that they had common ancestors, similar habitat, intertribal trade, and even some intermarriage. The hundreds of tribal cultures in Native America segregate themselves into several areas of reasonably uniform culture—the exact number depending on how finely one chooses to discriminate. These areas tend to coincide with areas of some degree of environmental uniformity, usually climatic and vegetational. Many anthropologists have described the "culture areas" of North and South America, and while most of them agree on the basic concepts, the different areas mentioned vary somewhat from theory to theory. One scheme divides the territory of North America north of Mexico (the area covered by this book) into ten culture areas as follows:

Northeast: Much of this area was heavily forested, so part of this section is also called the Eastern Woodlands. The people here lived in small settlements, sustained by hunting, fishing, gathering, and in those areas with a long enough growing season, farming. The Ojibwas and others around the western Great Lakes substituted the gathering of wild rice for maize cultivation. In the fifteenth or sixteenth century the Senecas, Cayugas, Oneidas, Onondagas, and Mohawks formed the League of the Iroquois. In the early 1700s the Tuscaroras joined the alliance, which was ultimately destroyed by internal disagreement about which side to support in the American Revolution.

Southeast: These people were primarily agriculturalists, although they also made use of a wide variety of wild plants. Diaries kept by men who were part of Hernando de Soto's expedition through the Southeast in 1539–1542 describe the Indian towns and temples in this warm, hospitable area. When the whites took over these lands, most of the southeastern peoples were moved to Indian Territory in Oklahoma.

Plains: This vast area harbored both farmers and nomadic hunters. The settled farmers, such as the Mandan and Pawnee, built fortified earth-lodge villages and cultivated maize, squash, and sunflowers. They supplemented their produce with buffalo meat and other game taken during summer and winter hunts.

The nomadic tribes, such as the Sioux and Cheyenne, lived mainly on the products of the buffalo. Most tribes enforced strict hunting laws designed to keep the great bison herds intact and the supply of food, clothing, and shelter constant. The Plains horseman endures as the stereotype of the North American Indian, though his culture flourished for less than a century (late seventeenth century to late eighteenth century).

Arctic: This is the land of the Eskimos, a people who were ingenious enough to learn to wrest an existence from a harsh, icy northern environment. The Eskimos were, and are, distinctive in physique, in speech, and in customs from other Native American groups. They hunted caribou where they could and fished in lakes and rivers, but their main subsistence was sea mammals. Eskimos generally lived in small bands, moving seasonally to follow game.

Subarctic: The great northern transcontinental area of coniferous forest was a land of scant food resources and consequent sparse population. The climate was too cold for agriculture and the people had to live widely scattered to take advantage of what game there was. Because there was little opportunity for people to congregate, there was no real tribal organization, little organized warfare, and not much public ceremony. And because these people had to focus so much attention on getting enough to eat, there was little time to spend on the luxury of artistic expression.

Northwest Coast: A bountiful supply of seafood made life easy for the tribes along the northwest coast. Because of their wealth and leisure, these people became very concerned with the collection of material goods. The main purpose for amassing great quantities of property was the chance to gain social prestige and influence by giving it all away at gift-giving feasts called potlatches.

Plateau: Widely scattered groups of foragers lived in this area, which ranged from semidesert to dense forests on snow-capped mountains. The growing season was too short for farming, so the people existed on fish, some game, berries, and roots. Plateau tribes lived a simple life in peace and harmony with each other. Both men and women sought supernatural experiences and often underwent long, lonely fasts in their quests for religious visions.

Great Basin: In their dry homeland with its searing heat and extreme cold, the Native American inhabitants of the Great Basin foraged for a somewhat meager diet of wild seeds, small animals, roots, and insects. Most tribes engaged in cyclic wandering to best exploit their harsh environment. The culture of these people was simple, and changes came very slowly.

California: Along the Pacific coast, west of the Sierra Nevada, the country was gentle and life was easy. Agriculture was unknown there, but so was famine, owing to the abundance of the sea life and the lush vegetation. The food staple of many of the California tribes was the acorn. The women made no pottery but were master basket-makers. Life was slow, easy, and generally pleasant for these coastal peoples.

Southwest: This area was for the most part very dry, especially in the lower desert regions. Those desert tribes who lived near large rivers were able to practice a little agriculture; otherwise the people lived a rather precarious existence by gathering the wild fruits of the desert. In the middle altitudes, summer rains made corn-growing possible in many stretches. The northern portion of this area was the land of the pueblos, large permanent towns made of mud bricks or stones. Pueblo religious ceremonies were highly developed. This area has been well-explored by ethnologists because many of the native cultures persisted well into the twentieth century much unchanged. In fact, several southwestern Indian groups still retain a high degree of native culture.

I feel I should make one final comment to guide readers in their perusal of this material. Many of the customs we will look at here are very different from those of modern Western culture. I have attempted to present the facts in a fairly straightforward manner, refraining as much as possible from judgment, though surely there are places where my politics must glare from between the lines. I ask readers to remember with me that any woman, living or dead, can be judged properly only by the way she conforms to the ethical and social standards of her people, not by the measure of our own ethical or social standards.

CJN

Daughters
of the Earth

Rose Emerson, a young Yuma mother, and her baby.
(*Courtesy of the American Museum of Natural History*)

1

The Dawn of Life

CHILDBIRTH IN NATIVE AMERICA

When the North American continent was younger and wild animals and dark mysteries still inhabited the woods and the plains and the mountains, women usually gathered unto themselves for the ritual of birth. For unusually difficult labors or when the time was right for certain necessary ceremonies, a medicine man might be called to render his special potions or incant powerful prayers, but, in general, males were infrequent participants in such business. It was the women who performed the practical and ceremonial duties that readied the infant for life and gave it status as an individual. These tasks were performed so often as to be commonplace, yet they were heavy with meaning at each new birth, for such rituals were elemental to the existence of women in early America.

Being a mother and rearing a healthy family were the ultimate achievements for a woman in the North American Indian societies. There was no confusion about the role of a woman and very few other acceptable patterns for feminine existence. Many Indian women attained distinction as craftswomen or medical practitioners, but this in no way affected their role as bearers and raisers of children.

Women's lives flowed into what they saw as the natural order of the universe. Mother Earth was fecund and constantly replenishing herself in the ongoing cycle of birth, growth, maturity, death, and rebirth. The primitive women of our continent considered themselves an integral part of these ever-recurrent patterns and accepted a role in which they were an extension of the spirit mother and the key to the continuation of their race. Not separate from, but part of, these deeply religious feelings was the practical consideration that many children were needed to help with the work and to take care of the parents as they grew older. In those simpler days, children were a couple's savings account and insurance.

SEX AND PREGNANCY

Women in most Native American cultures knew pretty clearly how they got pregnant, although even here beliefs varied when it came to the details.

The Gros Ventres of Montana and the Chiricahua Apaches of southern Arizona were among those groups believing that pregnancy could not occur as the result of a single sex act. One Apache explained that if a couple had intercourse three times a week they could have a baby started in about two or three months. But the informant also said, "I know a girl who had intercourse with a man many times in one night. If a girl did it at that rate, it wouldn't take any time at all to get a child started."[1] As another Apache related, "When a man has intercourse with a woman some of his blood (semen) enters her. But just a little goes in the first time and not as much as the woman has in there. The child does not begin to develop yet because the woman's blood struggles against it. The woman's blood is against having the child; the man's blood is for it. When enough collects, the man's blood forces the baby to come."[2]

Although many sexual encounters were believed necessary to create a child, as soon as an Apache woman noticed the first signs of pregnancy, she ceased her sexual activity to prevent injury to the baby growing within her.

The Hopi of northern Arizona, on the other hand, were convinced that continued sex was good for both the prospective mother and the baby; a woman slept with her husband all through her pregnancy so that their continued intercourse could make the child grow. It was likened by one Hopi to irrigating a crop—if a man started to make a baby and then stopped, his wife would have a hard time.

The Kaska Indians of northwestern Canada also maintained that repeated sex during early pregnancy developed the embryo, but warned that too much indulgence would produce twins. As soon as a Kaska woman felt the stirrings of life in her womb, she was warned to discontinue her sexual life. Mothers advised their pregnant daughters to use their own blankets and to sleep facing away from their husbands to avoid temptation.

Among most of the tribes, however, pregnant women continued a moderate sex life until the later stages of their pregnancy, much as many women do today. There were a few groups where custom completely forbade intercourse during pregnancy. In the area which is now Wisconsin, Fox women abstained from sex throughout pregnancy for fear their babies would be born "filthy," and down near where the Colorado River emptied into the Gulf of California, pregnant Cocopah women slept alone lest their babies be born feet first.

A BOY—OR A GIRL?

Most Indian mothers welcomed each baby regardless of sex and wished primarily that the child be strong and healthy. But it is universal for a woman carrying a child for nine long months to wonder whether her labor will produce a son or a daughter. Out on the Great Plains when an Omaha woman wanted to ascertain the sex of her coming child she took a bow and a burden strap to the tent of a friend who had a child who was still too young to talk. She offered the two articles to the baby. If the little child chose the bow, the unborn would be a boy; if the child paid more attention to the burden strap, the coming baby would be a daughter.

There were some societies, particularly those in the far north where life was hard, that did not welcome an abundance of daughters. But it is said that the Huron, who lived north of Lake Ontario, rejoiced more at the birth of a girl child, for girls grew into women who had more babies, and the Huron wanted many descendants to care for them in their old age and protect them from their enemies.

In the matrilineal societies of the Hopi in the Southwest, where the status of women was high, a woman wished to give birth to many girl babies, for it was through her daughters that a Hopi woman's home and clan were perpetuated. A boy was not unwelcome, for he also belonged to his mother's clan, but when he married, his children would belong to the house and clan of their own mother.

Generally the sex of the baby was left to fate, but among the Zuni, neighbors of the Hopi on the beautiful but arid and windswept deserts of the Southwest, if a couple desired a girl child they went to visit the Mother Rock near their pueblo. The base of the rock was covered with symbols of the vulva

3

and was perforated with small excavations. The pregnant woman scraped a tiny bit of the rock into a vase and placed it in one of the cavities. Then she prayed that a daughter would be born who would be good, beautiful, and virtuous, and who would display skill in the arts of weaving and pottery-making. If by chance a boy child was born, the Mother Rock was not blamed. Instead it was believed that the heart of one of the parents was "not good."

PRENATAL HEALTH CARE

In those early days, infant mortality was alarmingly high and many women died in childbirth. Prospective mothers used every means at their disposal to ensure safe delivery and healthy children, but because medicinal procedures were so primitive, these women relied on measures which today we label "superstition" and "sympathetic magic," including a vast and varied range of taboos. Pregnant Indian women were almost universally warned against looking at or mocking a deformed, injured, or blind person for fear their babies would evidence the same defect; being in the presence of dying persons and animals was likewise unhealthy for both the mother and baby. Among the Flathead Indians of Montana neither the mother nor father could go out of the lodge backward or a breech birth would follow, nor were either of the prospective parents allowed to gaze out of a window or door. If they wanted to see what was going on outside, they were to go all the way outdoors and look around, lest the baby be stillborn.

There were also taboos on certain foods. Some typical dietary restrictions for pregnant Indian women prohibited eating the feet of an animal, to avoid having the baby born feet first; the tail of an animal, to prevent the child's getting stuck on the way out; berries, so that the baby would not carry a birthmark; and liver, which would darken the child's skin.

The Lummi Indians of what is now northwest Washington were a fairly wealthy group whose home on the productive coastlands offered them a vast variety of foods. This bounty enabled them to place taboos on many foods, including halibut, which was believed to cause white blotches on the baby's skin; steelhead salmon, which caused weak ankles; trout, which produced harelip; and seagull or crane, which would produce a crybaby. The prospective mother also had to abstain from shad or blue cod, which would induce convulsions in the child; venison, which would lead to absentmindedness; and beaver, which might cause an abnormally large head.

Among some of the groups with less abundant food resources, restrictions

4

were limited to only certain parts of animals. Pregnant women were warned that eating tongue would cause the baby's tongue to loll, while the ingestion of an animal's tail might create problems during labor.

Though there were many foods that could not be eaten, there is some evidence that Indian women years ago, like many present-day women, did have cravings for special foods during pregnancy. The Reverend John Heckewelder, writing in the late 1700s, reported that he had witnessed what he called "a remarkable instance of the disposition of Indians to indulge their wives." Apparently, famine had struck the Iroquois in the winter of 1762, but a pregnant woman of that tribe longed for some Indian corn. Her husband, having learned that a trader at Lower Sandusky had a little of the desired commodity, set off on horseback for the one-hundred-mile trek. He brought back as much corn as filled the crown of his hat, but he returned walking and carrying his saddle, for he had had to trade his horse for the corn. Heckewelder continued, "Squirrels, ducks and other like delicacies, when most difficult to be obtained, are what women in the first stages of their pregnancy generally long for. The husband in every case will go out and spare no pains nor trouble until he has procured what is wanted. The more a man does for his wife, the more he is esteemed, particularly by the women."[3]

Each tribe had certain herbs and teas that were believed to relieve aches and pains and promote the health of prospective mothers. A Crow medicine woman named Muskrat used two roots which had been revealed to her by a supernatural who appeared to her twice while she was asleep. During the first vision she was instructed to chew a certain weed if she wished to give birth without suffering. Later she was taught about another plant and was told it was even better than the first. Another Crow woman paid a horse to a visionary who taught her a formula made from a combination of certain roots and powdered, dry horned toad. The resulting powder was used in giving backrubs.

Bear's Medicine for Pregnant Women

(H U P A)

While walking in the middle of the world Bear got this way. Young grew in her body. All day and all night she fed. After a while she got so big she could not walk. Then she began to consider why she was in that condition. "I wonder if they will be the way I am in the Indian world?" She heard a voice talking behind her. It said, "Put me in your mouth. You are in this condition for the sake of the Indians." When she looked around she saw a single plant of redwood sorrel standing there. She put it into her mouth. The next day she found she was able to walk. She thought, "It will be this way in the Indian world with this medicine. This will be my medicine. At best not many will know about me. I will leave it in the Indian world. They will talk to me with it."[4]

❀◇❀◇❀◇❀◇❀◇❀◇❀◇

But besides consuming herbal medicines, avoiding certain foods, and watching their own behavior, some Indian women had to be careful not to become victims of witchcraft during pregnancy. Matilda Cox Stevenson, who lived with and studied the Zuni Indians in the area of northwest New Mexico for many years in the late 1800s, wrote that she had helped a pregnant Zuni woman who was suffering from a cough and from pain in the abdomen. Although the woman felt better after taking the simple home remedies Mrs. Stevenson gave her, her family still thought it wise to call in the native surgeon. When he arrived and began to treat the pregnant woman, he appeared to draw from her abdomen two objects which he claimed were mother and child worms. Mrs. Stevenson wrote that one was about the length of her longest finger, while the other was smaller. The doctor pronounced this evidence that the woman had been bewitched and assured the family that it was well he had been sent for promptly, for in time these worms would have eaten the child and caused its death. Later, when trying to figure out who could have bewitched her, the Zuni woman recalled that some weeks before she had been grinding corn while kneeling next to the sister of a witch, and this woman had touched her on the abdomen. She decided it was probably then that the worms had been cast in.[5]

CHILDBIRTH CUSTOMS

Because in some groups the older women were unwilling to talk about the actual birth process, many young Indian women were remarkably unprepared for the birth of their first child. Pretty-shield, a Crow woman whose story is told in the book *Red Mother*, related how she was playing with some girl friends during her first pregnancy and felt a quick little pain. When she sat down laughing about it, one of her friends guessed what the pain meant and warned Pretty-shield's mother, who immediately consulted a medicine woman named Left-hand. The mother and Left-hand had to coax Pretty-shield to come with them to the special skin lodge they had pitched for the occasion. Outside the lodge Pretty-shield noticed that one of her father's best horses was tied up with several costly robes on his back—an advance payment to old Left-hand for her assistance. Pretty-shield described the medicine woman as having her face painted with mud, her hair tied in a big clump on her forehead and carrying in her hand some of the grass-that-the-buffalo-do-not-eat.

Inside the tipi a fire was burning and a mat made of a soft buffalo robe was folded with the hair side out to serve as a bed. As was customary, two stakes had been driven into the ground, and other buffalo robes had been rolled up and piled against them so that when Pretty-shield knelt on the mat and took hold of the stakes her elbows rested on the pile of robes.

First Left-hand took four live coals from the fire, spacing them evenly on the ground between the door of the tipi and the bed. Then she instructed her patient to step over the coals and go to the bed. Left-hand, wearing a buffalo robe and grunting like a buffalo cow, followed behind Pretty-shield, instructing her to "walk as though you are busy" and brushing the girl's back with the tail of the robe.

Pretty-shield concludes, "I had stepped over the second coal when I saw that I should have to run if I reached my bed-robe in time. I jumped the third coal, and the fourth, knelt down on the robe, took hold of the two stakes, and my first child, Pine-fire, was there with us."[6]

Anthropologist Ruth Underhill tells a somewhat similar tale in *The Autobiography of a Papago Woman*. Chona, a Papago woman of southern Arizona, described the birth of her first child, which occurred when she herself was but a teenager. She didn't know quite when to expect her baby, but when she felt a pain one day while stooping over to pass through the low door to her grass house, she surmised that the time had come for the baby's arrival. As was true for women among many North American Indian cultures, Papago mothers were required by custom to have their babies in a special segregation hut apart from the main dwelling. Chona knew that it was time to go to the "Little House" and did not wish to have such a dreadful thing happen to her as to be caught inside the regular house in childbirth. She announced her destination to her husband's aunt—her first mention of labor pains—and left to cross the wash between the main house and the Little House.

"When I reached the near edge of that gully I thought I had better run," Chona related. "I ran fast; I wanted to do the right thing. But I dropped my first baby in the middle of the gully. My aunt came and snipped the baby's navel string with her long fingernail. Then we went on to the Little House." Later one of her sisters-in-law asked her why she hadn't said anything about her pains. The other women hadn't known she was suffering because they had heard her laughing. Chona's response was, "Well, it wasn't my mouth that hurt. It was my middle."[7]

Chona and her baby had to stay in the segregation hut for a full month, during which time she was not allowed to bathe, for fear she would get rheumatism. Her family brought her food which she cooked with no salt. "When the moon had come back to the same place," it was time for the purification ceremony. Chona, her husband, and the baby went to a medicine man, or shaman, who was a specialist in child-naming. The shaman prepared a mixture of clay, water, and pounded owl feathers which both parents and the child were required to sip; then the shaman gave the child a name. If Papago parents neglected to have this ceremony performed, they risked the health of both themselves and the new baby.

Not all Indian women had births as easy as those of Pretty-shield and Chona, but they were nevertheless expected to endure the pain without crying out. Huron women who fussed while they were in labor were chided for being cowardly and failing to set a good example for others. A Huron woman proved her courage by her brave conduct during childbirth just as a man proved his courage in battle. The Gros Ventres of Montana believed that a woman who cried out drove the child back, and a mother who turned and twisted in pain might tangle the cord around the child.

During her labor an Indian woman was usually assisted by her female relatives or other women of her tribe who had special knowledge of birth customs. They supported the woman as she knelt or squatted, rubbed her back, pressed down on her abdomen to force the child out, encouraged the mother, and cared for her and the child immediately after the birth. A good example of how the women helped each other can be found among the Kwakiutl of British Columbia. In good weather a woman might deliver outside, but in bad weather she remained in the longhouse. Usually two professional midwives came to assist. They first dug a pit and lined it with soft cedar bark. Then one of them sat down on the edge of the shallow excavation, stretching her legs across it so that her feet and calves rested on the opposite edge. The pregnant woman sat on the midwife's lap, straddling the helper's legs so that both her own legs hung down inside the pit. The two women clasped each other's arms tightly, while the second midwife squatted behind the woman who was delivering, pressing her knees against her back, wrapping her arms around the mother's shoulders, and blowing down her neck in order to produce a quick and easy delivery. The baby dropped into the pit and remained there until the afterbirth was delivered. Then the mother went to bed for four days.

Some of the midwives were quite skilled at their profession, often being able to turn a baby in the womb to ensure a safer and easier delivery. They were also good psychologists, knowing just how to talk to, calm, and comfort a woman who was suffering a great deal. But sometimes, in very difficult cases, the power and skill of the midwives were not enough, and doctors with more power had to be called in. A Gros Ventre woman told of how she had been helped by such a doctor during one of her pregnancies. The man was old and blind and when called to help, he sat next to the suffering woman with a pot of medicine beside him. When the woman cried out in pain he touched her with the end of a stick and the cramps went away. When the woman complained that she was tired, the midwife assured her that it would soon be over, but the doctor disagreed. The labor continued for several more hours until the doctor predicted the baby would be born shortly, and he was right. It was believed that the medicine man's power allowed him to know what was happening without seeing or touching the laboring woman.

Although women generally gathered together for the birth of babies, in some North American tribes the expectant mother had to face the birth process alone. Women in the Caddo group near the border of what are now Mississippi and Arkansas were instructed, when the time of their delivery neared, to go to the bank of the nearest river and to build a little shelter, with a strong forked stick positioned in the center. Supporting themselves with this stick they gave birth all alone and then immediately waded into the stream, even if they had to break ice to do so, washed themselves and the baby, and returned home to continue their normal lives.

A report survives from 1790 of four Tukabahchee women (a tribe of the Creek confederacy located in Alabama) who came to sell horse ropes to some white men on a cold and rainy night in December. Because of the bad weather, the women stayed overnight, and about midnight, one of the women went into labor. Her mother instructed her to take fire and go to the edge of a

9

swamp about 160 yards away. She went alone, delivered her own baby, and the next morning took the infant on her back and returned home with the other women through the still-falling rain and snow.

Many of the native North American cultures insisted that, following birth, both mother and newborn child remain in seclusion, particularly away from all men, for a period of time ranging from a few days to as long as three months. The Nez Percé women in northern Idaho entered a special underground lodge two or three months before the baby was expected and remained for two weeks after the birth. For the most part, women in seclusion were well cared for. Life for them was hard, and rather than being chagrined at being excluded from the rest of the group, they no doubt welcomed a time of recuperation before returning to their strenuous daily duties.

CEREMONIES OF CHILDBIRTH

In some of the Indian societies, a great deal of ritual accompanied each birth. The Hopi infant began life in a society where elaborate religious ceremonials dominated much of village life. Each new baby was immediately immersed in the rich, sacred traditions that would so fully shape its life experience. In the Hopi pueblos a young mother was often alone at the moment of birth, but as soon as the baby had slipped out of the birth canal onto the patch of warm sand, the newborn's maternal grandmother entered the room to sever and tie the cord and to make her daughter and new grandchild comfortable. After washing the baby she rubbed its body with ashes from the corner fireplace so that its skin would always be smooth and free of hair. Then she took the afterbirth and deposited it on a special placenta pile at the edge of the village.

Very soon the baby's paternal grandmother arrived and began to take up her duties as mistress of ceremonies for all the rituals that would be performed during the twenty-day lying-in period and for the culminating dedication of the baby to the sun. Her first task was to secure a heavy blanket over the door so that no sunlight could enter the room where the mother and baby lay. It was thought that light was harmful to newborn children, and so the baby began its life on earth in a room almost as dark as the womb from which it had just emerged.

For eighteen days the mother and baby lay at rest in the darkened room. Each day a mark was made on the wall above the baby's bed and a perfect ear of corn laid under each mark. On the nineteenth day the mother got up and spent the day grinding corn into sacred meal to be used in the special ceremony the next day.

On the next morning the new mother's female relatives arrived at her home well before dawn, dressed in their most colorful shawls and carrying gifts of cornmeal and perfect ears of corn. When all the guests had arrived the solemn ceremony for the dedication of a new life was begun. First the mother was ritually purified. Her hair and body were washed in suds made from the root of the yucca plant, and then she took a steambath by standing over a bowl of hot water. Next all the grandmothers and the aunts each took a turn at bathing the baby in yucca suds and giving it a name.

While all this was taking place inside the home, the father, who since the birth had been living in his religious society's kiva, or underground ceremonial chamber, was stationed on the flat roof of the stone house watching for the sun. When the sacred Sun Father began to appear, the father alerted the women, who hastily took the child to the edge of the mesa. The grandmother who carried the baby crouched low so that no light would fall on the infant. Then, as the sun appeared over the horizon, the grandmother lifted the baby, turning her tiny bundle so the rays fell directly on the little face. Taking a handful of prayer meal she sprinkled some over the baby while reciting a short prayer. She flung the rest of the meal over the edge of the mesa toward the sun. The baby, now a full member of the family, was taken home and allowed to nap while the rest of the family enjoyed a breakfast feast.

Zunis recognized the sex of a baby in a special ceremony performed soon after birth: the newborn female child had a gourd placed over her vulva so that her sexual parts would be large, and the penis of a baby boy was sprinkled with water so that his organs would be small. Of course this ceremony was performed by the women attending the new mother so it reflected the feminine ideal for the physical proportion of the sexual organs.

Because of the extremely high infant mortality rate among the early Native Americans, ceremonials were often delayed until the child was about a year old.

Among the Omaha a newborn child was not considered a member of the tribe or kin group but just another living being whose arrival into the universe should be announced so that it would have an accepted place in the life force that united all nature, both animate and inanimate. On the eighth day of the baby's life a small ritual was held, and a prayer was recited to the powers of the heavens, the air, and the earth for the safety of the child, who was pictured as about to travel the rugged road of life stretching over four hills, marking the stages of infancy, youth, adulthood, and old age.

When the baby had grown and was able to walk, another ritual was held, during which the child was finally recognized as a real human being and a member of the tribe. The baby was given a new name and a new pair of moccasins. These moccasins always had a little hole in them so if the Great Spirit called, the baby could say, "I can't travel now, my moccasins are worn out."

❖◇❖◇❖◇❖◇❖◇❖◇❖◇

Prayer for Infants

(OMAHA)

Ho! Ye Sun, Moon, Stars, all ye that move in the heavens,
I bid you hear me!
Into your midst has come a new life.
Consent ye, I implore!
Make its path smooth, that it may reach the brow of the first hill!

Ho! Ye Winds, Clouds, Rain, Mist, all ye that move in the air,
I bid you hear me!
Into your midst has come a new life.
Consent ye, I implore!
Make its path smooth, that it may reach the brow of the second hill!

Ho! Ye Hills, Valleys, Rivers, Lakes, Trees, Grasses, all ye of the earth,
I bid you hear me!
Into your midst has come a new life.
Consent ye, I implore!
Make its path smooth, that it may reach the brow of the third hill.

Ho! Ye birds, great and small that dwell in the forest,
Ho! Ye insects that creep among the grasses and burrow in the ground,
Into your midst has come a new life.
Consent ye, I implore!
Make its path smooth that it may reach the brow of the fourth hill!

Ho! All ye of the heavens, all ye of the air, all ye of the earth:
I bid all of you to hear me!

Into your midst has come a new life.
Consent ye, consent ye all, I implore!
Make its path smooth—then shall it travel beyond the four hills.[8]

❀◈❀◈❀◈❀◈❀◈❀◈❀◈

The Omahas in eastern Nebraska believed that certain people had the gift of understanding the various sounds made by a baby, so when a little one cried persistently and could not be comforted, one of these persons was summoned. Sometimes the person decided that the child was crying because it did not like its name; in such case, the name would be changed.

NATURAL CHILDCARE

For a modern mother the thought of raising an infant without access to a drugstore full of powders, lotions, and disposable diapers would be appalling, but for centuries North American Indian mothers managed to raise babies with only materials supplied by Mother Earth and reliance on certain magical rites.

Because all Indian mothers breast-fed their babies, it was necessary that their breasts and nipples be in good condition. On the Washington coast Lower Chinook women spent the time of their confinement rubbing their breasts with bear grease and heating them with hot rocks or steam, while in northeastern Washington, Salish mothers heaped their sore breasts with heated pine needles. There seems to have been a feeling among many Indian groups that the colostrum, the yellowish fluid that precedes the appearance of the milk, was not good for the baby, and in some cases the babies were not fed until the milk appeared. Cultures that imposed such restrictions on new mothers had to come up with some way to relieve the painful pressure that resulted. Yurok women on the coast of northern California made the period bearable by softening their breasts over the steam of water mixed with herbs, which caused the colostrum to flow out. Gros Ventre mothers usually had someone else draw out the "first milk" and spit it out, whereas if a woman was alone when the child was born she often had a puppy suck out the colostrum. A Gros Ventre woman said that when her own daughter delivered her firstborn, an old woman offered to draw off this "first milk," but the daughter refused; as a consequence, the daughter could give milk only from one breast.

In the story of her life, Delfina Cuero, a Diegueno Indian from the southern California coast, explained the natural means she used to care for a baby's navel.

So that the navel will heal quickly and come off in three days, I took two rounds of cord and tied it (the navel) and then put a clean rag on it. I burned a hot fire outside our hut to get hot dirt to wrap in a cloth. I put this on the navel and changed it all night and day to keep it warm until the navel healed. To keep the navel from getting infected I burned cow hide or any kind of skin till crisp, then ground it. I put this powder on the navel. I did this and no infection started in my babies. Some women didn't know this and if infection started I would help them to stop it this way.[9]

Mothers powdered and oiled their babies with what was at hand. The Mandan, living on the northern Great Plains, pounded buffalo chips into a powder, warmed the powder with hot stones, and rubbed it on the baby's bottom, under its arms, between its legs, under its toes, and between its fingers. Mandan babies were also greased and painted with red ocher as a prevention against chafing. Down in the South, along the Mississippi River, Natchez babies were rubbed with bear grease to keep their sinews flexible and to prevent fly bites.

Women of early North America had their own forms of disposable diapers. Among the Natchez, Spanish moss was tied to a baby's thighs and buttocks before the infant was tied in its cradleboard. Up in what is now Saskatchewan and Manitoba, Cree babies were kept in a bag stuffed with dried moss, rotted and crumbled wood, or pulverized buffalo chips mixed with cattail down. When a child soiled the bag, the moss was shaken out, and a fresh supply of absorbant was stuffed in. Hopi babies were diapered with fine cedar bark which had been softened until it was absorbent and spongelike. When the diaper became wet it was rubbed in clean sand and put in the sun to dry. After the hot Arizona sun had dried and deodorized the diaper it was shaken clean, resoftened, and used again.

Reportedly, Huron mothers, living in southeastern Ontario, were a bit more creative. They swaddled their babies in furs on a cradleboard, wrapping them in such a way that the urine was carried off without soiling the baby; a boy was wrapped so that just the tip of his penis protruded, and for girls a corn leaf was cleverly positioned for the same purpose.

The cradleboard, practically a universal symbol of American Indian baby-hood, was the forerunner of today's widely used molded plastic baby carrier.

Cradleboard styles varied widely from tribe to tribe, but all provided a firm, protective frame on which babies felt snug and secure. A baby in a cradleboard could be propped up or even hung in a tree so it could see what was going on and feel a part of family activities. The Fox Indians thought it necessary to keep a baby in a cradleboard to prevent a long head, a humpback, or bowlegs.

After spending so much time in their cradleboards, Indian children became very attached to them. One Apache mother related that whenever her toddler son was tired or upset he would go and get his cradleboard and walk around with it on his back.

✿◆✿◆✿◆✿◆✿◆✿◆✿◆✿◆◇

Lullaby for a Girl

(ZUNI)

Little maid child!
Little sweet one!
Little girl!
Though a baby,
Soon a-playing
With a baby
Will be going.
Little maid child!
Little woman so delightful![10]

✿◆✿◆✿◆✿◆✿◆✿◆✿◆✿◆◇

INFANT DEATH

Sometimes all the special care and magic ceremonies were not enough to enable the vulnerable infant to survive. Even though Indian mothers could expect to lose at least half of their children in infancy or childhood, each death was a cause for sorrow. Most societies did not provide for dead children the full-scale mourning ceremonies presented for adults, but this did not temper the grief of the mothers, no matter how silently they had to bear their pain. In northern California, a Yokaia mother who had lost her baby went every day for a year to a place where her little one had played when alive or to the spot where the baby's body was cremated. At the cremation grounds she milked her breast into the air, all the while moaning and weeping and piteously calling on her dead child to return.

Young Hopi women often lost their first baby, since they all spent the first year of married life kneeling in front of the grinding stone producing many pounds of cornmeal as payment for their wedding robes. Babies who were born dead or who did not live past infancy were buried in crevices below the pueblos in the rocky slopes of the steep mesas. It was believed that soon after burial the little soul came out of the rocks and hovered near the mother until another baby was born. It could then enter the newborn's body and live again. The little knocks and cracks often heard around the house were thought to be evidence that the soul was near. If a woman's last baby died, the Hopis thought its soul stayed near her until she herself "went away" and took it with her on the trail to the sun.

THE PROBLEM OF INFERTILITY

There were some Indian women who were faced not with the problem of keeping their infants alive but of getting pregnant in the first place. When a Salish woman, in what is now eastern Washington and northern Idaho, did not become pregnant in a reasonable time after she was married, she would go to one of the old women of the tribe who were wise in such lore and would eat the herbs the medicine woman prescribed. If she remained barren her husband wouldn't divorce her, but he would probably take another wife if he could afford it.

The Mandan of North Dakota believed there was a Baby Hill which had an interior just like the earth lodges in which they lived, and many people claimed to have seen the tracks of tiny baby feet on the tops and sides of these hills. An old man supposedly lived in the hill and cared for all the babies that were there. A woman who had been married for a number of years and was still childless would go to one of the hills to pray for a baby, taking along girl's clothing and a ball if she wanted a daughter or a small bow and arrow if she desired a son.

The method used by Paiute women, living near the northeastern corner of California, was a little more risky. If a woman had a regular sex life and still didn't become pregnant, she sometimes resorted to drinking red ants in water. Views on just how effective this treatment was varied from reports of women getting pregnant this way to more skeptical accounts of the treatment which stated that the ants bit the woman all the way down to her stomach and usually killed her. A less dangerous method used by the Paiute women was to hunt for little gray birds that lived in the rocks of that area. If the birds were taken alive and worn near a woman's waist under her dress, they supposedly improved her chances of conceiving. And in what is now southwestern Arizona, a Yuma woman who was having difficulty conceiving might seek the help of a good doctor. Yuma folklore tells the story of one couple who went to such a doctor, who laid them both on the ground in an open space and lifted one after the other under the arms. Deciding that it was the woman who was lacking "seed," the doctor plunged his right arm into the ground as though it were a sharp stick and brought out some very coarse sand which he rubbed all over the woman, in addition to blowing smoke on her belly. Not long after this treatment the woman found herself pregnant.

Among the Havasupai, who live in the bottom of the Grand Canyon, it was so important for a woman to bear children that any barren woman could expect to be divorced. To avoid being cast off, a childless Havasupai woman would resort to rather extreme measures to conceive. One of the more radical cures for childlessness was drinking the water in which one had boiled a rat's nest, well-saturated with urine and feces.

On the other hand, the Ojibwa, of western Ontario, took a more enlightened attitude toward barren women. Like other early North American groups they considered a woman's chief function to be bearing children; sterility was a deviation from normal and always the fault of the female partner. Yet the sterility of a specific woman, while unfortunate, did not necessarily brand her in her husband's eyes. Ruth Landes, author of *The Ojibwa Woman*, cites many cases of women who had very happy marriages though they were infertile. Among the women whom Landes points out was Thunder Cloud, who did not have any children with her first husband during their ten years together, nor with her second husband during their eight-year union. Both men cared for her deeply despite her barrenness, and her third husband, with whom she finally conceived, did not seem concerned over her apparent sterility at the time of their marriage. Gaybay, another Ojibwa woman, was married five times and had only one child, yet she was never considered undesirable because of her infertility.[11]

BIRTH CONTROL

Although a large family was the goal of most Indian women, there were many situations in which women desired not to conceive. Perhaps a woman already had more children than she could feed and care for, perhaps she wanted to space her children so she could give more time to each baby as it came along, or maybe she had watched so many of her babies die that she wasn't able to undergo any more grief. And although it might be extremely rare, it was not unheard of for a woman to wish to remain childless, preferring to devote her life to other interests.

Primitive methods of birth control were largely magical and probably not too reliable. The manner in which the placenta was disposed of was widely believed to affect a woman's future childbearing. The Paiute believed that barrenness would result if the placenta was buried upside down or eaten by an animal, while an older Kaska woman, after helping her daughter with a difficult delivery, might fill the expelled placenta with porcupine quills and cache it in a tree out of compassion, to save her daughter the trauma of further childbearing.

Up in northwest Washington, a Lummi Indian mother who desired no more babies hung the afterbirth in a split tree in the hope that as the tree grew together her womb would also close up. Or she might hurl the afterbirth into an eddy in the river or ocean, so that her womb, like the placenta swirling in the water, would twist into a position to prevent conception.

A prevalent idea was that, in addition to preventing births entirely, the proper disposal of a placenta could also help to space the arrival of future babies. On the coast of British Columbia any Salish woman who wanted a few years' rest from childbearing directed that the placenta be buried with a scallop shell. Among the Cherokee in the Southeast, the father disposed of the placenta by crossing over two, three, or four ridges in the hills and burying it deep in the ground. He and his wife then felt confident that the number of years that would elapse before the birth of their next child would correspond to the number of ridges he had crossed.

Certain ceremonies were considered helpful in preventing conception. Often the rituals were known only to the old medicine women of a tribe who would secretly perform the rites for the desperate women who visited them under cover of darkness. Apache maidens who did not wish to have children could quietly seek out, at the time of their first menstruation, a woman to perform a rare and much condemned ritual that would prevent pregnancy. It was said that sometimes an Apache mother who knew the pain and suffering of labor had this ceremony performed for her daughter without the younger woman's knowledge or consent. A special variety of small prickly pear cactus fruit was said to be used in these ceremonies.

There were a number of preparations that Indian women took to avoid pregnancy. Quinault women brewed an abortive from a special thistle plant, while once a week southeastern Salish women made and drank a contraceptive of dogbane roots (*Apocynum androsaemifolium* L.) and water. If the dogbane didn't work, they could resort to an abortifacient tea made from the leaves and stems of yarrow (*Achillea millefolium* L.). Havasupais killed and dried a ground squirrel and pulverized it. During menstruation, a woman took some of the powdered meat in her hand, went to a place where she could be alone, and licked the powder from her hand bit by bit while praying that she would not conceive. Yuma Indian women relied partially on drinking a mixture made of mesquite wood ashes and water, but they also believed they could forestall pregnancy by regularly urinating on an ant pile or by strongly and persistently refusing to desire a child.

Among the Gros Ventre of Montana, persons who knew about contraceptives either received their knowledge directly from a supernatural or else had it handed down to them from within their family. Anyone who knew which roots or plants could be used to prevent pregnancy could command a large payment for this knowledge, often as much as two or three horses. A Gros Ventre woman named Coming Daylight confessed to Regina Flannery that she had been offered the power in a dream but when the supernatural had begun to show her how to make a medicine from a moss that grew on logs she had refused the knowledge.[12] The Gros Ventre acknowledged that their contraceptive medicines had certain limitations, and the woman who took them had to follow certain rules, such as not letting anyone who was a parent wear her robe, never sitting on the bare ground, never holding an infant, not sitting on anyone else's bedding, and not having sexual relations with anyone other than her husband. The breaking of any of the rules made the medicine ineffective.

Obviously, many of these contraceptive measures failed and when this happened there wasn't much a woman could do except try another herbal remedy or beat herself on the belly with stones—and even that didn't always work.

The leeway an Indian woman had in limiting the size of her family depended to a large extent on the society in which she lived. Generally, the groups living in the extreme north of our continent and in what is now the southeastern United States seem to have been the most broad-minded concerning the various methods of "family planning." Other groups were extremely conservative in their customs relating to birth control. The Cheyenne, who lived in the area of Wyoming and South Dakota, considered abortion out-and-out homicide, and a woman who killed her unborn child could expect to be prosecuted as a murderess. On the other hand, though the Papagos of southern Arizona severely criticized a woman who didn't want children, they had no officially sanctioned punishment for women who sought abortions. The only penalties were disapproval and criticism, and although sometimes the censure was so stringent that the woman was left friendless, no one would tell a pregnant Papago woman that she could *not* seek an abortion. Papagos felt that no one could rightfully interfere with what was really the business of the woman and her family.

INFANTICIDE

Infanticide was not unknown among the Native Americans, and there were many reasons why women had to resort to such an extreme measure of population control. Among the Eskimos living on the extreme northern fringes of our continent, each new child represented an enormous burden for the mother, especially during the summer when a mother was expected to carry the baby over and above her full share of household effects. It was nearly impossible to care for a newborn unless the previous child was able to walk long distances unaided. So if a second child arrived too soon or if a baby was born in a time of scarcity, it was exposed to die of the cold, its mouth stuffed with moss so its plaintive cries would not be heard.

The Kaska, who had a hard life in the subarctic forests of northwestern Canada, sometimes had difficulty finding someone in their group willing to raise a tiny orphan. The unwanted baby was placed in a little spruce-bark canoe that was launched on a large river. Tradition says that a child once survived such a voyage and was reared by a beaver from whose teats it nursed.

In the Creek nation all children belonged to the mother, who held the power of life and death over them during the first month of life. It was not uncommon for a woman who had become pregnant by a man who later jilted her to leave her baby to perish in the swamp where it was born. This was also a last resort for mothers whose families had grown larger than they could possibly support. But the baby had to be killed before it was a month old, for if the act was committed later, the mother would be punished with death.

Southeast Salish women occasionally went off alone into the woods to bear their children. A woman who did not wish to keep her baby might choose this option, for the privacy afforded her a chance to return to camp without the infant and to claim that her baby had been born dead. If it was discovered that the mother had killed the baby, the chief ordered her to be severely whipped, but apparently even so painful a punishment was not always enough to discourage this method of controlling family size.

Babies who were born deformed or diseased presented a special problem to Native American tribes, which in general could not afford to support a child that would never be a contributing member of the society. The Eyak, a people of the extreme north, kept their population free of unfit persons by openly burning deformed babies immediately after birth. This rule was rigidly enforced, and any mother attempting to save such a child was herself threatened with death.

The fate of an imperfect Comanche child was decided by the medicine women and the other women attending the birth. Comanches lived on the southern Plains, and if a baby was judged unfit to live, it was carried out on the prairie and left to die. Some families looked upon twins as a disgrace, and occasionally a mother who had two babies at once might dispose of one. An early white traveler named Dr. George Holley discovered and saved one such infant who had been buried in the sand by its mother.

The Hopi, generally a gentle and compassionate people, did not actually kill imperfect babies, but neither did the medicine men struggle to keep them alive, since they felt it would be cruel to subject a child to the taunts, neglect, and hardships that a physical defect would engender. These pueblo people had to work hard to eke out a living in their sandy, rocky, arid country, and unless they were old people who had spent their younger years working and who were currently paying their way by dispensing their wisdom, those who could not work could not eat.

Two Navajo girls in pre-Spanish and more recent traditional dress.
(*Roger Pfeuffer*)

The Indian Child

GROWING AND LEARNING IN EARLY AMERICA

As long as she was still a baby, an Indian girl would be cuddled and cared for and allowed to do as she pleased. But as soon as she had reached the age when she could understand and remember what was being said to her, her elders would begin to teach her, firmly but gently, about what it meant to be a woman in her society. There were no special educational complexes—the whole village and tribal territory were her school. Her lessons were not formal or structured, but went on all day long, encompassing not only economic pursuits such as the crafts, housework, wild-food gathering, and agriculture, but also the customs, etiquette, social obligations, and folklore of her tribe.

A girl's training was not always exclusively in the hands of her mother. In many tribes all the women in the family group collaborated in the raising of their children. The Navajos of northern Arizona were, and still are, a matrilocal society; when a young woman marries, she and her husband take up residence close to the wife's mother. Thus sisters usually lived very close to each other as adults and shared the childcare responsibilities. An outsider would have had a hard time guessing who was the blood mother of any of the children in these extended families, for although each woman had a favorite child, that child was usually not her own, but a niece or a nephew.

There were also very close ties between a Comanche girl and her mother's sisters. The girl called her aunt "Mother," and their relationship was one of mother and daughter, but with even less formality than between a real mother and daughter. The Hopi culture is also matrilocal, and sisters often lived their entire lives together in the same multiroom house. Hopi children used the same word for their mother and their aunts, and the women called all the children by the same kinship term. The ties were so close that it was reportedly not at all uncommon in more traditional times to find middle-aged persons who did not distinguish between their real mother and their maternal aunts.

In many cultures, children were raised by their grandmothers while their mothers were busy with jobs that required youth and strength. In these groups little girls usually felt closer to their grandmother than to their mother.

The extended family method of child raising was a good system for both the children and their mothers. The warmth and spirit of sharing that emerged from such a life-style made for happier children and left no room for the feelings of frustration and abandonment felt by twentieth-century American mothers, who are victims of the isolation of the modern suburban nuclear family.

EARLY TRAINING

Had the first white men on this continent any idea how meticulous the training of Indian children was in terms of "table manners" and personal cleanliness, they would never have considered calling these native inhabitants "uncivilized." Many groups required the children to bathe every day, no matter what the weather. In the Montana area, Gros Ventre children were roused at 3:00 A.M. in the summer and at seven in the winter, and all were required to bathe before they started the day. Even farther north the Tlingit and Salish groups insisted that the children arise at dawn and bathe in cold water, summer and winter. The Creeks, in the more moderate climate of what is now Georgia and Alabama, required all able-bodied men, women, and children to plunge into a creek four times or roll in the snow four times each morning before gathering near the fire. The Papagos in their arid desert habitat often had trouble getting enough water to drink, let alone to use for washing; but children were taught to rub themselves each morning with clean sand, which they thought was just as cleansing as water.

As for the behavior expected at mealtime, Chiricahua Apache mothers in the Southwest were reportedly very exacting. Youngsters were admonished to act like adults when they were eating, waiting until the various dishes were served instead of grabbing at them, and not drinking or eating until the older persons had started their meal. They were not permitted to move around or wiggle during a meal or to overeat, for food was a sacred blessing and never overly abundant.

The Yurok, of far northern California, were even stricter, with a rigid order of placement for each person sitting down to a meal. There was always a space left between the two parents for a potential guest. Girls sat near their mother, boys near their father. The mother taught the girls how to eat, telling them to take a little food with their spoons, putting it into their mouths slowly. There was to be no chatter during meals. If a child ate too fast, its food basket was silently removed and the child was expected to rise quietly and leave the house. If they had not been banished from the table for bad manners, the daughters had to remain seated after a meal until first the guest, and then the father followed by his sons, had left the room. They were not allowed to go outside and play until the mother had cleaned out the baskets with mussel shells, rinsed them with cold water, and swept toward the fire the floor over which the males had walked.

EDUCATION OF LITTLE GIRLS

Because the roles of Native American men and women differed so greatly from each other, it wasn't long before children had divided themselves according to sex. The age at which this separation was enforced varied; among the Salish of the northwestern United States and the Chickasaw of the Southeast it was as young as four or five years old. In other tribes the youngsters were allowed to play together until about eleven, or around the onset of puberty.

Learning the role of women by playing was the pervading method of education for very young girls, and mothers often took pains to see that their daughters had accurate miniatures of real household equipment to use in playing house. In some of the Plains tribes such as the Cheyenne, Omaha, Arapaho, and Crow, daughters of the more well-to-do families even had their own skin tents as playhouses, and when time came to pack up camp to follow the buffalo the girls got their own household—tipi, toys, and clothes—packed and ready to move.

The Crow woman Pretty-shield reminisced about such an experience of childhood in *Red Mother*:

Once several of us girls made ourselves a play-village with our tiny tepees. Of course our children were dolls and our horses dogs, and yet we managed to make our village look very real, so real that we thought we ought to have some meat to cook. We decided to kill it ourselves. A girl named Beaver-that-passes and I said we would be the hunters, that we would go out to a buffalo herd that was in sight and kill a calf. Knowing that we could not handle a bow, Beaver-that-passes borrowed her father's lance that was very sharp and longer than both our bodies put together. We caught and saddled two gentle pack-horses; and both the old fools went crazy before we managed to kill a calf. I helped all I could, but it was Beaver-that-passes who wounded a big calf that gave us both a lot of trouble before we finally got it down, and dead. I hurt my leg, and Beaver-that-passes cut her hand with the lance. The calf itself looked pretty bad by the time we got it to our play village. But we had a big feast and forgot our hurts.[1]

The transition from playing with dolls to full-time motherhood was gradual, since little girls frequently took care of their younger siblings. This was not too onerous a task, as the smaller ones could well fulfill the role of babies in the games of playing house. But one Gros Ventre woman admitted that some little girls got tired quickly when expected to babysit and would warn their mothers, "You'd better hurry up and take your baby or I'll drop it."

The spunky Crow Pretty-shield also had an exciting tale to relate about how she and several other young Crow girls "borrowed" a baby one afternoon. It was summer, and the village was moving. A group of about ten young girls was traveling together quite a way behind the main group, whose packhorses and travois were raising clouds of dust on the dry plains.

The children had stopped to swim in a creek when another Crow woman came along leading a packhorse which carried her belongings and a baby girl on a cradleboard. Seeing that the woman was anxious to catch up with the others, the girls offered to take the baby and the packhorse along with them. The young mother quickly accepted their offer and rode off. The girls had so much fun playing with the baby that they didn't pay much attention to the time until the afternoon sun began to wane. Pretty-shield explained: "The sun was already near to the ground when I spoke of the long way ahead of us, making quite a stir among the other girls. There were always Lacota (an enemy tribe) and buffalo herds to look out for, you see. We thought that we had better stop playing with the baby and catch up with our people; so we tied the baby, in its back-cradle, to the pack and started, riding moderately at first. I do not now remember who was to blame but anyhow it wasn't long before we were racing our horses. I could scarcely keep the others in sight because I was leading the pack-horse that carried the child. At first I kept looking back, until my neck ached, to see if the baby was there and all right; but when the racing started I forgot this for a long time. Then, when I suddenly remembered, and looked back at the pack, the baby wasn't there!"

Pretty-shield, her heart dropping, cried to the other girls to stop. Everyone was excited and crying and blaming each other for the loss. "We turned back," she continued, "dizzy with fear. Buffalo were coming. A great herd, headed so that it would cross over the very tracks our horses had made, was sweeping toward us. We ourselves were in danger. But what of the little baby? If it had fallen in the way that the buffalo herd would travel it would be trampled into the dry plains, leaving scarcely a mark upon them."

The girls hurried to retrace their journey. Farther and farther they rode without a sign of the baby. Finally, when the sun had almost set, they met some young men of their tribe, who had been out after buffalo. The girls explained their plight and pleaded for help. The young warriors of course found the tale hilarious and teased the girls, warning them that they would all be killed for their carelessness if the baby were found dead.

As it turned out, the young men had found the baby lying asleep and unharmed in its cradleboard. Pretty-shield scooped it up and rode to join the rest of the group. It was very dark by the time she rejoined the others, and the baby's mother was frightened and angry. "I never again tried to borrow a baby," Pretty-shield concluded, "and I never loaned one."[2]

Indian girls were gently led into the art of motherhood, and their introduction to other womanly tasks was gradual, too, at least for the littlest girls. They accompanied their mothers or big sisters while they gathered wild foods, weeded gardens, and went for water and wood. As the girls grew older, more was expected of them. A Fox woman, living in the area of what is now Wisconsin and Illinois, told how she was encouraged when she was about nine to plant a few things and to hoe the weeds. Then she was taught to cook what she had raised and was lavishly praised for her efforts. During the summer when she was ten, her mother allowed her to go swimming in the river only if she took along a few pieces of clothing to wash. Whenever she rebelled at being made to do these chores, her mother explained that it was because she cared about her daughter that she was making her work at such tasks, for she wanted her to be able to care for herself when she grew up.

❀◇❀◇❀◇❀◇❀◇❀◇❀◇

The Unhappy Woman

(OMAHA)

My daughter, if you do not learn to do well the things women must do and abide by the teachings of the elders, you shall stop at a stranger's house and your place will be near the kettle pole and without being told to go you shall go for water and when you have brought the water you shall look wistfully into the door of the lodge and they will tell you to open a pack so they may do their cooking. On opening the pack you will take a bit of the dried meat, thrust it slyly into your belt and take it with you and eat it stealthily but it shall not satisfy you. Food eaten in fear satisfies not the hunger.[3]

❀◇❀◇❀◇❀◇❀◇❀◇❀◇

Among the various southeastern Salish groups, little girls had a few chores they were expected to perform for their mothers but most of their time was their own to build little salmon traps and playhouses. The girls did not begin practical training until they were about nine. The Sinkaietk, a Salishan group, set up a girls' house in the permanent settlements, which served a twofold purpose: It kept the young girls away from the boys and provided a place where they could learn the skills useful for running a household. Girls went there during the day and the old women taught them how to make bags, baskets, mats, and twine, and to do bead and embroidery work. In some villages the completed articles were hung on bushes along the popular trails so they could be admired. Attendance at the classes was probably irregular, depending on what work the girls were expected to do at home, but each maiden kept going to the lessons until she had learned at least basic skills. Salish families also held a small family ceremony to celebrate the first roots and fruits gathered by their daughters. The women of the household were in charge of the feast, which included the foods the little girl had obtained. The little girl served the guests, primarily relatives, but she was not permitted to eat any of the food herself. Some of the older honored guests spoke to the child, emphasizing the virtues of hard work which lead to great success as an adult.

Jicarilla Apache maidens were constantly admonished by their elders not to think of themselves as children but as women able to do women's work.

Although a woman had to know how to gather food and grind corn, a young girl's lessons were not all connected with housework. A Jicarilla girl also learned how to take care of horses, and she could not only ride, but could stay on a horse as it jumped arroyos (dry washes) and other obstacles. Apache girls were also urged to develop their strength and endurance, particularly by becoming strong swimmers. They were warned that if they didn't swim every day they would develop lots of hair between their legs, an effective warning in a culture in which any body hair was repulsive.

DISCIPLINE

As a rule Native Americans were gentle with disobedient children, although discipline varied in harshness between groups. Among the Papagos living on the southwestern desert, children under ten years old had very little discipline of any kind, for the prevailing belief in that easygoing culture was that children should not be made to suffer. Ruth Underhill, an anthropologist who did a great deal of work with the Papago, wrote that even during sacred dances, children were allowed to run freely among the performers, talking and shouting. The adults just ignored such behavior, assuming the children didn't understand. Dr. Underhill explained that since noisy children did not shame the adults in charge of them, as they would in our culture, there was little cause for rebuke.[4]

The Cheyenne, and all Plains groups, expected more from their children, but they did not scold or slap their youngsters into obedience. When a baby's cries began to disturb the rest of the camp, the squalling infant was taken into the woods and propped in its cradleboard on a tree. It was left there all alone until it had finished crying, and only then was it brought back to camp. The important lesson the child was being taught was that control and self-effacement in the presence of elders brought the rewards of love and warmth, but that bawling only led to rejection and loneliness.

When a Crow child had cried and fussed for a long time for no apparent reason, her parents put her on her back and poured a little water down her nose. Usually it was necessary to perform the punishment only once or twice; thereafter just the threat, "Bring the water," was enough to hush a fretful child. Menominee, of the Great Lakes region, and Iroquois mothers also used the water treatment for a child who would not be calmed, throwing just a little water in the face of a crying child "to wash away its troubles." The Menominee thought that hitting a child, particularly in the head, would make it deaf and foolish. "Only white men are capable of such barbarities" was the opinion given by one member of that tribe.

Fox and Winnebago parents preferred to have a little girl who was disobedient fast for a short time, perhaps one meal, so that when hungry she would reflect on her misdeeds, apparently the early equivalent of today's "going to bed without dinner."

Beating of children was practically unknown among the Indians. The French, who were the first white men to visit the Huron Indians in southern Ontario, were shocked that these people never struck their children; they felt such parental restraint fostered disrespect in the children. But Huron mothers held a typical Native American attitude toward beating—that it usually did the child more harm than good. The Quinault, who lived on the Washington coast, regarded children as wholly irresponsible up to five years old, and children younger than that were never punished. Older children, though they might be rebuked, were never whipped, for it was believed that a little girl who was abused would likely grow up to be a mother who abused her own children.

In societies where harsher discipline was permitted, it wasn't the parents who administered it. These less sophisticated people correctly assumed that strong parental dominance bred resentment, so application of more forceful punishment was turned over to someone else. Among the Sanpoil, of northeastern Washington, an old man served as community disciplinarian; he lightly whipped not only the naughty children but their companions as well.

The Pueblo groups in the Southwest did not approve of mothers who punished their children too severely; there were many old stories of girls who were whipped or struck, causing them to leave the pueblo, never to return to their grieving and remorseful parents. Yet children had something to fear if they did not behave. All Zuni children knew of Su'ukyi, a frightful and wild-haired hag who had a packbasket on her back to carry children off. This bogeywoman must have had some communication with the mothers, for she accused each child of just the faults each had really committed. The mothers always pleaded for the children and promised they would do better, but the children knew if they didn't straighten out, the horrible old witch would be back. The Hopi living in the Second Mesa villages of Mishongovi and Shipaulovi have a similar character whom they call the "Black Lady." It is evident that her reputation still survives from the story "About the Black Lady" written by Janet Hyeoma, a modern-day Hopi child:

The Black Lady comes in February or March. She tells the boys to go hunt for her. She tells the girls to grind corn for her.

If you never help your mother wash dishes or sweep the floor you have to wash dishes or sweep in front of the Black Lady before she will accept your gift of sweet cornmeal. She goes from house to house picking these things up.

The Black Lady said that I never help my sister wash dishes. She said the same thing to my sister.

For older Indian children, the most widespread method of inculcating community standards was to appeal to the child's pride. A little girl was not presented with the hope of heaven nor the fear of hell, instead it was pointed out that the obedient child won the respect and approval of the rest of the villagers, while the naughty one risked condemnation and contempt. Flattery built pride in a job well done, and Indian children, like most people, were eager for the approval of others.

MYTHS AS TEACHERS

Indian children became acquainted with the less tangible parts of their culture—the morals, ideals, and ethics of their group—while the family was gathered together at night, often around a fire. It was then that the young ones heard all the stories of their tribe—how their people came to be on earth, where their food came from, and how their early ancestors learned all they knew. Many of the stories involved animals in the days when they could still talk. The story tellers were usually grandfathers and old men, but many old women were good story tellers, too. The long myths and legends they told served to illustrate practical lessons and point out what might happen if a child was disobedient.

❀◇❀◇❀◇❀◇❀◇❀◇❀◇

The Gossiping Girls

(TLINGIT)

Once there were two men of different houses but of the same clan. One became very ill and in his delirium dreamed that the other man was work- ing sorcery to cause his illness. The next day the sick man told his wife his dream. His small daughter overheard the conversation. Later this little girl got into a childish tiff with the other man's daughter, who

31

struck her. Angered, the injured girl told what her father had said, and the second little girl carried the tale to her own father. When he heard that his clan brother was accusing him of sorcery, he dressed in his war costume and went to the sick man, who, like himself, was a hard-bitten veteran of the war with the Haida Indians. The sick man also donned his war outfit, and since he was too ill to stand up, got the other man to sit on a box. With their respective nephews standing by as seconds, each man stabbed at the other until both fainted. When they regained consciousness, they resumed fighting until both died. The two nephews were about to carry on the fight when a person who was not related to either of them talked them out of it. The moral is that the daughter of the one was at fault for telling what her father had said; the other girl was at fault for repeating it. Both parents were at fault for not training their children better.[5]

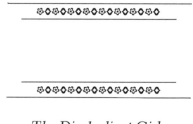

The Disobedient Girls

(SAN JUAN)

One day, long ago, the chief had sent word for all the young girls to go and gather onions, but the two Yellow Corn girls were playing and didn't get around to leaving until the others were already coming home. It was quite late and they were gathering their onions when along came one of the tsabiyu [*masked figures from Christmas folklore*] *with some long whips made from the sharp-edged leaves of the yucca plant. "You do not mind the chief," he said. Then he drew out his whips and beat one girl and then the other.*

Crying, the girls fled, but the masked figure ran after them, lashing them all the way. The laces of the girls' moccasins broke and their leggings fell off, but they left them where they fell and kept running. They lost their shawls and dropped their onions but still they ran, pursued by the fearsome supernatural. Finally the tsabiyu *used up all his yucca blades, so he called a warning to the girls, "Yellow Corn girls, next time you won't do this again. When people go out they should all go together.*

This is what happens to girls who don't obey the chief. Now go home."
The girls returned to their homes without onions, without moccasins,
and without their shawls.[6]

❀◈❀◈❀◈❀◈❀◈❀◈❀◈

SEX EDUCATION

Indian girls were generally very young when they were exposed to what we now call "the facts of life." The home was generally a single room, and close sleeping quarters did not permit a great deal of modesty within the family. Normally the hustle and bustle of village life allowed so little privacy that sex was largely a nighttime activity when the cover of darkness provided at least a suggestion of seclusion. But once a family was all in bed at night, parents usually did not go to great lengths to prevent their children from seeing them copulate. Some parents felt that young children who witnessed sexual activity wouldn't know what was happening and older children knew about everything anyway.

Among many groups, particularly the desert tribes, children went naked until puberty, and of course the universal game of "playing house," as popular with children then as it is now, led to sexual experimentation. Then, too, many of the myths told around the nightly campfires were rife with humorous and ceremonial sexual allusions, and these tales surely aroused the children's curiosity.

A few of the tribes were rather strict with their children in sexual matters, particularly regarding masturbation. The Kaska Indians, in what is now northern Canada, believed that masturbation led to insanity and blindness, and a child caught in such behavior had its hands whipped with a willow switch. The Apaches so severely repressed any tendency toward masturbation that many tribal members insisted that this otherwise universal behavior never occurred among their children. Even myths emphasized the misfortunes that might befall a girl who masturbated. Such severity in child training was the exception, however. The general Indian attitude toward children's sexuality was permissive and accepting.

❀◇❀◇❀◇❀◇❀◇❀◇❀◇❀◇❀◇

The Girl Who Abused Herself with Cactus

(JICARILLA APACHE)

There was once a girl who was very good-looking and many men wanted to marry her. But the girl always refused the men even though her relatives wanted her to marry. She was just not interested in any of the men. The people wondered about it.

One evening the girl took a rope and went out to get wood. A man who wanted to marry her followed her and hid in the bush, but she did not see him. After the girl had gathered quite a bit of dry wood and piled it up neatly, she carefully looked around in all directions. Then she uncovered a small round cactus which she had concealed with pine bark. The cactus had all the spines and outer covering peeled off, and the young woman sat down on the cactus and masturbated.

Then the man knew why the maiden would not marry him. Later this man came back to the same place and cut around the bottom of the cactus with a knife. Now it was very weak and ready to break off, though it still looked strong.

The next day at evening the man watched the maiden again. She went out for wood as before, and after gathering a full load, went over to the same spot. Soon after she sat down on the cactus, it broke off and stayed in her vagina. She tried to get it out but couldn't reach it.

The man came out of his hiding place and asked the girl what was wrong with her. The girl confessed her problem.

So the man said, "I'll cure you."

He made a small bow and some small arrows, then had her sit with her legs outspread. He shot two arrows into her vagina, one crossing the other. He held the arrows and pulled them out, and the piece of cactus came with them. Then the girl got better.[7]

❀◇❀◇❀◇❀◇❀◇❀◇❀◇❀◇◇

A Hopi maiden wears her hair in the traditional butterfly whorls that signify her unmarried virgin status. *(Courtesy of Arizona Historical Society)*

From Menarche to Menopause

A TIME FOR TABOOS

The appearance of a young Indian maiden's first menstrual period signaled the end of her happy, carefree days of childhood and the beginning of her life as a full-fledged woman of her tribe.

People of early native North American societies did not understand the complex physiological processes that cause menstruation, but they knew that they were related to fertility—even casual observation proved that a young woman could not become pregnant until she had begun to menstruate.

Even though the monthly discharge of the menses was experienced by all normal women, unsophisticated people found this regular appearance of blood—usually a signal of sickness or injury—difficult to explain with normal logic. In order to integrate this strange phenomenon into the accepted theory of beliefs, Native Americans incorporated an explanation into their myths and legends. These explained why a woman has menstrual periods and spelled out the proper behavior for her at menarche and during subsequent periods.

❀◆❀◆❀◆❀◆❀◆❀◆❀◆

Why Women Menstruate

(HAVASUPAI)

Long ago, when the world was still wet, before the human race was here and when the animals were like human beings, Squirrel lived in the San

37

Francisco Mountains. One day he took the tibia of a deer and painted on it a design. After sundown he threw the bone to the east with a prayer that a young girl would come to him with the next rising sun. The girl came just as Squirrel had prayed she would. She lived happily for a time there at the camp with her guardian, Squirrel, and her brothers, Coyote and White Dog.

One day Coyote called to his sister saying, "Sister, you must stay here while I go out to hunt." After the girl had waited a while Coyote returned carrying a fawn he had killed. The girl was glad to see the fawn and sat nearby thinking how good the meat would taste. While Coyote was butchering she felt of the fawn's smooth hair and touched its ears and face. Presently Coyote asked the girl to hand something to him and when she turned away to reach it, Coyote put his hand in the fawn's fresh blood and flipped it on the girl's thighs close to her vagina. Then Coyote cried out, "Oh, sister, you are menstruating. Now you cannot eat meat until you are clean, after four days have passed." The girl was angry because she couldn't eat the meat. Coyote said to her, "From now on it will happen like this to you once every month. After four days you must bathe."

The girl went to bed unhappy and the next morning when she awoke she was still angry with Coyote so she left the camp early saying nothing to her relatives. She ran away to a land in the west where she lived from then on.[1]

✿◇✿◇✿◇✿◇✿◇✿◇✿◇

PUBERTY CEREMONIES

The appearance of her blood—her life—flowing from between her legs is an upsetting experience for many adolescent girls, but for a young Indian woman the onset of menarche was also a time for her to play a brief but starring role in her puberty rites—often a heavily emotional drama.

In many societies the days or weeks following menarche were a special and dangerous time, with much of the girl's future hinging on the correct performance of certain duties and rituals. These rituals varied from tribe to tribe but all seem to have included one or more of three basic elements. In addition to performing these duties, a Native American maiden was expected to observe a great number of taboos, most of which were designed to protect her health, strength, and beauty, not only during the ceremonies but throughout her life.

A widespread custom, one of the basic elements, was the isolation of pubescent girls from the rest of society. A Fox woman remembers being warned as a girl: "You might ruin your brothers if you are not careful. The state of being a young woman is evil. . . . Whenever you become a young woman you are to hide yourself."² Young Indian women of many other tribes were told much the same thing—that with the appearance of their menstrual blood they must stay away from people, particularly men, so they would not harm others with their strong and potentially maleficent powers. This usually meant that at menarche a girl had to spend some time, usually four days to one month, in a small brush hut or tent erected away from the main dwelling. Some groups allowed the girl to remain in her home in a specially partitioned room, although she usually ate separately and did not interact with the rest of the family for fear of contaminating them.

Many tribes also included schooling or education in the puberty rite. Pubescent girls were taught what would be expected of them as women; often these lessons took place during the maiden's isolation.

The third element in the observances was a joyful celebration of the young maiden's change in status from a girl to a woman. Sometimes this was a private family rite and in other instances the celebration included the entire village.

RITUAL TABOOS

A great similarity in puberty taboos was found across the North American continent—even among those cultures that had few other customs in common. Many societies prohibited a pubescent girl from scratching herself with her fingernails during this time, believing that if she did so her hair would fall out, her face would be covered with permanent black streaks, or her body would be scarred. The maidens were taught to use a specially prepared scratching stick.

Another widespread taboo concerned the drinking of water, some tribes allowing the girl to drink water only through a reed or a hollow bone straw. For the Tlingit girls, living on the southern Alaskan coast, this straw had to be made from the wing bone of a white-headed eagle. The Tlingits also insisted that a pubescent girl, who might be isolated from the rest of the village for a whole year, leave her hut or room only at night, and then wearing a broad-brimmed hat so as not to taint the stars with her gaze.

Farther south, in Arizona, the Yumas enforced taboos against talking, to prevent garrulousness; laughing, to prevent light-headedness; and bathing, to prevent loss of strength. The Yumas weren't alone in their sanctions against bathing at this time, but among many groups, ceremonial bathing was part of the puberty ritual, even in cases when the ice had to be broken in a stream or lake to reach the water. A Lower Chinook girl had to bathe every day for five months following menarche to ensure future strength and regular occurrence of the menses. The Chinook girl who began her periods in the fall was unfortunate, for she faced a daily outdoor bath during the cold wet winter on the Washington coast. For the young Fox girl, the ritual bath included something more. As she stood in the middle of a stream, the skin on her back and sides was pricked and pierced until she bled freely—an attempt to ensure that she would not have an excessively heavy menstrual flow.

There were numerous other protective traditions in the various tribes: not stepping on a log or stick for fear of snakebite (Nisenan); not looking in the fire so eyesight would remain strong until old age (Quinault); not choosing one's own food for fear of becoming greedy (Flathead); not washing in or drinking cold water for fear of catching cold (Pomo); not washing in hot water for fear of wrinkles (Havasupai); not combing one's own hair for fear of scalp disease (Pomo); not smiling for fear of premature wrinkles, and refraining from touching the teeth so they would not fall out (Cocopah).

ISOLATION FROM SOCIETY

There are a number of accounts of what it was like for a young Indian woman while in isolation during her ritual initiation into womanhood.

According to Mountain Wolf Woman, a Winnebago, her first menstruation was traumatic. Her mother had told her what would happen to her some day and warned, "When that happens to you, run to the woods and hide some place. You should not look at anyone, not even a glance. If you look at a man you will contaminate his blood. Even a glance will cause you to become an evil person."[3]

It was a morning in very early spring and there was still snow on the ground when Mountain Wolf Woman realized that she was menstruating. Terrified at the powers she now possessed, the young girl quickly ran into the woods, pulled her blanket over her head, and sat crying alone. She was finally found by her sister, who had missed her and followed her footprints in the snow. The sister and another young woman built a small wigwam and a fire for the weeping girl and took her to them. The hut was about a quarter of a mile from Mountain Wolf Woman's home, and apparently she spent most of the required four days there crying, frightened, and hungry, for she was forced to fast.

Like other American Indian women, the Ojibwa maiden, in southern Ontario, was taught that at menarche she was a menace to herself and others and her presence blighted all young and living things. Dressed in very old clothes, she had to sit in a tiny hut in the forest, soot smeared around her eyes, obsessed and saddened with the terror of herself. She was expected to look always down, and whenever she left her special hut she was required to strew leaves behind her as a warning to men, pregnant women, and babies, who were thought to be especially susceptible to the evil forces surrounding her. As a "new woman" the only visitors she was allowed were women past menopause and other new women. The girls spent much time together discussing their new sexual eligibility and their emerging status as adults. If a young woman happened to be spending time isolated in a hut during the spring or summer, when Ojibwa families camped together in large groups, she could usually expect some unapproved visitors. Parties of young men regularly roamed the forest on warm nights. Finding a girl in a menstrual hut, they would disregard all the taboos and admonitions and crash in on her. Sometimes the boys just wanted to scare the girls and then stay and chat; other times they had lovemaking or even rape in mind. Although some might assume that the girl welcomed this as a pleasant distraction, we must remember she had been taught that at this time even her gaze was lethal. Few girls would dare risk the consequences of participating in the fun, and most buried their heads in their arms when illegal intruders approached.

Anthropologist Ruth Landes, comparing the Ojibwa maiden's puberty rites with similar rites held for young men, remarked with a touch of outrage, "His ceremony is a hopeful striving for broader horizons, but (the girl's) is a conscientious withdrawal of her malignant self."[4]

EDUCATION FOR ADULTHOOD

During her period of isolation a pubescent Indian girl was often attended by her mother, grandmother, or other elderly woman of good repute who taught her the skills needed by women of the tribe and the proper behavior for an adult woman.

This was the custom among the Flathead living in Montana. The mother of a Flathead girl nearing puberty would select a wise old woman to serve as a teacher and companion for her daughter during her first menstrual period. The old mentor, chosen because she typified the Flathead notion of the ideal woman, and the young girl spent four days together. During this time the two women became very close, and the special feelings of intimacy that developed during their days of ritual interaction usually continued for the rest of their lives. The younger woman was especially helpful to her guardian when the older woman grew aged and feeble.

The Flathead believed that this was a critical time in the formation of a girl's personality; therefore she was urged to exhibit no bad habits but rather to practice thrift and to develop skill in all the tasks she would have to perform as a woman. She was expected to get four loads of firewood each morning, to distribute some to each household in the village, and then to build a fire in her parents' lodge. She did all the cooking for her family during these four days, but she did not eat any of the food she prepared. Instead she ate her own meals at her old guardian's house. When she was not working, the girl was groomed by the old woman, who combed her hair and painted her face. Flathead Indians did not admire large feet, so a young girl was ordered to pound her feet with a rock so they would not get any larger. She was also told to pick a large louse from her head and impale it on a pine needle. The louse was slowly roasted over a campfire to prevent the girl from being afflicted with lice as an adult.

Education was also an important factor in the Diegueno rituals. "All that a girl needed to know to be a good wife, and how to have babies and to take care of them was learned at the ceremony, at the time when a girl became a woman," Delfina Cuero related in her autobiography. "We were taught about food and herbs and how to make things by our mothers and grandmothers all the time. But only at the ceremony for girls was the proper time to teach the special things women had to know. Nobody just talked about those things, it was all in the songs."[5]

But when Delfina reached puberty (around 1911 or 1912) the old ceremonies had begun to disappear, at the urging of the Christian missionaries, and she was not trained in the ways of her people. She was only thirteen when she married and became pregnant—she did not know what was wrong with her, and no one told her. Because of her total ignorance about childbearing she bore her first child, frightened and alone, while out picking wild greens. The missionaries, in their zeal to get rid of all heathen ceremonies, destroyed the educational, moral, and ethical system which was integrated into the religious ceremony, with the result that many of the Diegueno women of that era lost their first babies.

Although the vast majority of North American tribes incorporated the virtues of hard work into the girls' puberty rites, quite a different ethic pertained among the upper class of the slave-owning tribes along the northwestern coast of the continent. Here, girls were not allowed to do any work during their isolation; instead, they were cared for by servants, who were sometimes freed at the end of the ritual as a gesture of largesse on the part of the girl's father. Well-bred maidens of the Coast Salish tribes were taught to look on marriage with a rich gentleman as their ultimate goal, and the restrictions they faced during puberty were aids in accomplishing it. In some villages when a girl reached a certain age, whether she had actually experienced her first menses or not, she was secluded in a small compartment in the wooden longhouse in which her family lived. For several years she was kept incommunicado and allowed to go outside only at night, and then in secrecy, accompanied by her mother. She did nothing at all during the day; her continued inactivity and seclusion made her weak and pale and eventually unable to perform any physical task. These years of cramped-up sitting sometimes resulted in a partial crippling of the girl's legs, and upper-class women often had difficulty walking as adults. Yet these very defects were valued as marks of the ultimate aristocrat, and this was just the kind of girl noble families sought for their sons. These girls were so hidden away that an aura of mystery surrounded them, an additional attraction to an eligible suitor.

But, as mentioned above, such treatment of young girls required the luxury of slaves and was not widely found among the native North Americans, most of whom viewed industry and competence as the highest virtues.

JOYFUL PUBERTY FESTIVITIES

In many tribes the discipline and indoctrination period of a girl's puberty rite were followed by a festive ceremony. Chona, a Papago woman who related her memoirs to anthropologist Ruth Underhill, told about her experience.

As soon as she became aware of her condition, Chona moved into a very small brush hut, called the "Little House," behind the family dwelling. Her mother made her a special clay bowl and cup, her father made her a scratching stick, and an older and very highly esteemed female relative was chosen to be her teacher. Chona had to stay in the hut for four days, and each morning she was awakened before dawn by the older woman, who urged her to get up and go for water and firewood. Chona's village was not located near a water source, so the women had to run across the desert and to the mountains for the water and have it back in the village before daylight.

After the chores were done the older woman talked to Chona, telling her to be industrious and giving her lessons on how to run an efficient household. While the woman talked, other young girls came and sat near the Little House and listened to the lessons, too. The visitors were never allowed to come close to the girl who was confined, but they could get near enough to laugh and sing with her and help to while away the time.

When the four days were over and the Papago girl was not "dangerous" any more, her mother gave her a bath which was also a special ritual for protection against the cold. As the chilly water ran over Chona's hair and body her mother said:

> Hail!
> I shall pour this over you.
> You will be one who endures cold.
> You will think nothing of it.[6]

Then the real celebration began. All the people in the village knew that Chona had just been to the Little House for the first time, and they were ready for the dancing and feasting that would now follow. An old man who knew all the ceremonial songs was asked to officiate, and dancing went on every night for a month. Each evening after dark the villagers who weren't too sleepy from staying up the night before would join Chona and her family and dance until just before dawn. The dancers were arranged in two long lines facing each other, males alternating with females.

❀◇❀◇❀◇❀◇❀◇❀◇❀◇

Maiden's Song

(PAPAGO)

Poor little maiden!
In the evening you will clasp hands.
In the evening I arrive and hasten hither,
Hither I hasten and sing.
Songs follow one another in order.

*The shining mocking bird
At evening could not sleep.
When the moon was in mid-sky
He ran to the maiden's dance.
At early dawn
High did he raise his song.*[7]

❀◇❀◇❀◇❀◇❀◇❀◇❀◇❀◇

During the long nights of dancing the sexual mores of the village were relaxed, and it was common for women to slip into the darkness with men who were not their husbands. It was Dr. Underhill's contention that this time of licensed promiscuity had the connotation of fertility magic. But this was the privilege of adult women only. Chona danced every dance, through the long, dark, chilly nights. When the dancing stopped she would fall into bed exhausted, only to be awakened soon with orders to get the wood and water and to grind the corn. "If you sleep at this time, you will be sleepy all your life," she was warned. Chona remembered how she had listened to the songs of the maiden's dances when she was younger and how her father had refused to let her join in the dancing, but now that it was her turn to dance, she was so sleepy that all she wanted was to go home to bed.

Not all the Indian tribes required a time of seclusion for pubescent girls. To the Gabrielino of southern California, a girl's puberty ceremony was not a protection from malignant forces but a joyous presentation to society of a marriageable young woman.

The ceremony began with a test of the maiden's virtue—if she could swallow and not regurgitate a large wad of tobacco, she was considered chaste; if she couldn't keep the unpleasant mass down, her previous behavior came under suspicion. Following this trial, for three days the girl lay buried to the neck in a long pit warmed with hot stones. She could leave the pit only once every twenty-four hours, while the stones were being reheated. During the time she was lying in the pit, the Gabrielino girl was the focus of hours of dancing and singing.

The Havasupai Indians, living in the depths of the Grand Canyon, "roasted" pubescent girls in a warm pit as the Gabrielinos did, but here the ceremony was a private family rite. Anthropologist Carma L. Smithson, who studied the Havasupai, suggests that this ceremony was psychologically very important to the young woman, who was experiencing so many changes in her body and in her status in the tribe. The rites served to dramatize a difficult experience for the girl, making it one of importance and minimizing the possible unpleasantness of physiological change by directing attention toward ritual and symbolism and the importance of future womanly duties.[8]

Both the Navajo and Apache puberty dances are festive ceremonies and are still being held almost in their traditional forms. The Navajos celebrate a four-day ceremonial called kinaalda. Each day the pubescent girl arises at dawn and races to the east, repeating the run at noon. And each day she is given the molding ceremony while she lies on a blanket in front of the hogan, or family home. An older woman kneads her body and straightens her hair to make her shapely and beautiful. During the first three days of the observance, the girl grinds corn, and on the fourth day the corn meal she has produced is used to make a large round cake, which is baked in an earthen oven. A man who knows the traditional songs comes to lead the singing, which goes on all night while the cake bakes. The singers, the girl, and all the other persons in the hogan where the ceremony is taking place must stay awake all night or bad luck will come to the girl. In the morning the cake is carefully uncovered, and the maiden distributes large pieces to the singers and smaller pieces to all her other friends and relatives who have attended the ceremony and stayed awake all night.

The Apache four-day puberty rite is a time of happiness and sociability. A small observance is held when a girl first menstruates, but a larger event is scheduled for the following July or August. The celebration is always very expensive, costing anywhere from one to six thousand dollars today, and all the girl's relatives are expected to contribute money and food. It is always convenient if a girl's first period occurs in the fall or winter, because this gives her family a few extra months to save up money for the summer ritual. Today not all Apache families can afford to give their daughters the traditional puberty ceremony, and in some cases a girl refuses to have the ceremony because she is too bashful or is disdainful of the old traditions.

During the months of preparation for the summer ceremony, a medicine man is chosen to conduct the singing, and an older woman of impeccable reputation is asked to be the girl's sponsor or godmother. Intense preparations start four days before the ceremony, when the girl's family and relatives and the sponsor and her relations move to the campground and begin building brush shelters, clearing the dance ground of grass and stones, and gathering wood for the huge fires.

On the night before the main ceremonies are to begin the guests have all arrived, some of them having traveled many miles to participate in this popular Apache ceremony. The maiden is introduced to the guests, and then the singing and drumming begin. The people link arms, forming long lines, and dance four steps toward the fire and four steps back. The girl for whom the ceremony is being given dances side by side with another young girl about her age who has been chosen to be her companion during the ritual. Although the rest of the people are in a gay mood, dancing and greeting friends, the celebrant must dance with downcast eyes and a serious expression.

The main ceremonies begin at sunrise. The function of the celebration is mainly educational, and through symbolic actions the young woman is taught the four Apache life objectives: physical strength, good disposition, prosperity, and a sound, healthy, uncrippled old age. The ceremony can be trying for the maiden. In several parts of the rite she is required to dance in place with a little bouncing step for two or more hours while wearing a heavily beaded buckskin costume; she faces the rising sun as she dances.

During the singing and dancing, both sacred and social, the young girl gains the power of Changing Woman (also called White Painted Woman), one of the legendary founders of Apache culture. Changing Woman has never died, and thus part of the power she grants is longevity.

How Changing Woman Stays Young

(APACHE)

When Changing Woman gets to be a certain old age, she goes walking toward the east. After a while she sees herself in the distance looking like a young girl walking toward her. They both walk until they come together and after that there is only one. She is like a young girl again.[9]

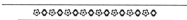

Throughout most of the ceremony the girl's power is used for her own benefit, but for four days following the main rites she is believed to be able to cure the sick and bring rain.

❀◇❀◇❀◇❀◇❀◇❀◇❀◇

Puberty Rite Dance Song

(APACHE)

I

I come to White Painted Woman,
By means of long life I come to her.
I come to her by means of her blessing,
I come to her by means of her good fortune,
I come to her by means of all her different fruits;
By means of the long life she bestows, I come to her;
By means of this holy truth she goes about.

II

I am about to sing this song of yours,
This song of long life.
Sun, I stand here on the earth with your song;
Moon, I have come in with your song.[10]

❀◇❀◇❀◇❀◇❀◇❀◇❀◇

Although an Apache maiden knew that her life would be much more difficult as a woman than as a child, her introduction to her adult role was accompanied by so much ritual and festivity that she had little desire to return to her previous status.

IMPORTANCE OF THE RITUALS AND TABOOS

All the tribes with puberty ceremonies and regulations considered them very serious matters. A girl could bring grave danger not only to herself but to her family and the rest of the villagers if she disregarded the traditions and taboos.

Papagos tell the story of a girl who "became dangerous" and did not begin the required observance. All the villagers were out in the fields planting, and she was right there with them, laughing and having a good time. When it began to rain, the girl and her sisters ran home to take in the family bedding, for it was warm weather and they had been sleeping outside. There was a crash of thunder, and from the girls' house came a long sigh. The people in the field ran to help and found the family lying stunned on the floor with one sister blind and the one who had violated the taboo dead. The brush house then burned to the ground.

Lower Chinook girls were warned never to go out of the house while menstruating if there was a southeast wind with signs of rain. It was believed that Too-lux, the south wind, would be so offended at finding such a girl in his path that he would send Hah-ness, the thunderbird, to shake his wings, causing roaring thunder, and to blink his eyes, sending forth flashes of lightning. All thunderstorms in the area, and their consequences, were attributed to girls' going outside during their season of purification.

The tales tend to reinforce the taboos. Among the Quinault, of coastal Washington, and their neighbors, the Queet, girls were to abstain from fresh fish and meat for five months. The story is told of a Queet couple and their pubescent daughter who came and stayed with some relatives at a Quinault village near a lake. Soon the sockeye salmon stopped running, and the people guessed that the visiting girl had broken her ritual fast by stealing and eating fresh salmon. The fishermen were angry and upset that their nets and traps remained empty. What threatened their food supply, threatened their lives. So they grabbed the suspected young girl and started down the river in boats, taking her with them. Coming to a big log jam, which they attributed to the violation of the taboos, they attached large stones to the girl's body and threw her in the water. It is said that no one commented on the occurrence, but after that everyone was very careful to carry out the puberty ritual.

THE MONTHLY RETREAT

Ideas of the foulness and dangerousness of menstrual blood were so strong in some societies that women were forced to seek isolation every time they menstruated from menarche through menopause—some twenty-five to thirty years. Because Native American women were so often pregnant or nursing they generally did not menstruate as regularly as modern women, and so the appearance of a menstrual period was something more of an event.

Chickasaw and Creek women in the South who did not seclude themselves during their menses committed a crime on a par with murder or adultery. They were expected to retire to brush huts called "moon houses" located outside the village. This was sometimes a dangerous practice because warriors from unfriendly neighboring tribes would lie in wait near the huts for the women and kill them. But if a woman remained in the village during her period, she had to answer for every misfortune that befell her neighbors.

Before returning to her village after each sojourn in the brush hut, a Creek woman was required to bathe in deep running water, even if she had to break ice to get to it. While walking to the water, she had to pass downwind of all men, and it was also necessary for her to bathe downstream from any man who happened to be in the creek.

The fear seemed to be that this so-called horrid and dangerous pollution would affect the success of a hunt, ruin garden crops, and diminish the spiritual powers of a man. Widespread taboos forbidding the eating of fresh meat by menstruating women were tied to the fear of future unavailability of game, although additional reasons for the sanctions were usually given. Creek women had to avoid meat from large game animals; the Kaska, in the north, had to avoid moose head and moose marrow in particular. Other groups held that sterility would result from eating meat (Yokut) and fish (Cocopah). Menstruating Iroquois women were not to touch meat intended for preservation or general household purposes, and menstruating Eyak women weren't even supposed to see fresh meat.

Hunters carefully avoided any contact with a menstruating woman. In Washington, Lummi husbands believed that menstrual odors would cling to their bodies and would be detected by the deer they stalked. Among the Chipawyans, in the subarctic, it was considered potentially harmful if menstrual blood came into contact with male hunters, because game and fish were thought to dislike any contamination of this sort. A Quinault wife had to stay in her house for five days during her menses, and if her husband was hunting at the time, he moved out and camped in the woods. If he so much as saw a menstruating woman, he had to bathe and purify himself for ten days before resuming the hunt.

In contrast to the general custom of avoiding a woman during her period, a certain group of Mandans in North Dakota required the services of a menstruating woman during eagle trapping. This atypical practice was based on a tribal myth about the capture long ago of the leader of the eagles, who, in return for having her life spared, promised unusual hunting success if her song was sung when a menstruating woman was brought into the ceremonial lodge.

In many tribes, not only the hunting success but also the health and power of a man depended on his wife's circumspectness during her menses. If a

Nisenan woman living near the Sacramento Valley in California touched or stepped over her husband during her period, it was believed that he would become paralyzed. In Texas, Comanches thought menstrual blood nullified a man's power, so each month a woman had to move out of her husband's tipi for several days. If she had no tipi of her own, she could move in with her parents; the medicine of old people was considered too weak to be harmed by her presence.

The Assiniboine, living along the midwestern United States–Canada border, handled the problem of possible contamination a little differently. A menstruating woman was not permitted near a certain medicine bundle containing sacred objects. But instead of the woman having to leave home each month, her husband merely moved his bundle out of the lodge. When a menstruating woman approached another lodge, she announced her condition so the bundle could be removed if necessary. If a menstruating woman entered a lodge that contained the medicine bundle, it was believed she would continue to menstruate indefinitely.

In Arizona, Navajo women could come and go freely from their hogans and do their usual chores during their menses, but the menstrual discharge was considered extremely dangerous, and great care was taken by men to avoid seeing it, touching it, or eating it. Contact with this blood was thought to cause one to develop a hunchback, and there was fear that a woman might deliberately put the discharge in food to cripple someone. A menstruating Navajo woman was not allowed to enter the hogan of a sick person or to attend a sand-painting ritual held for someone who was ill, for it was believed her presence would make the patient even weaker. Strangely, it was also thought that if a menstruating woman stepped over a man, he would become pregnant. When questioned about this by anthropologist Flora Bailey, a Navajo woman affirmed, "It's true. You must be very careful this way."[11]

Zuni women, in northern New Mexico, were not segregated during their monthly periods but were given special consideration instead. They generally didn't walk much at this time and were not expected to perform their usual chore of bringing water from the well. They did mainly indoor work, usually weaving or grinding. If they were uncomfortable, they wore a heated stone under their belts and drank hot juniper tea.

Although there were many taboos governing the conduct of a menstruating Indian woman, some societies provided methods of getting around the taboos. Paiute men in Nevada never approached the menstrual lodge, as illness and death were thought to follow contact with a menstruating woman; however, if the woman was really needed in her home, perhaps to attend a sick child, a shaman could neutralize the ill effects of a menstruant by smearing red paint around her wrists or making a circle of red paint on the floor and singing. A Pomo woman, on the coast of northern California, was not supposed to weave baskets while menstruating, but if she happened to be working on a basket when her period started and she didn't want to stop, the insertion of a few short pieces of yellow hammer bird quill at the point she was working would permit her to continue with her task. Flathead women in Montana inadvertently breaking a taboo could hide a weapon under the lodge entrance so that they might unconsciously step over it and thus alleviate the infraction.

Husbands were sometimes forced to obey restrictions each month along with their wives. This was particularly true among the Pomo Indians. When a married Pomo woman had her period, she moved to one side of the dwelling, and her husband cared for her and fed her. Believing that if another man touched him or talked to him it would bring bad luck, the husband stayed indoors at home for the four days of his wife's confinement. On the fifth day he bathed before rejoining the rest of the populace. If a Pomo man started out with a war party and his wife began to menstruate, a messenger was sent out to report this to the group, and they immediately called off the war.

A Papago male was also believed to be weakened while his wife was menstruating, and he was forbidden to join any war parties during that time. Apparently some Papago women who did not want their husbands to go to war would tell them they were menstruating when they were not. This did not set well with the men of the tribe, who would be more angered by this deceit than by any other injury, including unfaithfulness.

Sexual intercourse was almost universally forbidden while a woman was menstruating. Many tribes, including the Hopi, Havasupai, and Navajo, thought women were most likely to conceive while menstruating. Margaret Mead found in her study of the Omaha that the "no sex during menstruation" taboo was originally intended to protect the power and skill of the men but later was used as a form of (supposed) birth control.[12] Although Navajos were afraid to have sex during menstruation, they might take the risk if they wanted a baby very badly. However, the man had to be certain to take the superior position during intercourse—otherwise he might become pregnant!

HYGIENE AND MEDICATION

Methods of menstrual hygiene varied. A special knee-length dress and a breechcloth padded with dry moss was used by the Kaska woman, of British Columbia; the Navajo woman wore a piece of sheep pelt attached to her waist with a rope. Women of the southeastern Salish tribes, of northern Washington, staunched the flow with cattail down, and among the Washo women near Lake Tahoe, sagebrush bark was used.

A Zuni woman spread heated sand in a thick patch on the floor of her home. She sat over the sand, her robes caught up around her waist. A blanket fastened around her shoulders fell loosely to the ground, covering her body and the sand.

Various plant preparations were used to treat menstrual pain and irregularity. The women at San Ildefonso Pueblo along the Rio Grande in New Mexico drank an infusion of corn smut in water and also thought corn meal made from black corn with streaks of red was beneficial. A Cheyenne woman whose period was continuing longer than it should made herself a strong tea from the powdered stems and flowers of a weed (*Eriogonum subalpinum*). A tablespoon or two of the tea reportedly acted at once.

Sometimes a woman who was not pregnant ceased to menstruate. Apaches considered this a serious if not fatal disease called "blood is in her." The treatment, which could be administered only by a person with special knowledge, consisted in part of making a tea with chips of wood from a branch that had been struck by lightning. The tea was blessed with sacred pollen and drunk by the sufferer.

Literature reports that a Cahuilla woman living on the desert in southern California went to a medicine man when she had not menstruated for many months. The medicine man waited until the next new moon and then inserted a long stick in his nose until it bled. Catching the blood from his nose in his hands, he rubbed it all over the woman's abdomen. The next day she got her period and had no further trouble.

MEANING AND ORIGIN OF THE TABOOS

The myths and legends concerning the reason for menstruation and the attendant taboos may have sufficed for the early Native Americans, but modern anthropologists aren't satisfied with these explanations.

A number of experts have sought more scientific theories for the origin and perpetuation of menstrual taboos, but there are few undisputed conclusions. According to some anthropologists, the more the sexes are separated into exclusively male or female activities, the more likely that society is to enforce menstrual taboos. Other scholars have reversed the logic of this observation, postulating that primitive man's horror of menstruation is the cause of the pronounced sex dichotomy found in most tribes.

Opposing both these theories, others who have written on the subject believe that there is not necessarily a relationship between the physical facts of menstruation and the taboos because menstruation is known in all societies, but not all societies have such taboos. Very simply stated, the next logical step is that menstrual taboos are actually an institutionalized way for men in unsophisticated societies to discriminate against women, and although any number of reasons might have been chosen to justify such discrimination, the taboos were attached to menstruation because of its convenient universality among females.

Other possible reasons for menstrual taboos have been studied and discarded. For example, statistical correlation studies (a favorite tool of scholars) have shown no relationship between menstrual taboos and disgust for the feces or between the severity of the customs and the status of women in a society. One revealing study compared the strictness of the taboos to the amount of inconvenience caused by a woman's temporary absence from the home. The study showed, speaking nontechnically, that if there weren't other wives or other related women in the household to keep up the chores while one of them was confined to a menstrual hut the society would be less likely to insist on this custom.

At any rate, once a culture had developed its taboos for women to the point of excluding women from tribal initiation rites—on the basis that one of them might be menstruating and ruin the whole ceremony—then a separate puberty rite for girls became a necessity. (There is a feeling among some anthropologists that the puberty rite is so widespread among hunting and gathering societies in North America as to indicate an ancientness stretching back to the proto-Amerinds of Asia.)

The female initiation rite seems to have been most important, and therefore occurred most often, in cultures in which the husband went to live in the bride's home with her after marriage. Because the girl went from child to woman to wife all in the same house, some special measure was needed to proclaim her changes in status. Girls' puberty rites were also common in those societies which accorded women a role of great economic importance.

Through the various parts of the rite, both the girl and the society were assured of her competence to fulfill her new duties as an adult. Some evidence suggests that the severity of the training during the puberty rite may have been related to a society's treatment of its children. If boys and girls were treated the same, a maiden would not have received much training in what would be expected of her as an adult. Therefore it would be necessary to stress the importance of the adult female role at puberty.

But what of the women themselves? How did they view the menstrual customs which ruled their lives for so many years? To us the practice of banishing women from hearth and village because of a natural and healthy occurrence seems harsh and cruel. But men made up only half of the population of each tribe, and there is no way they could have enforced such traditions without cooperation from the women. Why did the females not rebel and refuse to go off to the forest once a month?

Let us take a brief look at the life of a Native American woman. Hard work was the daily lot of any group in early times, even though Mother Earth was rich and provided well for her children. There were fields to plant, maintain, and harvest; wild foods to gather, dry, and store; meat to prepare for jerky and hides to tan and sew into clothing and tipis.

When an Indian woman prepared a meal, she did so all the way from the planting of the corn kernel and the butchering of the buffalo or deer to the ladling of the food into pottery bowls or baskets she had made—all the while bearing and minding children. Is it any wonder that a four-day rest each month seemed an acceptable tradition? Aside from the fear of being attacked by the enemy while away from the protection of the village, staying alone in a hut with peace and quiet or with a few other women for company, cooking only her own food, and bathing in a stream was not a bad vacation.

One anthropologist reports that Chipawyan women, in subarctic Saskatchewan, seemed to keep the true nature of the menstrual cycle a secret from the men. When a woman wanted to avoid her husband, which might be several times a month, she simply crawled out of the tent and went to the menstrual hut.[13]

Mrs. Antelope, a well-to-do married woman of the Coeur d'Alene tribe. (*Courtesy of the American Museum of Natural History*)

Sharing a Life

FROM COURTSHIP THROUGH WIDOWHOOD

As soon as an Indian maiden reached puberty and adult status she and her parents began making plans for her marriage.

The maiden didn't have much choice whether she would marry or not. There was simply no place for a single woman in early Indian societies. Most tribes viewed woman as the natural complement of man; neither was complete without the other. A woman depended on a man for food and protection and a man needed a wife to process the meat and dress the skins of the game he killed and to cook his food and make his clothing. A spinster was an oddity and a rarity.

In some Native American societies there was no courtship. Because the elders in these tribes knew it was difficult to keep young men and women apart when their sex urges were strongest, many Indian maidens were married off immediately after reaching puberty to assure that they would enter marriage as virgins. In these societies it was difficult for the girls to have even the most casual contacts with young men. Two examples are the Fox of Illinois and the Papago of southern Arizona. A Fox girl could not have any male friends, for even talking to a male other than a relative or her fiancé was considered suspect behavior. A Papago girl was taught that if she talked to boys or daydreamed too much about them before marriage, one of them would appear to come and make love to her, but in reality it would not be the boy but a snake. After marriage was time enough to talk to a man.

Other societies held off marriage for a few years, allowing the young women time to mature before they had to take on the full responsibilities of adulthood. This interim also allowed time for the maidens to be courted by the young men of their village.

COURTSHIP

Courtship customs varied widely throughout early North America. In some tribes young people were always fully chaperoned and in other societies they were left to do pretty much as they pleased.

The Cheyenne of the Great Plains closely protected their young women. Immediately after her puberty ceremonies a Cheyenne woman began wearing a protective rope tied around her waist, passed between her thighs, and wound around her upper legs almost to the knees. She was expected to wrap herself up like this every night and at all times while traveling. Any male who even touched her rope could expect punishment—even by death.

But it wasn't only sex between unmarried young men and women that worried Cheyenne elders; even casual friendship was unacceptable behavior. Girls were warned not to exchange too many glances and smiles with young men for fear of being considered easy and immoral. After puberty, boys and girls were prevented from socializing, and girls weren't even allowed to spend much time with their female friends. Because of such restrictions, the courtship of a young Cheyenne couple was a very bashful and long drawn-out affair. It might take a year for the boy and girl to get up the nerve to speak to each other, and then another three or four years before the young man had the courage to request his old aunt or grandmother to ask for the girl's hand.

Among the most sexually straightlaced of all the North American Indians were the Apache groups. The girls were trained to be reserved and bashful, and the boys were taught that it was unmanly to pay too much attention to women. Any show of affection in public between males and females was laughed at.

Apache girls were expected to remain chaste before marriage. A maiden who didn't—and was discovered—could expect a public whipping with a rope or a stick, delivered by her father. The father was very vocal in his chastisement as well, and because the whipping was performed in full view of the rest of the camp, it was supposed to serve as a lesson to the other girls. An intact hymen was proof of virginity, and a marriage could be called off—

bringing great disgrace to the girl's family—if the bride was found to be unchaste.

But even with all these restraints and warnings, Apache girls did manage to be with young men occasionally. Interestingly, it was the girl who was expected to make the public advances to the boys. Those who weren't too bashful might get together and invite the youths they liked best to go hunting for wild plant foods or to help them with harvesting and planting. Maidens invited only youths who would make suitable marriage partners for them. One Apache told of working side by side with other young people all day in a field and being too bashful to leave to relieve herself.

If an Apache maiden and a youth were really attracted to each other and were willing to risk a scolding from their parents, they might set up a rendezvous. Usually two couples met together. At the first few meetings the young men and women would sit about ten feet apart and smile at each other self-consciously, trying to avoid showing their teeth, perhaps tossing pebbles at each other. After several meetings they might sit closer together and chat of commonplace things, or the couples might separate to talk more privately. The very farthest a suitor might go was to touch his beloved's breasts or squeeze her thighs, and most girls probably did not allow such attentions even from their fiancés.

The culturally approved way for Apache young people to meet was at the tribal social dances. Apache parents were happy to have their daughters go to these gatherings, but they always watched them very closely. Unmarried girls were usually accompanied by an older relative, or they might be put in charge of a younger child so they wouldn't have time for any exploits. If a young man were interested in a particular girl, he would always arrange to be at any dance she attended. But the first move was up to the girl, for every dance was ladies' choice, though some girls were so shy they wouldn't face the boys when asking them to dance, and even avoided looking at their partners during the dances. There were others who were not so shy, however. Consequently the young people were forbidden to leave the dance place, and chaperones continually policed the outskirts of the grounds to prevent clandestine adventures, herding youngsters lurking in the shadows back into the light of the fire.

The lyrics of the songs sung during the dances usually had to do with romance, and sometimes they were funny. The old men who beat the drums and sang thought it amusing to compound the embarrassment and awkwardness of the young people by throwing in a suggestive tune now and then.

❖❖❖❖❖❖❖❖❖❖❖❖❖

Dance Songs

(APACHE)

Young woman, you are thinking of something,
Young woman, you are thinking of something;
You are thinking of what you are going to get:
The man of whom you are thinking is worthless.[1]

I

I see that girl again,
    Then I become like this;
I see my own sweetheart again,
    Then I become like this.

II

Maiden, you talk kindly to me,
    You, I shall surely remember it,
I shall surely remember you alone,
Your words are so kind,
    You, I shall surely remember it.[2]

❖❖❖❖❖❖❖❖❖❖❖❖❖

Most Indian societies, however strict their sexual mores, provided some socially acceptable way for young persons to meet. As was the case with the Apaches, the meeting ground was often a dance. The only time Nisenan Indian girls, of the Sacramento Valley, were permitted to talk to boys was at the tribe's annual dance ceremony held to allow young people a chance to choose mates. In the ceremony the young men and women danced in a ring around a fire, which did not allow opportunity for advances much beyond smiling at each other.

The Sioux also arranged a "formal" social ball for their young people. The Night Dance took place on a summer evening in a large tipi set up near the center of the camp. The sides of the tipi were rolled up so that spectators could join in the fun. As is typical of young people's dances even now, the girls sat on one side of the lodge and the boys congregated on the other side. When the drumming began, each girl walked over to the boys' side and chose a partner by kicking the sole of his moccasin. The couples, holding each other by the belt, formed a line and danced in a two-step motion around the fire. The next dance it was the boys' turn to choose partners. Midway in the dancing a feast was served—usually boiled puppy.

If two young people became attracted to each other during a Night Dance, the girl might invite the young man to come and meet her in front of her family's tipi. It was not uncommon in a Sioux camp to see a young couple standing in front of a skin lodge at dusk, their heads covered with the young man's blanket in an attempt to find a bit of privacy in the middle of the busy village. A girl might have several boyfriends who would actually wait in line during the evening for a chance to embrace her beneath the blanket. In some groups only young men who were already warriors, and so eligible for marriage, were allowed to take part in such tête-à-têtes. These formalized little chats didn't allow much chance to get to know each other; with curious little brothers and sisters romping around and an ever-present chaperone just inside the lodge, conversations tended to be stilted and brief. Most of what a girl learned about a young man came to her from the boy's sister or female cousins.

Crow young people gathered for an outing at berry-picking time. They all came dressed in their best clothes, each boy offering to carry the berry bag of his favorite maiden. Gaily, the group of young people all rode off together for the day. When it was time to return to camp in the late afternoon the couples exchanged horses and rode back home, laughing and singing. A similar party was held when the wild rhubarb was ripe.

A popular time for young Hopis to get together was a sort of picnic held after the sacred kachina dances. The boys went out first to a prearranged meeting spot, hunting rabbits as they went. The girls, accompanied by their little sisters, followed later, carrying along special food they had cooked, including a traditional corn dish called somiviki. When the maidens arrived at the picnic spot they sent their little sisters to bring them the boys they liked best. The boys roasted the rabbits, the girls unpacked their lunches, and all had a good time. This was often the time that later, private visits were arranged.

Daughters of the Earth

When a girl had decided she wanted a certain man for a husband, she would prepare a special food called *qomi*, which was a large loaf of sweetened cornmeal. If the man agreed to picnic with her, she handed him the qomi, which meant she was formally proposing marriage. Because the boys were aware that a proposal could be sprung on them at any time, they were careful to picnic only with maidens they might be willing to marry. Of course, as in other Indian cultures, the ultimate decision to marry did not lie with the young people themselves but with their families. There were several other special events during which a maiden might offer a young man a qomi or a plate of the special wafer bread called piki, but in each case it was necessary for the young man's family to rule favorably on the match before the marriage could take place. The young men did not have to accept the proposals, even if their parents approved, but they were careful not to humiliate the young women in public.

In addition to the properly chaperoned dances and approved outings, young Indian girls managed to meet young men in several fairly standard surreptitious ways. In hunting and gathering tribes the young women were usually responsible for getting water and firewood. Thus the nearby spring or stream and the woods around the camp were areas where a young man might hope to catch a private word or two with his beloved.

Because Omaha girls knew they might be approached by young men, they never went to the spring alone, always in twos or threes. They were very timid; rather than constantly watching their daughters, Omaha mothers cultivated such a state of bashfulness and fear of men in them that a girl would not only be too frightened and inhibited ever to approach a man, but she could even be counted on to flee if advances were made toward her. The customs of the Omaha did not allow young people to visit each other in their homes, so the only means a young man had of letting a maiden know he liked her was to signal her when she was doing errands away from camp. He would get dressed up and hide in the bushes near a spot he knew she would pass. There he would await an opportune time to let his beloved know of his presence by whispering a few words or composing a tune on a flute. The tunes were original, and whenever a girl heard her boy friend's special tune, she knew he was near.

‡◇‡◇‡◇‡◇‡◇‡◇‡◇

A Brother Came Courting

(OMAHA)

Once there was a young warrior who was highly respected, industrious, and thrifty. He had never married. He had a younger brother who wished to marry a certain maiden, but this brother had never had much success at wooing the young women of the village. The elder brother decided to help the younger man to court the girl of his desires. He began to go down to the spring when he knew the young woman would be there. She was surprised at his attentions but eventually she consented to elope with him. At a prearranged time the maiden slipped away and met the warrior, and together they rode off to the lodge of one of his near relatives where the younger brother was waiting. When the two arrived the bachelor explained to the girl that he had been wooing her for his brother, and the girl, having already compromised herself by running away with her supposed lover, could do nothing but agree to become the wife of the younger man. As it turned out, the two liked each other and had a pleasant marriage.[3]

‡◇‡◇‡◇‡◇‡◇‡◇‡◇

In some societies, flute music was considered particularly seductive to women and so was widely used in courting. A special bird-bone whistle summoned a Flathead maiden to an evening tryst. Each girl knew her lover's tune, and there was a nightly battle of wits between the young girls who were whistled for and their parents, who wanted them either at home at night or at least properly chaperoned. Sometimes a boy without a girl friend would stroll through a village whistling a tune just to see who would answer.

The flute was part of a rather complicated bit of courting tradition among the Crow. If a young Crow woman rebuffed a man's amorous attentions, perhaps during the berry-picking outing described previously, perhaps at some other time, he might grieve for a few days, but then he would attempt to have a supernatural vision of a man playing a flute and attracting all the female animals. The young man would then try to make a flute exactly like the one he had seen in his vision and play it so the young woman he desired would come to him. If the tune actually charmed her into spending the night with him, and provided he was still angry at her for her previous refusal of his attentions, he could take revenge on the maiden by publicly casting her out of his lodge in the morning. If the young woman liked him after all that, she could prepare a special charm of her own to win him back.

Other love charms were used by both men and women in Indian societies. If a Pomo girl on the coast of northern California wanted to gain the love of a certain boy, she made a charm from four white feathers with four of the youth's hairs tied to each feather, then placed the bunch of feathers high in a tree where the wind blew. An Apache girl could go to a special woman practitioner who knew how to cast a love spell using the symbols of sun, water, and sacred butterfly. A common type of Zuni love sorcery allowed a man to gain control of a woman by getting a fragment of her clothing, such as a bit of the fringe of her shawl or belt, and carrying it constantly in his headband or pocket.

Winnebago girls were warned to reject suitors gently, for it was not unknown for a young man who had been humiliated by the girl of his choice to seek out someone who had a special magic medicine which could be used against the girl. The medicinal charm could change a girl from a chaste young woman to a loose one or even a whore.

The practice of love magic was apparently most elaborate in societies where there was a great deal of separation between the sexes. Because the young men and women spent so little time together on a casual basis, sexual anxiety was unduly high in these societies, and institutionalized methods of courtship helped bridge the social distance between men and women. For example, a girl would indirectly find out that a boy was interested in her when his female relatives saw him practicing love magic and mentioned the fact to her aunts or sisters, who would no doubt tell the girl about it or at least discuss it within her hearing. Of course that would make the young man more attractive to the girl, and she might begin to pay a little more attention to him, perhaps shyly returning his smiles and acknowledging his greetings.

SEX AND COURTSHIP

For the majority of tribes, premarital chastity of young women was a cultural ideal not often realized. Young people were allowed a certain amount of dalliance that had nothing to do with seeking a permanent marriage partner. In fact, among the Kaska, of northern British Columbia, premarital intercourse was so common that they believed a young girl did not menstruate until five months after her first sex experience. (The theory that internal injury also brought on menstrual bleeding served as a rationalization for the appearance of menses in girls whose chastity had been closely guarded.)

South of the Kaska, the Kutenai, of southern Alberta, did not demand premarital chastity, but they preferred it. Their daughters received copious moral instruction, including the admonition that a girl who had illicit sexual intercourse or tried to steal other women's husbands would turn into a frog just before her dead relatives came back to live with her at the end of this world. Although this tale probably didn't scare many of the girls, premarital intercourse among the Kutenai was usually part of serious courtship rather than just flirtation, and a girl generally married the man with whom she'd had her first sex experience.

Navajos held a squaw dance, somewhat parallel to the present-day debutante ball, to show off the marriageable young women of the tribe. The young men appeared with their best horses or wagon, and the girls bedecked themselves with jewelry and other finery—even borrowing items. The Navajo girls had the privilege of choosing their dance partners and the right to expect a present in exchange. These maidens were quite bold and forthright, even to the point of leading a reluctant boy off into the bushes with them.

Some particularly strict Navajo parents would not let their daughters attend the squaw dances because they were not well-chaperoned, but in general the Navajo attitude toward premarital sex was liberal, a girl receiving advice about sex from her older female relatives around the time of her first menses. After that, Navajo girls found ample opportunities for clandestine sexual activities if they wished during the long days spent herding sheep on lonely mesas and in hidden canyons. An unmarried Navajo girl was considered a virgin unless she said otherwise or was caught in the act, but her defloration was not considered a great change in status.

A common courting institution in many Native American tribes was "night crawling" or "the creeping lover." A young man would wait until the village was quiet and all were asleep and would then stealthily enter the lodge or tipi of a girl he fancied. If the girl accepted him, he would lie with her until just before daybreak, when he would silently return to his home. A Crow maiden might awake to find an arm thrust under the edge of her tipi and a hand groping for her genitals. A Kaska girl, feeling such a wandering hand, might either squeeze it, in which case the young man would slip under the blanket with her, or scream, so that the boy would be caught and punished. Tlingit parents, on the coast of southern Alaska, forestalled this type of courting by insisting that any unmarried daughter past puberty sleep on a shelf above the parents' bed. Apaches, the archconservatives, considered night crawling disgraceful, and if a man was caught at it, he would be beaten and all his horses killed.

Such nocturnal meetings were popular among the Hopi young people; however, as was typical of the people of the southwestern pueblos, the Hopi were quite accepting of the part sex played in the courtship of the young. Generally a young man would sneak across the village, late at night, wrapped with a blanket to conceal his identity from anyone who might be about at that hour. After stealthily making his way to the girl's side, taking care not to awaken the other members of her household, the boy would gently shake the girl. "Who is it?" she would inquire, but his only answer would be a whispered "It is I," for the girl was supposed to be able to identify the young man by the sound of his voice. If the suitor was acceptable to the Hopi maiden, he would spend the night with her, leaving before morning to avoid detection.

This custom was a source of instruction to younger girls sleeping with older sisters who received secret midnight visits from their lovers. A Hopi girl told an early woman investigator that once when she was about thirteen she spent the night at her grandmother's house, sleeping with her female cousin who was about eighteen. In the middle of the night she was awakened by a disturbance and discovered to her horror that there was a young man in the bed and that he was lying on top of her cousin. The younger girl was just about to scream for help when the other two hushed her, her cousin promising to explain everything in the morning, which she did. The girl who was relating the incident admitted that she felt very strange the next day, "kind of queer all over."[4]

When a Hopi mother discovered that her daughter was receiving these visits—and it was impossible to keep anything a secret very long in the small, tightly knit society—the maiden wasn't even reprimanded for her conduct unless her mother considered the young man unworthy of her daughter's attentions.

At Cochiti, another southwestern pueblo, engaged couples slept together every night, often in the presence of the girl's parents. This type of intimacy was not considered sinful or immoral—in fact, among some groups premarital chastity was more a sign of extreme shyness or unattractiveness than a mark of virtue.

Some tribes accorded young women the privilege of making sexual advances toward the young men. At the Southern Ute bear dances, which ushered in the spring season of sociability, a Ute girl might make a pass at a man by throwing a stick or stone into his lap, as a signal that she wished him to visit her later that night.

It was proper for a Comanche maiden to approach a man seeking a sexual encounter, but it was not acceptable for a youth to be so forward. Comanche custom prevented young couples from being seen together in public, so most courting was done when the girl slipped out of her tipi at night to meet her lover in a prearranged place. Bolder girls, usually a bit older, might crawl into a boy's tipi to initiate love-making. The tipis were dark and the maidens tried to keep their identity secret. Although premarital sex was not subject to heavy moral censure, it was not encouraged, and Comanche girls wished to preserve good reputations.

Among the Natchez, who lived along the lower Mississippi River, maidens did not even attempt to conceal their sexual exploits. In that society the chastity of unmarried girls held no value and as a consequence was nearly nonexistent. An early French explorer wrote, "I am not at all astonished that these girls are lewd and have no modesty since their fathers and mothers and religion teach them that on leaving this world there is a plank very narrow and difficult to pass to enter into grand villages where they pretend they are going after death and only those who have disported themselves well with the boys will pass this plank easily."[5]

Natchez maidens expected and received generous presents from all their lovers, and a girl's reputation rested not on her chastity but on the size of the dowry she was able to amass by her freedom and desirability in her various sexual liaisons.

A report of what sounds like truly open and joyous sexuality came from a traveler among the Mandan in the late 1800s. He was "astounded" when, in a Mandan village, he was awakened about midnight by noises. Looking out from his lodging, he saw about twenty-five stark naked teenagers parading around the village singing and dancing. At times couples retired into the darkness but soon rejoined the others. This traveler must have followed some of these young couples into the woods because he wrote that he found them enjoying one another "with as little ceremony as a common call of nature." After about two hours of revelry, the group went skinny-dipping in the nearby stream, then sat around a fire to dry off.[6]

It is written that among the Huron, who lived north of Lake Ontario, maidens vied for who should have the most lovers. Although these people accepted premarital sex as normal, no overt expressions of sexuality, such as hugging and kissing, were allowed in public, and all trysts took place outside the village, which allowed for some measure of privacy. Anticipating by a few hundred years the liberated youth of today, young Huron men and women sometimes lived together as "companions" without a marriage ceremony. They stayed together as long as they wished, freely seeing other friends, male and female, without fear of reproach.

Yet as free as the Huron appeared to be in comparison to other groups, they apparently still felt some degree of repression from being forced by custom to conduct their sex lives in utmost privacy. In a clear example of how cultures often erect elaborate social structures to allow themselves to transgress other restrictive norms, the Huron devised a curing ceremonial that allowed a public mating of young men and women. A Huron man or woman who was ill could have a dream which prescribed its own cure, and it was not unheard of for someone, particularly an old person, to dream that she would become well if all the young people of the village participated in a special sexual ceremony. All the young unmarried women were called to assemble in the sick woman's house and each was asked whom she wanted for her partner. The men were then notified, and the next night they all arrived at the woman's cabin to have sex with the maidens. The party went on all night, accompanied by the music of two older men stationed at either end of the dwelling who sang and shook tortoise shell rattles until dawn. The sponsor of the ceremony was propped up at one end of the longhouse so she would have a good view of the proceedings.

Of course all of this sexual activity sometimes ended in pregnancy. When an unmarried Huron maiden discovered that she was going to have a baby, her various lovers came to her, each saying that the child was his, and from among them she picked the man she liked best to be her husband.

In the permissive Southwestern pueblos, where illegitimacy was not considered sinful or degrading, the unmarried mother was not looked on with pity or condemnation. Her status was similar to that of a widow with a child.

But such was not the case among all the Native Americans. Very often the unwed mother's bride price was diminished and she and her parents lost prestige. If a pregnant girl's lover married her, the problem was usually soon forgotten. But if the accused father denied the baby was his or if the young woman had had several lovers, the situation might become unpleasant for her.

When an unmarried Ojibwa maiden became pregnant, malicious talk began in the village, and the girl's whole family was acutely embarrassed. The brothers of Ojibwa maidens were particularly concerned with the sexual honor of their sisters: the disgrace of an unmarried sister who became pregnant would force an Ojibwa brave to leave his village for another locality where he was not known. The girl's mother either killed the baby when it was born or else raised it herself, even though another mouth to feed was not always welcome. Young women finding themselves in such a situation probably began to appreciate the advantages of their tribe's "ideal" womanly conduct.

If an unmarried Quinault girl became pregnant, she was forced to name her lover, and her male kinsmen sought him out to force a marriage, killing the young man if he refused. The Hupa of northern California were very strict with their young maidens, but even such a severe cultural tradition did not prevent an occasional seduction. To avoid disgrace a Hupa girl sometimes tried to induce a miscarriage. If she died in the attempt, her seducer, if he was known, was strangled beside the girl's corpse by her male relatives.

ARRANGED MARRIAGES

Marriage in most Native American societies was less a matter of romance than an arrangement for sound economic advantage. The conventional union of a young woman to a man of her tribe was usually arranged by her family with great attention to what was best for the prosperity of the families, the tribe, and, only incidentally, the young woman herself. It often happened that a young woman did not agree with her parents about who would be the best husband for her. Perhaps she was in love with a young man who had been secretly courting her, or maybe her family had in mind for her a wealthy, prestigious man, who unfortunately was quite old and ugly. People today might think that young women subject to arranged marriages generally accepted their lot because "that was all they knew," but nearly every society in which arranged marriages were the rule included in its mythology a legend which strongly reinforced this custom and which warned against infractions. The stories told of the terrible plights which would befall a young woman who did not accept her parents' choice of a mate, and how such disobedience could affect the welfare of the entire tribe.

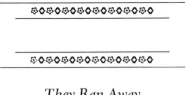

A Snake Comes Courting

(TUNICA)

Long ago among the Tunica [who lived on the banks of the Mississippi River in what is now northeast Louisiana] there was a maiden who was visited by a handsome youth who came every night and left before daybreak. Finally the young man appeared to the girl's parents, asking for her hand in marriage; but the parents refused to give him their daughter because they did not know who the man was. The maiden was foolishly in love with the young man and so one night the youth, having been once again refused by the girl's parents, convinced his sweetheart to run away with him. After the old people were in bed the girl went off with her lover to his house. The house was very nice and his relatives were very good-looking. The couple chatted for a while with the other people in the house and then went off to bed. The girl awoke at daybreak and discovered that instead of lying in the nice house she had seen the previous evening she was now in the middle of the ugliest kind of briar bush. It was a rattlesnake nest and the young man she had married was a rattlesnake. She tried to move but every time she did, all the snakes rattled their tails and she had to lie still all day long. She was so frightened that she held her hands over her eyes so she wouldn't have to look at the snakes. When night came the briar bush turned into a lovely house once more. She quickly walked out and returned to her parents, glad to escape from that place. When she told what had happened all of her relatives gathered together to go out and kill the bad snakes.[7]

They Ran Away

(OMAHA)

There was once a family of three brothers and one sister. Their father was not a chief, but he was respected and honored by the rest of the tribe for his bravery and hospitality. Although the girl had many suitors, there was one man she preferred, and she wished to be his wife. The girl did not communicate her desires to her parents for they had promised her to an aging warrior. When the time came for the wedding the parents led her to the lodge of the older man and the usual ceremonies took place. The maiden did not protest rudely but went along and outwardly acted her part graciously, while vowing never to be the old man's wife. When night came she quietly slipped away into the forest and was gone. Her mother grieved at the loss of her daughter and the disappointed bridegroom and his relatives looked all over for the girl. The maiden's father was silent for he had noticed that a certain young man was also missing from the camp. One day a messenger arrived to the girl's family saying that the runaway had been found and the aging warrior was flogging her to death. The father asked the eldest brother to go and see what was happening but he merely bowed his head. The youngest brother ran for his bow and left immediately to defend his sister. The whole village was watching the old man beat the girl and the young brother was angry that no one had rescued the poor girl.

After the brother had shot the old warrior, a battle started between those who sympathized with the scorned husband and those who sided with the girl. In the ensuing battle father fought son and brother fought brother. When night put an end to the battle many had been slain. In the morning those who had fought on the side of the maiden left the village with the girl's brother and traveled eastward. The opponents picked up their belongings and moved toward the south. There was no wailing or any outward sign of mourning. Silently the living separated and the village was left with the unburied dead.[8]

(There is no mention of what happened to the girl. This is no doubt a function of the fact that the emphasis of the myth is on what can happen to a village or a tribe when conventional customs are flouted.)

In two published autobiographies of Indian women, accounts are given of the anguish felt by both when they learned they were to be married to men they did not know or care for. In *Autobiography of a Fox Woman*, the anonymous story teller recounts how she fell in love with a young man she met surreptitiously while picking berries with a girl friend. The youth was good and kind, but the young Fox woman's parents forbade her to marry him, believing that he would become a lazy wife-beater just like his father. In fact, they threatened to disown their daughter if she so much as spoke with her sweetheart again.

71

The maiden could not forget her beloved, but she did begin to go places with a man her parents had chosen, and gradually she became acquainted with him. After their marriage the young woman's husband treated her nicely, but she never loved him nor did she forget her sweetheart. After their first baby was born the husband's behavior changed, and eventually our narrator divorced him. Shortly after that the wife of her former sweetheart died. After a suitable mourning period of several years they married. They lived blissfully together until the man died suddenly after they had been married a few short years.

Mountain Wolf Woman, a Winnebago who lived along Lake Michigan in Wisconsin, also was forced to marry against her will when her brother gave her away to a man who had done a small favor for him. Mountain Wolf Woman's mother sympathized with her plight but admitted there was nothing she could do, as her son had already arranged the marriage. The frightened and upset young woman was advised that if she did not comply with her brother's wishes he would be embarrassed and disgraced—he might even experience "something unfortunate." Because Winnebago girls were taught to have the highest respect for their brothers, Mountain Wolf Woman finally was swayed. She married the unwelcome suitor but clung to her mother's words, "When you are older and know better you can marry whoever you yourself think that you want to marry." After the birth of her second child, Mountain Wolf Woman left her husband and married a man she liked better.

Among the Coast Salish tribes in Washington a young woman's preference was not considered when her parents selected a mate for her. She was told what was best for her, and, convinced either of the wisdom of her parents' judgment or the futility of resisting, she yielded and was duly lauded for her obedient and respectful behavior. It was maintained that girls were not forced into distasteful alliances; however, when young women married into tribes other than their own, their heads were covered on the journey to the new village so they would not know the way home.

Not every young Indian woman consented to her parents' choice of a husband, threats and tales of what might happen to her notwithstanding. Among the Kaska, in the far north, children were sometimes betrothed as infants. If both children survived but developed a distaste for each other so extreme that they could not be cajoled into acceptance of their chosen mate, a sister or brother was substituted for one of the partners. Elopement was another way young women contrived to escape an arranged match. Some southeastern Salish families of extremely high prestige might agree that their very young children should marry. The father who suggested the union took a present of horses or hides to the other father and immediately received a gift of equal value. From then on it was accepted that the youngsters were married, although they did not live together until after the girl's first menstruation. The only way out of the situation was for one of the pair to elope. Usually the young person who had run away was welcomed back after a short time, for it was said, "What could the parents do?"

Sometimes, however, the couple was found and brought back, and it was not uncommon for a young woman so disgraced to commit suicide by hanging herself or by falling forward on a sturdy pointed digging stick. The story is told of a maiden who had been away with a man for several days. On her return her older sister reprimanded her and told her never to see her lover again. The younger woman took a tumpline and left the house, as if she were going for wood. Later it was discovered that the distraught maiden had hanged herself in the woods.

Sometimes a father might give his daughter as a gift to a man in honor of his valorous conduct. One story tells of some Santee (Eastern Sioux) who were out hunting and found themselves surrounded by their enemies. They all fled to hide in the woods. One of the young women who had accompanied the hunters was protected by a young man in her party, and after the group had returned home the girl's grateful parents offered her to the man who had saved her. The woman belonged to her hero just as her scalp would have belonged to the enemy. This story sounds similar to some of our fairy tales—handsome brave rescues young maiden, they marry and live happily ever after—and apparently the young woman was happy with the arrangement, because a Santee maiden could flatly refuse to subordinate her personal wishes to family arrangements.

Sometimes an Ojibwa father, in southern Ontario, might organize a war party, announcing that he was taking along his daughter and would award her at the end of the campaign to the boldest warrior. He knew that more men would join him in hope of love than in dreams of glory. Of course, this only worked when the maiden was desirable—beautiful and of good reputation. The maiden was closely chaperoned while on the warpath, but as soon as victory was achieved she became the bride of the most outstanding brave.

In cases where a young woman had been very ill, Ojibwa parents might arrange to hand her over to the doctor that cured her. The rationale was that since the daughter would have died without the medicine man's services and since he had brought back life to her, she belonged to him. Because the girl

73

was often very desirable, she was also a munificent reward for the shaman's aid. The story is remembered of one such liaison which had a tragic outcome. An Ojibwa medicine man named Pahwah was generally very successful in his doctoring and could command high fees, but whenever he saved the life of a young woman, he asked for her hand as payment. He acquired three wives in this manner. The third wife was about eighteen when he cured her; he was forty. Now it happened that one of Pahwah's grown sons was already in love with the maiden, and the son became very resentful of his father for marrying all the young women, suggesting that perhaps it might be kind if he were to share with his sons. His father's reply was that if the son wanted a wife so much, he should go and save one for himself. The romance between the son and his young stepmother did not end; in fact, they became more and more attached to each other. After a month of marriage to the old doctor the young woman became desperate. She didn't like the old man, yet she didn't feel it proper to wrong him. Her solution to her dilemma was to hang herself with a leather strap. The grieving young suitor warned his father that henceforth he should get his payment in goods and food, for young girls did not like to marry old men.

Of course there was much individual variation in the pressure put upon a young woman to marry a man of her family's choice. Traditional, autocratic fathers or mothers might not give their daughters any choice at all, while other parents would not consider arranging a marriage for their daughters unless they knew the young man was to her liking. The actions of the more authoritarian parents were probably tempered by the many myths which described in vivid detail the suicides of young women forced to marry men they did not care for. It must be remembered that marriage relationships did not have the heavy overlay of romance and pledges of undying love that they do in our culture; yet there was still room for individual choice even among two or three men, all of whom were excellent hunters and providers.

A Leap to Death

(SANTEE)

A Santee maiden was in love with a young man who was courting her, but her parents would not allow her to marry him. To get away from her suitor, they moved from the village to a place to the north. There they chose a rich old shaman to be the girl's husband. Their daughter warned them that she did not like the man and that she was so desperate she would commit suicide if they insisted on the union. The parents did not heed her remonstrances and insisted she marry the old man anyway. The bride stayed with her new husband for a short time, but she never spoke to him. One day she secretly packed her best dress and went into the woods. Her unhappy husband was watching her, although she did not know it. He trailed her and saw her go to the top of some rocks near a waterfall, where she painted her face, dressed in her best clothes, and undid her braids, letting her heavy hair fall over her shoulders. She sat forlornly for a time, finally hearing a sound and noticing her husband's presence. Speaking to him she said, "I don't want you, yet you follow me."

Then she sang a death song, picked up her shawl, wrapped it over her face, and leapt from the rock. The husband leaned out from the rock to see what had happened to her. About half way down, a spruce tree grew out from a ledge. She had fallen on it and hung there in space. In a few minutes the young woman swung off the limb, and the man saw her smash against the rocks in the water. For years if anyone passed there and mentioned the leaping of a woman, the waves dashed so high that no canoe could pass.[9]

It was not uncommon for an Indian maiden to be paired off with a man much older than she. The theory was that an older, more experienced man would be able to support the young woman better, and she would have an easier life. Young Omaha braves derided this kind of marriage saying, "An old man cannot win a girl, he can only win her parents."

Among the Iroquois nations in the Northeast, it was the mothers who arranged marriages for their children. Both sons and daughters were married to persons older than they, as it was felt they needed a companion experienced in the affairs of life. An experienced woman of thirty or forty sometimes became the wife of a young warrior, while a young girl was married to a widower, who might be over sixty. The arrangements were entirely in the hands of the mothers and other wise women of the village—the young persons receiving no intimation of their impending marriage. It was extremely rare for a young Iroquois woman to reject her mother's choice—she just accepted the older man as a gift from her parents. On the day following the announcement of the marriage the maiden was conducted by her mother and female friends to the home of her intended husband. She took some corn bread or other plant food she had prepared as a symbol of her ability to provide garden produce. In return she received some game from the man, to show that he was a good hunter. This concluded the marriage ceremony.

In Montana, the Gros Ventres also married young women to older men. The girls were wedded before they had even reached puberty, usually to an elderly man with an independent household. This meant that the child bride was widowed early, and a remarriage was quickly arranged for her, perhaps to another older man. By the time she was ready for her third marriage—probably around the age of twenty—the men who were her age would be eligible for marriage and able to benefit from her greater experience in married life.

This experience was also felt to be necessary among the Pawnee of the northern Plains. It was believed that a young maiden was in no position to take on the responsibilities of a household, so she was given a mature man as a husband, while the young Pawnee warrior who needed a capable woman to guide his development was married to someone older. As the young persons matured and entered into other marriages, the situation reversed. A woman who had become competent in the duties of running a home was at last in a position to claim a handsome young brave as her husband. This arrangement was more congenial to the Pawnee culture than it would be among us, for a special joking relationship existed between Pawnee young persons and their grandparents. In fact, the word for grandparent had the connotation that physical familiarity was allowed and that sex relations were a possibility. Not that a young woman would have a sexual relationship with her own grandparent, but the term was used to refer to other persons in that generation as well. Because women bore children fairly soon after puberty, there was not a great age difference between a child and its grandparent.

Even in groups in which young women were allowed quite a bit of choice about whom they wished to marry, it was not generally considered good form for them to refuse too many suitors, especially if these young men were well thought of in the tribe and would be good providers. A maiden would be berated by the rest of her village if she thought no one was good enough for her. There was always a possibility that the young man might be so angered when his attentions were not returned that he might seek the aid of a shaman to bring illness or bad luck to the girl in return for her refusal.

✿◇✿◇✿◇✿◇✿◇✿◇✿◇✿◇✿

The Feces as Suitor

(ASSINIBOINE)

There was once a maiden who refused to marry any of the men who were courting her. She was a very particular maiden, not only in the men she would see but also in the food she ate, for she consumed only the white meat from the neck of a buffalo. Whenever she defecated, her feces were white. Her mother, worried that her daughter was too thin, finally persuaded the girl to eat some of the tongue, considered a choice portion of the buffalo. After the girl ate the tongue her feces were black. She was angry and called them "bad feces."

In the spring the camp moved. The black feces were still angry at the girl for calling them bad names so they called together other feces and all decided to get together in a heap as big as a man. Whenever the people moved in search of buffalo, these feces marched after them in human guise. Whenever the dung-man found a little piece of skin or cloth he picked it up and began to make himself a suit of clothes; after that he found some paint and painted himself up and began to look like a handsome young warrior.

The dung-man finally caught up with the camp and was noticed by the girl's father, who invited the young man into his tipi. He began to question the good-looking stranger, asking him where he came from and what were the names of his people. The suitor answered, "One of the chiefs is called Standing-Hat, another Lie-down-on-the-ground, a third is called Quick and another Big-Ball." The father offered the man some hot soup, and the dung-man, who was frozen into his shape, knew that he would melt if he drank it. Pretty soon he got heated inside and began to soften, so he excused himself to go outside and hunt. Now the girl, who was confined in a menstrual hut, had heard the talking and had taken a peep at this stranger, thinking he was handsome indeed. As the dung-man prepared to leave the camp he threw a stick at the girl's hut. When she came out he asked her to accompany him so she ran and got her clothes in a sack and took off to follow the man. Soon a warm mountain wind came up and the dung-man began to melt. The girl, tracking him, found one of his otter-skin gloves on the ground, put it on, and found it filled with dung. "This glove is full of feces," she said to herself. She*

---

* These terms were explained to be descriptive of feces.

found his moccasins in the same condition. At last she caught up with her suitor. He was lying on the ground, face down, all melted by the heat. His clothes were still in fine shape, but they only covered dung. The girl went home crying and began to sing, "I have followed my own feces."[10]

Carma Smithson, in studying the Havasupai Indians who live in the bottom of the Grand Canyon, attributed their women's reluctance toward marriage not only to an expression of culturally required shyness but also to genuine fear. She saw the timidity of the young women as arising from two conditions: the first was that they were vulnerable to physical abuse from their husbands because the men were usually stronger than the women; and the second was that if the relationship did not turn out well there would be little chance of improving it either by working things out with the man or by leaving him in favor of another man. According to Mrs. Smithson, if a Havasupai woman tried to escape from her husband by running home, her relatives would usually send her back to the man. So the easiest course for a woman would simply be to accept whatever treatment she received. Interestingly the Havasupai women who talked to Mrs. Smithson always spoke of these conditions as objectionable in their own case, while the same women would condone the right of a man to beat a woman if a generalized example of wifely misdoing was presented.[11]

WEDDING CEREMONIES—LAVISH AND SIMPLE

The forms of traditional and acceptable marriage rites varied greatly among Native American societies. The wealthier families usually insisted on a more lavish celebration, while poorer people were no doubt content to let their daughter announce her marriage by simply taking up residence with the bridegroom. In any case, the marriage rite was not a religious sacrament but a contract between the two persons and sometimes their families. Any public ceremony or celebration served to publicize the union to the rest of the village, like today's written records.

It has been reported that the Huron, living north of Lake Ontario, did not attach the same importance that we do to the distinctions between being married and unmarried; instead they recognized various stages of experimentation and growing commitment between a man and a woman that did not stabilize into a permanent union until children were born. The parents of the young people helped to arrange the first "marriage," but the typical arrangement was at first just an agreement to remain together so long as each provided the services the other had a right to expect.

Among the Cherokees, who lived in the area of what is now eastern Tennessee, the whole town gathered to provide young couples with a ceremony heavily symbolic of what their roles would be as mature members of the society. On the day of the wedding the bridegroom feasted with his male comrades in a lodge a little way from the council house while the bride was joined by her companions for a feast in another building. Later they met with the rest of the community in the council house where the groom's mother gave him a leg of venison and a blanket and the bride received from her mother an ear of corn and a blanket. Then the couple exchanged the gifts of food and enclosed themselves together in the blankets. (Cherokees called divorce the "dividing of the blankets.")

It was often expected that the bridegroom would give valuable gifts to the young woman and her family; in many societies the bride's family was expected to reciprocate with goods of similar value. Although the gifts given by the bridegroom have been called the "bride-price," they signified a transaction much more meaningful than the purchase of the sexual and household services of a woman. The payments and reciprocal payments legitimized the marriage, created social and political alliances, and served as surety that the husband and wife behaved properly toward one another. As anthropologists Dorothy Hammond and Alta Jablow commented in their perceptive article on women's economic role, "The argument that brideprice makes [a woman] chattel is irrelevant. For her the issue is the legitimacy of her marriage. As a matter of fact a woman does take pride in the high price paid for her because this attests to the high status of her family and her husband. So long as there are no alternatives to consider, and there are few in intact traditional societies, women accept this situation and indeed derive satisfaction from their success within the established system."[12] A wife "purchased" in this way was really not a commodity, for she had the right to expect her husband to provide some services, such as protection from the enemy and economic support. Actually it was the young men who had reason to object to the brideprice. It was difficult for a young man to amass a great deal of property, and although his kin usually helped provide him with the goods he needed to get a wife, he was left heavily in debt.

As a general rule, the customs relating to marriage ceremonies and gift exchange pertained only to a young woman's first marriage or to those sub-sequent unions which occurred when she was quite young. As a woman became older she was usually given more leeway in arranging her own mar-riages. If custom did not entirely eliminate the giving of gifts in a second or third marriage, at least the quantity and quality of gifts were reduced.

The importance of the bride-price was greatly stressed among the Yurok, who lived on the coast of northern California. The social ranking of the entire family—husband, wife, and children—depended on how much was paid for the woman. Wealthy men paid large sums for their brides so that their own status and that of their future children would be high. When the daughter of a wealthy man was sent to the village of her new husband, her father usually sent a considerable amount of property with her, voluntarily returning part of the payment made to him. This large payment on the part of the bridegroom constituted "full marriage," and the man was entitled to take his bride to live in his town and to keep the children if the marriage ended in divorce. When his own daughters matured and married, their bride-price would go to him, and if his sons were killed, he would collect the blood money paid by the culprit. A poor man who could not afford such high payment was not barred from marriage, however. The bride of a poor young man entered a "half marriage" in which her husband paid about half her rated value and went to live with her in her father's house. The husband remained under his father-in-law's direction, working for him and contributing to his household. The children belonged to the wife and her family, with any marriage payments or blood money staying within her family. Half marriage was legitimate but obviously connoted relatively low social rank.

The following is an account of a typical Cheyenne wedding, which was similar to those in most other Plains societies during the height of the buffalo culture in the 1800s. Usually the marriage of a Cheyenne maiden was in the hands of her parents, but in some cases they might give their daughter over to a particular brother or cousin, who would then have charge of her marriage. When a young man fell in love with a girl, he did everything he could to ingratiate himself with the person who controlled her marriage. After he was fairly sure that he would be accepted by both the maiden and her family, the suitor told his own family about his plans. If they approved, they helped him gather together presents and load them on horses which were led to the tipi of the girl's father or brother by one of the young man's relatives. The horses were staked outside the lodge while the emissary went inside to smoke, make small talk, and finally state the purpose of his mission. It was understood that the proposal would be accepted or rejected within twenty-four hours. If the family council decided that the marriage was unacceptable for some reason, the horses were led back to the young man's lodge. But if the decision was favorable, the young woman's relatives unloaded the goods from the suitor's horses, everybody taking what they wanted, including the horses, with the understanding that within one or two days they would have to return other goods equal to or exceeding the value of what they had taken.

When the return gifts had all been accumulated, the bride was dressed in fine new clothing and mounted on the best of the horses being sent to her new husband. Her mother and other women relatives led the rest of the gift-packed horses, and they all set out for the lodge of the young man's father. When they arrived, all the bridegroom's female relatives came running out, helped the bride to dismount, and carried her into the lodge so she would not have to step over the threshold. Her husband's sisters and cousins removed the clothing she was wearing, dressed her in new clothing they had made, combed and rebraided her hair, and painted her face. Then the newly married couple sat side by side, and a small feast was served. The couple lived with the bridegroom's family until the two mothers and their relatives, assisted by the bride, had gotten together enough household goods for the newlyweds to live alone. The bride's mother pitched the new tipi near her own, and a new family was begun.

When a young couple eloped, the parents would hasten to legitimize the marriage by making the usual exchange of gifts as soon as the youngsters had returned to camp.

Marriages in the societies that lived on the northwest coast of the continent also involved much reciprocal gift giving, particularly among wealthy and aristocratic families. Among the Coast Salish, of British Columbia, the formal marriage proposal was always made by the boy's father or other near male relative. If the family had sent out discreet feelers and were assured of acceptance, the young man and his family set out in canoes loaded with gifts, paddling up to the young woman's door. The door was always barred to them, and then there began long and repetitious speeches praising the families and stressing the desirability of the match. When the door was finally opened, negotiations immediately stalled, and the boy's relatives and speakers departed for a while, leaving the young fellow alone inside the door sitting on a pile of blankets. He sometimes had to sit there for several days, nearly motionless, eating nothing, leaving only to relieve himself. The prospective bride was nowhere to be seen. When the boy's relatives returned, there were more speeches, and after each flattering speech the girl's family presented the speaker with a blanket, making no other comment. It was a matter of prestige for them to be able to boast later of how difficult they had made it for the young man's people.

─────────────────────

The Proud Father

(TLINGIT)

A great chief had a daughter who was desired by many men as a wife, but he was too proud to give her to anyone but another chief. He owned an ugly dog who one night in the guise of a man went to the daughter and asked her if she would have him as a husband. Since he had a handsome appearance the girl agreed and later she gave birth to eight puppies, seven males and one female. The father flew into such a rage that he and his whole tribe abandoned the young woman, destroying the food supplies and putting out the fires in order that she might starve to death. However, one of the chief's relatives, who was sympathetic to the young woman's plight, hid some food and embers under the threshold so that the chief's daughter could make a fire and have some food until she could catch salmon. The hidden provisions helped during the first difficult days, but the mother still had to be away from her children for long hours trying to get enough food for them to live. As long as she was away from the house her children played with each other in human form— the seven little boys danced around the fire while the little girl watched at the door for their mother's return. As soon as the little girl saw the mother approaching, all the children returned to their dog forms. Once the mother suspected something and quietly sneaked up on the house. Seeing her children in human form with their dog clothing hanging on the wall, she ran into the house and immediately threw the dog clothes into the fire. From then on the children remained human.[13]

─────────────────────

The day after the proposal was accepted all the villagers were invited to a feast. Speakers from both families paid flattering tributes to all and admonished the young couple to do all they could to have a good marriage and bring honor to the family name. Then the canoes were unloaded and the gifts were given to the bride's family, who distributed them among the assembled guests. The bride and groom left for the young man's home, accompanied by substantial gifts from the bride's father, including food, blankets, and canoes. These gifts made from the bride's father to his new son-in-law were not an unencumbered asset; the son-in-law had to pay out some of the goods at a marriage announcement celebration when he and his new wife got back to his village, and some of his relatives who had contributed to the bride-price might demand compensation for their gifts.

Among the Tlingit, another northwest coast group, if the bride's father was very wealthy and owned a number of slaves, he might assign one of them to carry the bride's gifts to her new home—he might even give her the slave. This act substantially raised the status of the families involved, and for years it was remembered that "a slave carried her possessions." If two women were quarrelling, and one of them wanted to outdo the other in a discussion of family prestige, she might taunt, "In your family did a slave carry a daughter's possessions?"

The newlyweds visited back and forth between their two families until they had accumulated enough to build their own home. The young woman always returned to her mother's home for the birth of her first child, after which the young couple usually established their own household.

Of course all this ceremony pertained only to the upper class. Among common people, when a young man wanted a wife, his parents talked to the girl's parents, a few friends were invited in for a meal, a small amount of property was exchanged to formalize the marriage, and the couple lived together as man and wife.

The Rejected Suitor

(QUINAULT)

The daughter of the chief of a certain village was being courted by a worthless young fellow who was something of a wastrel. The girl was attracted to him because he had a powerful guardian spirit. The maiden was sequestered in her puberty cell in the family home but the young man used to come and talk to her through the outside walls. The girl allowed herself to be persuaded to elope with the young man, and one night he loosened two of the wall planks so she could escape. He had brought with him a large bag made of cattail rushes which he had stuffed with moss, but he told the girl it was full of furs and blankets and should make an acceptable present for her parents. They left the bag in the cell and started off.

One of the chief's slaves, who had been suspicious of the girl's conduct, saw her escaping and followed her, finally persuading her to return. The hapless suitor was warned to stay away after that, but he kept lurking around. In a few months the maiden was married to the chief of a neighboring village. He gave her parents four ocean canoes, five slaves, and a quantity of dentalia (shell money) before he took her away to live in his own village.

A year later, just before the birth of their first child, the couple returned to the young wife's village so her mother could attend her during her labor. The former suitor heard she was back and came to the village. The young woman was frightened of him, remembering that he had vowed to use his strong guardian spirit to prevent her being anyone else's wife. Because of her fear the young woman persuaded her mother to go with her to another place for the birth. As they went down the river in a canoe, the rejected suitor watched them go from a bluff. The pregnant woman hid under a blanket, but he knew she was there, and he shot his power into her, and soon the young woman felt a pain in her back. That night the woman was delivered of a stillborn child. She bled profusely, blood even running from her mouth. In her last moments she told her mother what she surmised was the cause of her death.

Her grieving father immediately dispatched two of his slaves to find the young man and kill him, which they did by ripping open his abdomen and stabbing him in the back.[14]

❀◇❀◇❀◇❀◇❀◇❀◇❀◇❀◇❀◇❀◇❀◇

Marriage was a particularly traumatic experience for young women who grew up in societies which did not allow any friendly interchange between adolescent boys and girls. The Papago, of the southern Arizona deserts, rigidly separated boys and girls. A girl, who was rarely out of her mother's sight, was not allowed to speak to any man unless he was a relative. If a man stopped by her home when she was there alone, she was instructed to offer him food and then leave the house. So it was a frightful ordeal for a girl when her parents noticed that her breasts were beginning to swell ("They should be used for something," it was said) and began to arrange a marriage for her. The maiden's extended family gathered to discuss who might be a good match, and when a young man had been chosen, the girl's parents paid a visit to his family with the proposal. It was necessary that the prospective bridegroom live in another village, for persons living in the same village were always too closely related to marry. There might be a slight interchange of gifts, as a courtesy, but unlike the people of the Plains and the rich northern coast, the desert people were poor and did not have any means of accumulating large amounts of property for lavish gifts.

If the proposal was accepted, the maiden's parents returned home and devoted the next month to further instruction of their daughter. As she would be living with her new husband's family, she was told to work industriously for them and to consider the new village her home for the rest of her life.

When her parents felt their daughter was sufficiently prepared for marriage, they notified the other family. The new couple spent their first four nights together at the bride's home, so that the young woman could have her mother near during what was for her a difficult time. The mother instructed her daughter not to fear the young man, saying, "If he wants anything, don't be afraid of him," adding that she should try to comply with his wishes without restraint. The bridegroom would arrive after the family had bedded down, sleep with his new wife, and leave before dawn, for he would have been ashamed to be seen leaving in daylight. The morning following the bridegroom's four nocturnal visits the bride's mother led her to her new home, taking a little present.

The terrified brides would sometimes run away and have to be caught by their mothers. One, named Rustling Leaves, hid in a large granary basket and had to be dragged out. Chona, the Papago woman we met in previous chapters, told how afraid she was of her husband. She had never talked to a man before and did not know what to say. "Maybe I never would have talked to him; I don't know," she related. "Only one night when we went to bed there was a rattlesnake in our bed. I screamed. He said: 'Get up and we'll shake our bedding.' After that I felt more at home."[15]

Apparently some young Papago women were even more recalcitrant. The story is told of some parents who appealed to the headman of their village, complaining that their daughter, who had just been married, would not sleep with the man they had given her. The headman knew that the husband was an old man but that he was all right, and so he assumed that the girl was just scared. The chief threatened the girl with a whipping, even going so far as to tie her hands to the post. Then she began to cry and consented to go off with her husband.

Apache maidens had also been taught to be very shy around men and consequently were usually terrified of their husbands during the first days of their marriage. Generally a young Apache suitor first sought his family's approval of his prospective bride and then sent an intermediary to the maiden's family to plead his cause. The go-between spoke of the young man's fine qualities and mentioned the gifts he would give his future in-laws. One or two horses or their equivalent was an average gift. If the proposal was accepted, the youth's mother or another female relative went to fetch the girl. Sometimes the maiden was expected to sleep with her new husband from the first night, but usually she was so shy that she slept with his mother or sisters for the first three or four nights, leaving before dawn to avoid embarrassing contacts with her new in-laws. She also ate and spent the day in her own parents' camp. After the first few days she remained in her new husband's camp for perhaps a month, until her mother had constructed for the couple a new wickiup, or grass house, near her own home.

An alternate method of arranging marriages, sometimes used by the Western Apaches, was for a maiden's parents simply to send her to the camp of a youth they admired. This was considered a great honor to the youth and his family, but the young woman in question usually found such a mission extremely distasteful, for there was no assurance that she would be accepted, and a refusal would be a cruel blow to her pride. To lessen the young woman's embarrassment, she was often accompanied by a companion—a sister or intimate friend. When the two girls arrived at the youth's camp, they stood in the doorway and the companion told his mother they had come to spend the night. If they were not welcome, they were simply told to go back home, and they left immediately, the humiliated maiden no doubt extremely angry with her parents for putting her in such a shameful position. If the two young women were accepted, they spent the night sleeping with the youth's sisters or mother.

Apache newlyweds had usually not lost their self-consciousness with each other when it was time for them to move into their own wickiup, so sometimes a companion couple was sent along to ease their discomfort for a while. The companions did not have to be married or even courting but were usually relatives of the newlyweds. The bride slept next to the wall, her companion beside her, the groom's companion next, and then the groom, next to the fire.

An old Apache woman recalled her shyness the first night she slept all alone with her husband: "I lay there stiff with fright and embarrassment, hardly daring to breathe. I was cold all over and my body shook. My heart was beating very fast. I don't think I moved the whole night long. I guess my husband was the same way."[16] Apparently she was not the exception.

Among the Jicarilla Apache, the young people were strongly pressured to marry within their own tribe. The elders warned that any Apache who married a Ute would become an owl after death; marrying a Navajo would cause reincarnation as a mountain lion. Worst of all was marrying a Mexican, which would lead to rebirth as a burro, or an Anglo, which would ensure return as a mule. It was thought that mules and burros would give a loud hee-haw whenever they saw a Jicarilla Apache who had married or had had sex with a Mexican or an Anglo.

The marriage customs among the Hopi of northern Arizona were in keeping with the general Hopi emphasis on individual freedom. We have already discussed the ways in which a Hopi maiden might directly propose marriage to a young man, although it was permissible for a young man to initiate marriage plans. Once a union had been approved, the elaborate marriage rites were mainly the responsibility of the bride and the female relatives of both the bride and groom. The ceremonies varied in minor details from village to village, but in general they closely paralleled those at Old Oraibi, where the girl began wedding preparations by first grinding cornmeal and making piki (cornmeal wafer bread) for several days at her mother's home, then going to her future mother-in-law's home and spending the next three days, grinding cornmeal from before dawn until late at night. She was not only demonstrating her competence but also in a way compensating the boy's mother for the loss of the young man's services around the house and in the fields.

At some point during the three days the paternal aunts of the youth arrived and staged a mock battle, which usually included an uproarious mud fight. The aunts berated the young bride, calling her stupid and lazy, while moaning that she had stolen their sweetheart. The whole episode was really a good-natured ribbing and indicated that the older women liked the young bride and thought she was making a good choice for a husband. On the fourth morning, long before sunrise, the young woman's female kin came to the groom's house, bringing all the cornmeal and piki the bride had previously prepared. The bridegroom's female relatives came too, and the two mothers, assisted by their women kin, washed the heads of the newlyweds in one basin, finally twisting the hair of the young couple into one strand to unite them for life. When their hair was dry the couple went to the edge of the mesa to pray to the rising sun.

After the wedding breakfast the bridegroom and his immediate relatives, often assisted by other men of the town, descended to a kiva (underground ceremonial chamber) and began to weave the bride's wedding garments.

(Men do all the weaving in Hopi towns.) Two white wedding robes, one large and one small, were woven first; then a long wide belt. White buckskin leggings and moccasins completed the outfit. During the preparation of this outfit the bride remained with her mother-in-law industriously grinding corn-meal and doing other housework.

It took a long time for the bride to grind enough cornmeal to pay for her wedding garments; sometimes her new husband actually had to plant and raise some corn before she could begin. As was mentioned in the chapter on childbirth, many young Hopi women lost their first child due to the excessive amount of grinding they were expected to do. Yet it was most important to have the wedding garments, for they were a woman's passport to paradise. When a Hopi woman died, her body was wrapped in the small wedding robe, which had been preserved in a reed case, and tied with the wedding belt. The robe served as wings to carry her soul to the House of the Dead, and the belt guided her in her spiritual flight. It was necessary for a woman to have only one such robe, so the ceremonial weaving was usually omitted in the case of a subsequent marriage. Some women, concerned for their afterlife, married simply to get the special robe.

When the weaving was finished, the bride was dressed in the completed garments and led back to her mother's home. Her new husband joined her there, and the couple took up permanent residence in that household, perhaps in time adding another room to the rock and mud pueblo-style dwelling. From then on the bride and her mother could expect the young man to work their fields, supply them with wood, and in other ways contribute to the support of the household. The bride's mother was a matriarch and ruled the household, but she usually got along well with her son-in-law, even though they all lived in one house.

MOTHER-IN-LAW TABOO

In many societies in which newlyweds took up residence near the bride's parents, it was necessary for the young couple to have a separate dwelling, for there was a rigidly enforced taboo forbidding any contact between the bride's mother and her son-in-law. Commonly called the "mother-in-law taboo," this custom no doubt eliminated much strife in Indian families.

The upholding of this taboo was so important to the Navajo that the bride's mother was not even allowed to be present in the hogan during her daughter's wedding, although sometimes a curious mother might sneak a quick peek at the ceremonies through a crack between the logs of the hogan. If the mother did not know her new son-in-law, she would have to take a hasty look at him so she would be able to recognize the person she had to avoid. The taboo was observed until the death of the mother or the son-in-law; even if a woman's daughter divorced and remarried several times, the older woman would have to avoid all her previous sons-in-law. It was felt that persons who broke the taboo would become ill or would be seized by a type of insanity that would force them to jump into the fire.

Surprisingly, although the Navajo husband and his mother-in-law were forbidden to "see" each other, they strove to be particularly helpful to the other. The avoidance and helpfulness combined to build up a special sort of respect between the two. Among the many other societies insisting on mother-in-law avoidance were the Apache, the Sioux, the Cree, and the Cheyenne.

The Blackfoot people also observed a strong mother-in-law taboo, but there were socially acceptable ways of adjusting the restriction when necessary. If a woman's son-in-law was ill and there was no one else to care for him, she could do so; upon his recovery the taboos were permanently removed for them. Or if a man went out to war or was missing, his mother-in-law might pray for his safe return, vowing that if her prayers were answered she would shake hands with him, give him a horse, and no longer feel ashamed in his presence. However, even if the taboo against meeting and talking was removed, custom did not allow the man and his mother-in-law to live in the same tipi; instead, a small tipi was set up for her outside her daughter's dwelling if she were a widow.

AFFECTION AND ROMANCE

Marriage partners in early America did not have to be in love with each other to have a satisfactory life together. In many societies, especially those in which parents arranged the marriages, a woman did not expect to have her needs for companionship and intimacy fulfilled by her husband. Marriage was seen more as a vehicle for economic cooperation and child rearing.

An example is found in the Kuskowagamiut Eskimos, of the far North. There marriage partners probably remained silent and cool toward one another during the first years of marriage, and normally would not talk together in the intimate way modern husbands and wives do. Husbands didn't even live with their wives; instead they worked, played, and slept in the men's house, or kashgee. The wife, her daughters, and young sons lived in the family home. When a daughter grew up and married she remained in her mother's house raising her children there. Under these circumstances we would not expect to find the husband and wife forming a close-knit partnership, although as time went on the couple became closer and developed affection for each other.

There were of course many couples who were very much in love from the beginning of their marriage and others who developed deep and abiding affection for each other after years of living and working together. As one Papago woman put it, "I had grown fond of him. We had starved together so much."

❀◈❀◈❀◈❀◈❀◈❀◈❀◈

The Buffalo Rock

(ASSINIBOINE)

In Montana, where the buffalo were once thick, there was a rock which looked very much like a buffalo lying down. The Assiniboine tribe considered the rock sacred and whenever a band passed by the rock they would camp nearby, making offerings to the boulder in thanksgiving for their wealth or health or to ask for success in hunting or warfare.

One time a group of Assiniboine were traveling in search of buffalo; it was a time of famine, for the great beast on which the tribe so depended had seemingly vanished. When the group passed the sacred Buffalo Rock they laid offerings there, asking for food. Toward the rear of the band of Indians was a young newly married couple. They were traveling very slowly because the husband was weak from illness and lack of food. He walked with the aid of his wife, for his feet were sore from hunting on foot and his moccasins were worn through. The man crawled to the rock alone, since no women were allowed near the shrine, and laid down his offering, remaining for a while in silent prayer. Then the two continued their journey, but because they were traveling so slowly the rest of the group soon left them behind.

The young couple camped alone near a small creek where many willows grew. The wife gathered willows, and together the two constructed a small shelter for the night. They built a fire, but there was no food to cook. After a while the man began to speak with much effort, recalling their plans to build themselves a fine skin tipi—plans that were now dashed because the buffalo had disappeared and he was not able to collect the hides that were needed. He continued, "We are still together, but alone. Our people have gone on. We still wish much to always sit beside each other, although seven moons have passed since you became my sit-beside-me-woman." He urged his wife to leave him behind—to continue on alone and join the others, but she refused, saying she had come to stay with him forever.

Their conversation was cut short by a crash of thunder, followed by much wind and rain. The storm did not last long. It was the kind of storm carried on by young restless Thunder Birds who delighted in coming suddenly on prey to destroy it and also to cast fear into people who have not made their sacrifices to the Thunder Birds. They did not always come to destroy but sometimes completed a mission for good. But the rain almost put the fire out, so the woman went out to gather more dead wood to build it up again.

She soon came running back, breathless. She had found three buffalo who had taken shelter from the storm in the woods near the creek. The husband was grieved that he was not able to go out and kill the buffalo, but the wife had a plan. Seeing that her husband was still strong enough to draw a bow, she would carry him on her back. It was dusk when they crept toward the buffalo, who were huddled together, their backs to the wind, unmindful of the strangely mounted hunter.

A kill was made, and the two butchered the animal, carrying the choicest parts back to the shelter for a joyous supper. Before eating they gave thanks to the Sacred Buffalo and the Thunder Birds who had driven the buffalo close to their camp.

The next morning the young wife caught up with the rest of the group, and several hunters went back and killed the other two buffalo who were still nearby. Many pipes were filled and offered to the Buffalo Rock.[17]

POLYGAMY

Sisters in some Indian societies were so close that they spent their entire lives in each other's company—sleeping on the same mat as children, working together at women's tasks, even sharing the same husband. The widespread custom of one man marrying all the sisters in one household is called sororal polygyny. Sometimes the custom included cousins, nieces, aunts, or other female relatives as eligible co-wives. Although there were societies in which a woman might find herself the co-wife of a woman not her sister, generally it was believed that co-wives who were related would form a more harmonious household.

Even in those societies which permitted polygamy—or rather polygyny, since we are talking only about multiple wives—a man could have only as many wives as he could support, so the practice was usually limited to the headmen or very good hunters. Among the Gabrielino, of southern California, monogamous marriages were the rule for everyone except the chief. Because he was expected to dispense large quantities of food and property to visiting officials and guests on public occasions, he needed the help of two or more wives to gather enough food to fulfill his ceremonial duties.

A similar custom was found among the Omaha, where it was usually only the prominent men who had more than one wife. The wife of a man who was a public figure had much extra work, including cooking for many guests and manufacturing fancy gift items. There was no serving class, so if the work got too much for her, it was not possible to hire any help. A man who noticed that his wife was becoming overworked, or even a man who just wanted another woman, might reason with his wife, saying, "I wish you to have less work to do, so I am thinking of taking Pretty Moon [or whoever] for my wife. She can then help you with the work." It was necessary for a man to obtain his first wife's permission before he could marry any other woman. The first wife always retained control of the household affairs, including the distribution of food.

The first wife usually maintained a higher status than any of her co-wives. In fact, sometimes a Sioux woman would suggest that her husband take a young wife, realizing that this would relieve her of some of the burdens of housekeeping while giving her added status as the senior spouse of a well-to-do man, since it was common knowledge that a man had to be fairly wealthy to afford more than one wife. Although in most of the tribes living on the Great Plains the junior wives had to do most of the chores, sometimes they didn't mind for they were not watched very closely by their husbands. If they were young, it was generally assumed that they had lovers among the young men of the tribe.

This customary dominance by the older wives was reversed among the Eyak, of Alaska. Although it was said a man would not sleep with an old or barren wife, he would not divorce her. Instead, he would marry a young woman and relegate the older wife to practically the status of a slave.

Polygamy was extensively practiced by the Southeast Salish tribes. There a woman with several co-wives not related to her usually continued to live with her own family, receiving her husband whenever he cared to visit. Salish women placed great emphasis on physical appearance, and a woman was envied and respected if she had a handsome husband, whether he supported her well or not. Since these people lived in the Northwest, a region of comparative plenty, it didn't matter too much if a woman had the support of a man or not, for an able-bodied woman was capable of taking care of all her personal needs. She could always trade some of her roots and berries for salmon or venison, and she was welcome in the home of her parents or other relatives. Nevertheless, it was nice to have a husband of one's own, and this led to considerable quarrelling among co-wives, and subsequently to a high rate of divorce.

There were many cases where co-wives, particularly sisters, got along beautifully, enjoying each other's company as well as sharing the chores, but the greater number of stories pertain to the jealousies and arguments that arose. In fact, among the Papago the joking term for a co-wife meant "one with whom I have a relation of jealousy," and Gros Ventre co-wives addressed each other as "rival" unless they were sisters.

❖◇❖◇❖◇❖◇❖◇❖◇❖◇

The Bluejay and the Deer

(Y U R O K)

The panther had two wives—the bluejay and the deer. As was the custom among the people, the panther slept in the sweathouse rather than with his wives. Every day the deer sent her daughter to carry some acorn soup to the panther. It was very good soup, but every day the bluejay would waylay the daughter, take the soup away from her, and eat it. One day the panther realized what was going on and took the soup and ate it himself. It was the best soup he had ever tasted, and from then on he always made sure that he received the deer's soup. The bluejay got jealous, so she sneaked over to where the deer was making the soup and tried to find out how she made it so delicious. She saw the deer take a rock, hit her front leg with it, and let some bone marrow run into the soup. The jealous bluejay, thinking that she could do likewise, went home and hit her own leg, but only slime came out. (You can still see the knot on the bluejay's leg.) When the panther ate the bluejay's soup it tasted so terrible that he paid no more attention to her. The poor bluejay got so

93

jealous that she jumped all around all the time. The panther noticed her odd behavior and one day he asked her what was wrong with her. The bluejay got so angry that she pulled out her clitoris and stuck it on top of her head.[18]

❀◈❀◈❀◈❀◈❀◈❀◈❀◈❀◈❀◈

In the Muskogee tribe, part of the Creek federation in the Southeast, a man had to have his first wife's permission to take additional wives, and the secondary wives were in a position of handmaidens. If the first wife refused her permission and the man took another wife in defiance of her wishes, the first wife would often ask her female relations to help her fight the new wife. The goal was disfigurement, the original wife using her nails to claw the face of the interloper and whipping her with switches. One early observer reported seeing a wife lashing another woman, crying, "You think it is honey, but I will make it vinegar before I am done with you." But a woman who fought in this way ended up the loser, for custom decreed that she yield her rights and move away while the new wife took over her position.

Great shame was felt by any Ojibwa woman whose husband took another wife, and her wounded self-esteem was only aggravated by the talk of the rest of the villagers, who openly speculated on just what qualities the woman lacked that forced her husband to take another wife. Most wives left their husbands when they came home with another woman, and most refused to come back even if the man promised to return the second wife. Even women who were married to shamans and had reason to fear their power and wrath sometimes felt so humiliated that they gathered their courage and left.

The story was told to anthropologist Landes of an Ojibwa woman named Giantess whose husband, Walker, had a second wife in another village. Walker managed to keep the two women apart until one day both villages had to meet to sign a treaty. During a fit of spite, the younger wife, Grey Girl, threw boiling blueberry jam in Giantess' face, burning her badly. Giantess was, of course, very angry, and made Walker promise that he would not return to his second wife; he consented on the provision that she would not gossip about the quarrel. Some months later, Walker was getting ready to go to a dance and, upset that Giantess had not made some new moccasins for him, he went to Grey Girl's tipi and got a pair from her. Later Giantess saw Grey Girl going to the dancing place.

The anger that Giantess had been nursing for months was fanned. She gathered her belongings and packed them in a canoe. Then she sharpened a butcher knife. The dancing was in a lodge made of birch bark, and Grey Girl was sitting with her back to the wall. Giantess lifted out a piece of bark and addressed the other woman saying, "My, you hurt me badly the time you burned me. Now it's my turn to hurt you." With that she raised the butcher knife and slashed Grey Girl's face, cutting her cheek open and removing a piece of nose and ear. Then she said, "I am leaving you with my husband. You can have him all to yourself. I can go and get a man who is not some woman's husband." Then she got into her canoe and paddled down the river.

Polygyny served several functions in Indian societies. For example, in many tribes sexual intercourse was taboo for a woman from the beginning of pregnancy to the time she weaned the baby—a period of up to three or four years. Polygyny provided a socially sanctioned outlet for the man whose wife was sexually restricted and also for the man who just couldn't restrain his appetite for a variety of women. The "other woman" was put into the role of "another woman," and what might have become a disruptive situation for both the family and the tribe was integrated into the social structure.

Polyandry, or the practice of one woman having more than one husband, was unheard of over most of the North American continent. The Kaska Indians, of extreme northern British Columbia, were one of the rare tribes in which this type of marriage was found. The Kaska restricted polyandry to old men who were unable to hunt sufficiently to support their families. The old man, with the consent of his wife, invited a younger brother or other close relative to come and live with him. The auxiliary husband was allowed to have sex with the wife only when the older man was gone on a trip; and it was expected that the woman would report the younger man's attentions to the senior husband when he returned. It was also expected that when the older man died, the younger husband would continue to look after the widow.

A story that illustrates how such a practice might have developed is told by the Tlingit, western neighbors of the Kaska. Two sisters were married to a man named Tiget. Tiget's nephew, JD, came to live in the household when he was a small boy. Tiget much preferred the younger of his two wives, rarely sleeping with the older wife and never having sexual relations with her. During cold weather the elder sister often asked JD if he were cold and invited him to her bed where she would cuddle him like a child. The years passed and JD became a young man. One day when JD was about eighteen, Tiget and the younger wife and their children went on a trip. When JD returned to the camp later that day the elder sister was taking a bath. It was the first time JD

95

had seen her naked. She told him that she was "man hungry" as her husband never came near her. Later that night the two enjoyed each other sexually. The woman knew immediately that she was pregnant. The next day they decided that when Tiget returned, his wife would tell him what had happened and suggest that he give her to his nephew as a wife, for that was sometimes done. The older man wasn't angry and told JD that he and the woman could set up housekeeping any time they wished. But JD decided that people might tease the uncle for losing his wife to a younger man, so the matter was just left at that. In nine months the woman gave birth to a child, but JD never slept with her again, since he did not wish to have any more children before his uncle died (and he came into his inheritance). After a few years she died. When the old man died, JD, being the man's full heir, wished to marry the younger sister. The young widow refused because JD had previously been her older sister's lover.

DIVORCE

Divorce was common and easy for most Native American women. If a woman was living with her husband's family, she simply took her belongings and perhaps the children and went home to her parents. If the couple was living with the wife's parents or if the dwelling was considered hers, she told the man to leave, throwing his clothes and paraphernalia out after him. Common grounds for divorce were sterility, adultery, laziness, bad temper, and cruelty.

One reason for the frequency of divorce may have been that many couples were the victims of mismatings caused by arranged marriages. While a woman might accede to such an arrangement in her youth, as she gained maturity she was granted more power over her life and was then able to satisfy her own inclinations as far as a husband was concerned.

The early Christian missionaries were concerned about this lack of marital stability. In 1624, Father Joseph Le Caron wrote about the Labrador Eskimos of northern Quebec: "One of the greatest obstacles to their conversion is that most of them have several wives, and that they change them when they like, not understanding that it is possible to submit to the indissolubility of marriage. 'Just see,' they tell us, 'You have no sense. My wife does not agree with me and I cannot agree with her. She will be better suited with such a one who does not get on with his wife. Why, then, do you wish us four to be unhappy the rest of our days?' "[19]

In some tribes it wasn't quite as easy for a woman to obtain a divorce as it was for a man. A Gros Ventre woman could expect to be received back into her family only if her husband had grossly neglected her; otherwise it was assumed that a wife usually deserved whatever treatment she had received. The Flathead, neighbors of the Gros Ventre in Montana, were likewise intolerant of husband desertion. If a woman thought her parents might be likely to return her to the deserted spouse, she might visit another camp for a while. It was part of Flathead hospitality to kindly receive a woman in that position. On the other hand, a Flathead man who wished to divorce his wife merely tied a horse near her door. This was not only a gentle hint for her to move away but also made it easier for her to do so.

Although most women in the Plains tribes could divorce their husbands easily by going home to their parents, the men had the option not only of divorcing their wives but of publicly disgracing them at the same time. At a public dance a husband could hit the drum and announce that he was throwing his wife away and whoever wanted her could have her. This signified that he considered her so much rubbish to be swept out of his house. Women who were "drummed out" did remarry, but the incident was not forgotten. Such a woman could expect to have the incident thrown in her face at any time by someone looking for a way to discredit her, perhaps in an argument. Among the Crow, it was also possible for women to shed their husbands in this manner.

Divorce became a little more complicated in those tribes where the marriage included a great deal of property exchange. Divorce was not common among the Tlingit, but if a couple separated by mutual consent the marriage gifts were not returned. If a man sent his wife home simply because he didn't like her, he was obligated to return the gifts her father had given him at the marriage. However, if the marriage broke up because a wife was unfaithful to her husband, he could keep the gifts he had received and demand the return of those he had given.

A Yurok woman could leave her husband at will provided her kin would refund the bride-price. The relatives weren't too eager to give up all those presents unless the woman had really been abused. A man, also, was not expected to divorce his wife without good cause. If he couldn't come up with a reasonable allegation, the woman's relations would refuse to return the bride-price. While he was still free to divorce the woman, it would mean a great economic loss. One implied condition of the marriage was that the wife bear children for the man; if she was sterile (and it was always assumed the problem was hers), she did not fulfill the contract, and the man was entitled to a return of his goods and money. The average middle-aged woman who had raised several children to adulthood had theoretically paid back her bride-price and was free to leave her husband if she wished.

For the Ojibwa and Cree, who lived north of Lake Superior, divorce was nearly as common as marriage, and some women divorced and remarried seven or eight times. A marriage was ended when one party deserted the other, either in a surprise move or as the result of mutual agreement. Sometimes a man abandoned his wife under cruel circumstances. Ojibwa tell the story of Hawk-Woman, who was a kind and gentle wife. Her husband treated her badly, beating her and leaving her periodically for other women. She always took him back, remaining quiet and faithful. One spring they went moose hunting together, traveling up the lake for two days by canoe. They soon killed two moose, and Hawk-Woman did the butchering and hung the meat up to dry. At one point she and her husband went separately into the woods to get some birch bark to make a wigwam and also another canoe. When Hawk-Woman emerged from the woods, bringing back her first load of bark to the camp, she saw the gun there so she took it and went back for another load. When she returned, the canoe and her husband were gone. But her kettles, knives, clothing, and bedding were still there. When her husband did not return after two days, Hawk-Woman knew he had left her there to die. Resolving to save herself, Hawk-Woman tanned the hides, pounded meat, sewed, made mats, and built a wigwam. She even shot a moose and began to construct a canoe. She was rather lonely but getting along fine when she was discovered by a young man whom she later married. He told her that her husband, who had since remarried, had told her relatives that he had lost his wife and had not been able to find her even after three days of searching. Her relatives went out to search for her, but her husband had not sent them to the right place, so they had presumed her to be dead.

Women also deserted their husbands if they wished to live with another man. Marsh-Woman was a Cree who was married to a mean and jealous man. Once when a party of Ojibwa were visiting her camp she met a man named Chief White Place, and they became lovers. When it was time for the Ojibwa to return home, Marsh-Woman and Chief White Place did not want to be separated. One morning she pretended to go out and check her fish net. Instead she tipped over her canoe and threw the paddle and the dress she had been wearing into the water, attempting to simulate her death. Then she took off with Chief White Place, and they paddled all the way back to his people without stopping. The people of her village assumed Marsh-Woman had drowned—all except her mother, who Marsh-Woman had confided in to spare her grief.

In the southwestern part of the country, Hopi customs of divorce were in keeping with the rest of that culture; divorce was allowed without formality and at the desire of either party. Actually, divorce changed a Hopi woman's life very little. She remained in the same household where she had been since childhood. She was entitled not only to a share of her clan's land but also to a portion of whatever was produced on the land. The fields allotted to her household were worked by her father, unmarried maternal uncles, bachelor brothers, unmarried sons, and sisters' husbands, all of whom contributed indirectly to her support. A divorced woman could remarry at will, but it was only proper for her to marry someone who had been married before. Hopis believed that they would spend their afterlife in the company of their first mate, so a woman's second or third husband was considered "borrowed" for this lifetime. It was thought that a divorced or widowed Hopi who married someone who had not been previously married would be condemned to carry a large burden basket filled with rocks during the afterlife. This custom served to preserve the stability of marriages by discouraging unmarried persons from seducing those who already had a husband or wife.

WIDOWS

When an Indian woman was widowed she was expected to be utterly and completely grief stricken—or at least to make the culturally required motions for expressing her sorrow.

The Plains tribes required a widow to make an ostentatious display of her grief. A typical example can be found among the Sioux. At the instant of her husband's death a widow seized a flint, later a knife, and began to demonstrate her grief—first cutting her hair and then slashing the flesh of her arms and legs. Occasionally a woman was so anguished that she gashed clear to the bone and had to be restrained for fear she would commit suicide. The theory was that this custom of self-mutilation not only allowed a woman to express her grief but also made her feel better by distracting her from the intense psychological pain. When the widow had finished cutting herself, she rubbed ashes into her wounds. The resulting mixture of dried blood and ashes remained caked on her body until the end of the mourning period—about a year. During this time she also gave away all her property and that of her dead husband and went around camp unkempt and joyless. Regular stylized wailing was also part of the mourning duties of widows, who often did their lamenting under the scaffold on which the rotting body of their spouse lay.

Victor Tixier, an early French traveler among the Plains tribes, described the ritual mourning wail of his Osage cook: "She started her song in a very low tone; she gradually sang more excitedly, her voice growing louder, her breathing irregular, her eyes filled with tears, her body trembling; she uttered ear-splitting cries and big tears rolled down her cheeks. She reached a condition of extreme excitement and sang with a frenzy. She seemed to have become insane, but little by little she grew more calm, wiped her tears and resumed her work."[20]

A Cheyenne widow who was really bereft might also gash her forehead and go off to live alone and destitute in the brush. Sometimes a woman isolated herself for a full year, after which her relatives gradually began camping close to her, slowly reincorporating her into the life of her family and community.

Another conventional way for a Plains widow to express her grief was to organize a vengeful raid on an enemy tribe. This was particularly appropriate for a woman whose husband had been killed in battle. Sometimes the women themselves accompanied the war party, but more often they outfitted one of the warriors, providing him with moccasins, food, and the like. If the brave she had sponsored brought back an enemy scalp, the widow could rest assured that she had sent a soul after her husband's to wait on him in the afterlife.

An elderly Sioux woman who had been married to only one man and had been faithful to him was eligible to conduct a special ceremony when she was widowed. Preparing a feast, the widow would invite other honorable women to come and eat with her. Each woman gave a short speech to the others, telling how faithful she had been; after her declaration each woman bit down on a knife, an act of swearing that she spoke the truth and a vow always to be faithful to her husband. After a widow gave this feast she was forbidden to remarry lest a curse befall her and her family—she had "bitten the knife."

Although few tribes outside the Plains culture required widows to slash their bodies, the customs of wailing, cropping the hair, and wearing dirty and ragged clothing were widespread throughout the North American tribes. In many cases, widows were also forbidden much social contact, especially participation in feasts or other joyous occasions. In most Indian cultures, a widow was expected to remain in mourning—and single—for a period of one to seven years; the customs requiring her to be dirty, shabby, and subdued no doubt grew up to reinforce her separation from society. It does not seem likely that men would be attracted to a woman who was smeared with dried blood and dressed in clothing so old and dirty it was falling to pieces.

A Menominee widow, of the northern Great Lakes region, was expected to mourn for a year, and during this time she maintained the fiction that her husband was still with her. When the corpse of the dead husband was taken to the grave, the widow placed beside the body a new suit of clothing. One of the burial attendants snipped off a lock of the dead man's hair which the widow wrapped in the clothing. She put the bundle in her bed, referred to it as her husband, and offered it food, drink, and tobacco from time to time. When her period of mourning was up, the widow went to her dead husband's parents, taking them gifts in order to redeem herself. Because by that time the eyes of her dead spouse had rotted and he could no longer take pleasure in seeing her, the parents released her from further mourning. Had she not observed these customs, her brothers- or sisters-in-law would have had the right to slash her cheeks or cut off her nose or ear, the same punishment meted out to an adulteress.

Some of the tribes who lived in the Southeast, particularly the Chickasaw, Cherokee, and Creek, also had stringent requirements for widows, but in those societies the women did not have to leave home to wail—the dead man was buried in the house, under the bed where he had died. A Creek widow was bound to remain with her late husband's parents for four years.* Her hair hung loose and she was forbidden to comb it, but once every four months or so her sister-in-law would groom it for her and occasionally a little girl would check her head for lice. When the years of mourning were over, her husband's sisters dressed her in fine new clothing, fixed her hair, and led her to a dance, perhaps arranged especially for the occasion or sometimes just the next public dance. Later the widow had to spend the night with a man whom her husband's clan had selected as a good husband for her. If she liked the man, she could marry him, but if she didn't she could choose a man for herself, as she had been released from her widowhood by sleeping with her in-laws' choice.

A Chickasaw widow was also required to lament her late husband for a period of three to four years. But if it was known that she had sincerely grieved for a full year, and if her husband's elder brother spent the night with

* In 1840 the Creek National Council reduced the period of enforced widowhood to one year, but so many tribal members opposed the new law that the original custom was reinstated the following year.

her, she would be exempt from mourning. It was said that young widows who were chafing under the restrictions frequently attempted to ply their brothers-in-law with liquor to induce them to lie with them, thereby releasing the young women from further mourning.

REMARRIAGE OF WIDOWS

A young widow who had completed her required period of mourning was not always free to make a completely new life for herself. In many Native American societies she was expected to become the wife of one of her late husband's brothers or other kin as soon as she was free to marry. This custom was called the levirate. (The corresponding custom in which a widower was expected to marry a sister of his dead wife was called the sororate.)

As was typical for many first marriages, this left the widow little personal choice in whom she would have for a husband. To society as a whole it was more important to stress the concept that the first marriage was perpetual and could not be terminated even by the death of one of the participants. A brother or cousin of the dead man could just step in and fill the place of the departed. Some societies also considered it better for a brother to become the stepfather of the dead man's children, fearing that if the widow married a stranger he might mistreat the children or move them far away from their grandparents.

Although some women were not fully satisfied with the husband chosen for them, the practice was not entirely unfair to widows, for it provided bereaved women and their children a type of economic security they might not have found elsewhere.

A Navajo widow was required by custom to marry a brother or close relative of her late husband, but if there was more than one male who was eligible, she was free to choose among them. If for some reason the man she picked could not or would not marry her, she was free to marry anyone she wished.

Customs were similar among the Apache. A widow might indicate which of her husband's male relatives interested her, but if the man did not take her, and if none of the dead man's other kin showed an interest in her after a reasonable period of time, she was released from any obligations to that family.

On the Northwest Coast when a Tlingit woman had completed the required mourning ceremonies she announced to her husband's relatives that she was ready for them to furnish her with a new spouse. The dead man's heir was his sister's eldest son, and it was expected that the widow would request this nephew for her new husband if he was not already married to her daughter. If the nephew had his eye on a younger woman and did not wish to be tied to his old aunt, he could refuse to marry her, but such behavior was considered extremely disrespectful. If a Tlingit widow was still young enough to bear children, she could end up married to her own grandson. Her family saw it as a convenience for her to have someone to catch salmon and bring wood and water for her and also keep her from having affairs. There were also advantages for the young man. He would have a wife who could bear one or more children and then be free of menstrual taboos. In addition an older woman was thought to be less sexually demanding, so she would not interfere when he had to be continent for hunting or war. If a young man made such a marriage his own father called him "stepfather."

In northern Quebec, Labrador Eskimo widows had no difficulty remarrying because in that society the women controlled the hunting territories. If a widow had inherited claim to a good hunting ground, she was a desirable marriage prospect, no matter how old she was or how many children she had. She was courted not only by men her own age but by younger men wishing to acquire a hunting district or to improve what claims they did have.

Among the Copper Eskimos, however, widows had a hard lot. Although they could expect some support from their brothers and other kinsmen, a man seeking to eke out a living for his own wife and family did not care to be burdened with a widowed sister or sister-in-law. Young widows were claimed as brides without much trouble, but middle-aged women had more difficulty finding husbands. Often a widow who did not remarry became a public woman, offering herself to any man for a day or a week in the hope that one of her lovers would decide he liked her enough to keep her as a permanent wife.

Sometimes an old woman who had lived long and faithfully with one man did not wish to survive her husband, especially in light of the kind of life she would be obliged to lead. Stories are told of Omaha shamans who were able to use their sacred power to take their wives with them when they died. One old woman whose dying husband dusted her with a powdered root from his medicine bundle died two days after he did.

Papago women with their carrying baskets, in which they transported everything from foodstuffs and firewood to children. *(Courtesy of Arizona Historical Society)*

Making a Home

WOMAN'S ECONOMIC ROLE

Gatherer, planter, harvester, cook, tanner, tailor, potter, weaver, and home builder—the early American Indian woman filled all these roles as she transformed the bounty of Mother Earth into the products she and her family needed for survival.

While the man was the hunter and the warrior, an essentially destructive orientation, an Indian woman's activities were turned to the conservation of life. As she wandered the countryside gathering the seeds, roots, and fruits of the land, as she labored in her garden, coaxing the plants to grow, and as she provided clothing and shelter for her family, she felt her oneness with the earth, and her constant concern with growth and life reinforced her unity with the womanly principles of universal motherhood.

Of course, our sister of long ago did not intellectualize her role in this way. She saw the duties that filled her day as simply the tasks that women did—as her mother and her mother's mother had done before her and as her daughter and her daughter's daughter would do after her.

The rhythm of her tasks was the rhythm of the seasons—anticipation of the appearance of the first edible greens in spring, planting of the gardens, harvesting, storage for the long winter, indoor labors during the cold and the dark. This cycle repeated and repeated through her life, yet what gave it meaning was its position in the much larger cycle of birth, growth, maturity, and death. The Native American woman could see her daily drudgery transformed into the rhythm of eternity as she gave birth to children, raised them, and helped her daughters in turn give birth to and raise their children.

Survival was often a struggle for the early Americans. Yet no matter how difficult and wearisome her work, the Indian woman did not begrudge the time spent at her labors. In general, Indian women performed their traditional tasks in the company of other women. In most societies there was a clear line dividing routine tasks into men's work and women's work. Although tasks which revolved around the home—child rearing, food preparation, housekeeping—usually fell to the women and the dangerous and risky jobs—hunting and warfare—were considered the realm of the men, there were some duties, such as clothing making and house building, that were allocated to men in some societies, to women in others.

In spite of the fact that women's role in the early American tribal cultures was somewhat subordinate to that of men, Indian women were not mere slaves or drudges. That myth grew up out of the ignorance of early white explorers who visited Indian villages. They saw the women bustling around the camp, cooking, tanning skins, caring for the children, while the men in evidence lounged about, gambled, or chatted with their cronies. Of course it looked like the women were doing all the work. What the early travelers did not take into account were the late nights the warriors spent on guard duty, and the days, sometimes months, they spent away from the fireside in perilous and wearying pursuit of game or the enemy. Surely the white man's somewhat lopsided view of native life was heightened even more when he saw an Indian family on the move. The picture of an Indian woman burdened by a huge bundle on her back, leading one or more children by the hand while she was flanked by her warrior husband atop a fine steed, roused the ire of many a pioneer, unless he realized that it was the duty of the man to protect his family from the enemy and to find game for them along the way, tasks which would have been impossible had he been burdened with household goods. Indian women did not enjoy full equality with men; but they were not so downtrodden as they have often been portrayed.

There was very little specialization of labor within the men's or women's sphere of activities. A woman might be a good potter, or she might have the special skills to cut out a tipi, or perhaps she was a good herbalist. But although she might be sought out for aid by the other women, she still had to perform all the tasks that were necessary for the functioning of her household. In return for sharing her skills she might receive small gifts, but never in sufficient quantity to release her from those other daily tasks.

WOMEN AND FOOD

The Native American woman's housekeeping duties were simple. Sweeping the floor, straightening the blankets, and scrubbing one or two pots was pretty much the extent of her housecleaning. Of course she often had to build the dwelling in the first place—be it skin tipi, grass hut, or adobe house—and manufacture every item she used—horn spoons, baskets, pots, needles, woodenware, and clothing. Yet her major tasks still revolved around providing food for her family.

It has been estimated that in some Native American hunting and gathering societies, women contributed as much as eighty percent of the labor needed for producing the family food supply. This included not only the time they spent gathering and raising plant foods, but also the labor they contributed toward butchering, drying, and cooking the game brought in by the men. To be able to provide for her family adequately, a Native American woman had to be a good botanist. For example, Cherokee women knew and used more than eight hundred species of plants for food, medicine, and crafts.

In fact, it is felt by some experts that agriculture was the invention of women. This theory will never be authenticated by archeological evidence, but it is generally accepted that among Stone Age peoples it was the women who did the gathering. It would follow then that women would be most likely to experiment with domesticating the wild plants they were using for food.[1]

But even in light of this important historic contribution to the stabilization of the food supply and in view of a woman's overwhelming importance in day-to-day food production, her work was overshadowed by the glamor of hunting. Whatever the economic value of her labors, a woman could never expect to gain excitement or prestige through her gathering, farming, or cooking. Though her tasks fed her family, the only reward for a competent and hard-working woman was social approval and the affection of her healthy family. But that was her universe and that was what she expected.

Although the Indian woman rarely had an official voice in tribal affairs, she exercised almost complete control in her own sphere—the home. One area where the Native American woman wielded a great deal of power was through her close relationship to food, for in many tribes it was the wife who controlled the family food supply. Among the Cree, who lived in the northern Great Plains as they extend into what is now Saskatchewan and Manitoba, the woman had absolute say in the disposition of anything around the tent except those few possessions which were her husband's personal property.

Once game in the form of hides and meat entered the family tipi, they were the property of the women, and the men would not think of interfering with their wives' use of these products.

In other tribes the game was the property and responsibility of the women from the moment it was killed. Along the lower Mississippi a Natchez wife did not expect her husband to bring home whatever large animals he killed near the village. Instead, when he arrived home and threw at her feet the tongue of a deer or a bison, she followed his directions to the spot where the animal had been felled. With the help of her slaves, if she had any, she brought the game back to the cabin, cooked what was necessary, and prepared the rest for storage.

An Iroquois wife had control not only of the food supply but also of her husband's appetite, for males never asked for food. Whenever the husband returned, at any hour of the day, it was the duty of his wife to set a meal in front of him. And among the Blackfoot Indians, of southern Alberta, it was actually a disgrace to both a man and his wife for him to cook food at home or to own food or provisions. Young, unmarried men were allowed to cook food, but they never did so when they could be seen. The story is told about a Blackfoot maiden who surprised her warrior sweetheart while he was cooking some meat. Before she could see what he was doing, the young man threw the hot meat onto his bed and lay back so as to hide the fact that he had been cooking. As the maiden embraced the young fellow the searing meat was burning into his flesh, but he did not wince or reveal his secret.

John J. Honigmann, who studied and wrote about the Kaska of subarctic British Columbia, felt that the numerous folk tales concerning a wife who hoards food while the husband starves might indicate that men felt insecure in the face of the wife's household dominance. In the tale "The Wife Who Hoarded Meat" we see that although a wife might control all of the family food she faced censure and even death if she was stingy.

❀◇❀◇❀◇❀◇❀◇❀◇❀◇

The Wife Who Hoarded Meat

(KASKA)

Once there lived an old woman and an old man. The husband was very thin as he was starving to death. One day the woman's brother came along to visit. He was anticipating a good meal as he had seen the head of a bear near his sister's home. When the visitor saw his sister's husband, his brother-in-law, he said, "You have game. We saw the head back there." The old man protested that he knew nothing about any meat. The woman overheard the conversation and was afraid and didn't know what to do. So she took some of the bear meat she had kept hidden and cooked it in a spruce-root kettle. When she offered the food to her brother he refused to eat it. Later that night he said, "I thought you treated my brother-in-law right. You don't. I can't eat that meat. I'm going home."

When this man got home he spoke to his younger brother saying, "I don't think our sister will live much longer. I feel it. If anything happens to our sister don't think anything about it until we see our brother-in-law."

When the man returned to his sister's house a week later he found the old woman dead and her husband gone. So the man went looking for his brother-in-law. In the meantime the widower had found a beaver den and set a net. He caught two beaver and was in the process of butchering one for his dinner when the man came along. When the widower saw his brother-in-law he began to weep saying, "Have you seen what I have done? You can kill me if you want."

"No, I'll wait until you have eaten," the wife's brother said. So the widower cooked the meat, holding it over the flame with his bare hand (a show of courage in that culture). Then his brother-in-law said, "I'm not going to bother you. I still have a younger sister at home. You can have her for your wife."[2]

❀❖❀❖❀❖❀❖❀❖❀❖❀❖❀

Although women had absolute control of the food supply in many societies, it did not give them license to withhold provisions from those who were hungry. Quite the contrary, for most Indian cultures highly valued generosity and hospitality not only as requirements of sociability but also as a necessary form of welfare and unemployment benefits. For those families who had more than enough to eat, food was not only nutrition but a road to popularity as well. One of the main reasons for gaining wealth was to be able to share and win friends by one's generosity, and the status of a woman in a community depended to a large extent on the manner in which she chose to distribute the extras in the family larder. In fact, it was an almost universal custom among the Native Americans that as soon as a visitor entered one's home, he or she was immediately offered food. It didn't matter what time it was or how many callers a woman had, offering food was the first act of attention. The visitor had to uphold his or her end of the bargain by eating something, even if only a mouthful.

Singer, a Gros Ventre woman, told anthropologist Regina Flannery about an incident that happened to her one day when she was hungry and went to the lodge of a good hunter to beg for some meat. The man had three wives, but when Singer arrived at the lodge two of the women were out gathering wood. The wife who was at home did not greet her visitor nor speak to her, but sat with her head bowed.

Singer told the woman she had come because she was hungry, but still she received no recognition, and the two women sat for some time in silence. Later, a woman who lived nearby and was the daughter-in-law of the man of the house came back from a wood-gathering trip and stuck her head inside the tipi. Seeing Singer sitting there she called her over to her own lodge and asked her what had been going on. Singer explained what had happened, and the woman got to work immediately, cooking up some food for her. She also gave Singer a piece of meat to take home but warned her to hide it under her arm as she left, explaining that although the other household had plenty of meat, they only gave her a little bit and then became angry when she shared it with others.

When Singer was leaving her benefactor's lodge the other two wives of the good hunter came home and asked the third wife what Singer was doing in the neighborhood. The stingy wife said Singer had come to beg and admitted that she had not fed her. The other two wives upbraided her, explaining that she should have fed her at least a little bit to preserve their good standing in the community.[3]

The necessity of dispensing such hospitality was one of the first lessons taught to an Indian girl. Young Winnebago maidens who were being lectured on the art of womanly conduct were told, "When you have your home, see to it that whoever enters your lodge obtains something to eat, no matter how little you yourself may have. Such food will be a source of death to you if withheld. If you are stingy about giving food, someone might kill you in consequence; someone may poison you."[4]

A newlywed Cahuilla wife, living on the desert of southern California, experienced the first test of her hospitality as soon as she and her new husband began living together. The old people who lived near the new couple went to see them, one by one. If the new wife gave the old women some flour or meal to take home with them, she was considered a good woman. But if she sent them away empty-handed, the crones could not say enough bad things about her in their daily gossip rites.

Thoughts of generosity and sharing permeated even the smallest daily activities. When an Omaha woman borrowed a kettle from her neighbor, she was expected to return it with a portion of what had been cooked. When a white woman beautifully scoured a borrowed kettle before returning it to its owner, she was resented as showing a lack of respect and courtesy toward the owner.

Hospitality and generosity with food was particularly important to the desert people, who were not able to build up large food reserves to tide them over lean times. Papago women continually shared whatever they had cooked with their neighbors, who were all relatives of one degree or another. At the close of every day, about the time the evening meal was being prepared, children could be seen scurrying around the village going from brush house to open-air shade, helping their mothers to distribute portions of meat stew or vegetables. No one ever went hungry if there was food in the village. If a homemaker had not cooked on a particular day, either because she had nothing to cook or even if she was too busy with other things, her family would still have something for dinner, for a dish would be sure to come from some of her relatives.

Of course whoever received a gift of food was expected to reciprocate as soon as she was able, so certain equivalents had to be worked out. Papago women usually made baskets in standard sizes and decorated them with black lines running parallel to the rim. A housewife who received a basket of food carefully measured the amount of food she received according to the black line on the basket and was sure to return a fair portion. For a woman to return more than she had received was considered virtuous, but to reciprocate with less was social suicide. Food hoarding was a serious offense, and offenders were ostracized from the social group. A woman who was not generous soon found that the food she had saved could not make up for the consequent loneliness, humiliation, and lack of help when she needed it.

LIFE ON THE GREAT PLAINS

A Native American woman's life was dominated by her society's mode of subsistence. For example, a woman living in any one of the Great Plains tribes during the height of the buffalo culture spent most of her time dealing with the enormous amount of meat and hides her husband provided. To fully understand the lives of the Plains women, we should first attempt to fit the flourishing buffalo culture into historical perspective. Around 1650, many of the groups which eventually moved out onto the Plains were still living in the Eastern Woodlands around the Great Lakes and subsisting on products of the chase and wild plant foods. As the white man began taking over the land on the East Coast the Indians there were pushed further into the interior of the continent, and they in turn pushed other groups west in a sort of domino effect. So by 1750 some of those Eastern Woodlands groups, including the Sioux, were beginning to move out onto the Plains and beginning to exploit the huge shaggy beasts they found there. As time went by they made the adaptations necessary to a nomadic hunting existence, such as developing lightweight skin tents and training dogs to carry some of their goods while they were on the move. The eventual accumulation of large numbers of horses enabled the Native Americans to take full advantage of the plentiful meat supply they found.

The number of buffalo that roamed the Plains at this time is apparently beyond the imagination of one who never witnessed them first hand. In 1871 a white man who was considered a reliable witness reported seeing a herd of more than four million animals near the Arkansas River. The main herd was fifty miles deep and twenty-five miles wide, and this was only one of the many herds in existence during that period. At one time during a northward migration a huge herd extended to more than one hundred miles in width and was of unknown length. A conservative estimate numbered the animals at one hundred million head.

William Hornaday, in his report on the extermination of the American bison, also examined the Native American's use of the animal. He estimates that fifteen to twenty-five Indian hunters working together could kill about one thousand buffalo in a fall season, which averages out to more than fifty head each. It took a woman of average skill about three days of labor to dress a hide. This meant that a woman could tan about twenty robes a season in addition to her other household duties, which included processing a great deal of meat. By combining these two estimates, it can be seen that it took the labor of more than two women to process the meat and hides provided by one hunter.[5] There were always extra women around to help the wife of a successful hunter—a co-wife, an older widowed relative, the wife of a man not so skilled or lucky at hunting—yet even with help, such a housewife had to be tremendously industrious and energetic to keep on top of her work. Among the Crows, practically every housewife was assisted by an otherwise unattached elderly woman, sometimes the wife's mother, who slept beside the entrance to the lodge, warding off stray dogs or taking care of the more routine tasks, such as making up the beds or straightening up the other household goods.

A Plains woman's responsibility for the buffalo carcass began as soon as it was killed, if she had accompanied the party of hunters, or when her husband dumped the dead beast at her door, if she had remained at home.

If an Assiniboine woman's husband had been out hunting on the plains near their home, on the northern border of what are now Montana and North Dakota, she went out to meet him on his return. If he came home with game she lovingly led him to the tipi, unpacked the horses, staked them where they could graze, and gave the carcasses whatever immediate attention they needed. Then she began to care for her husband, removing his clothing, washing his feet, and fixing food for him, all the while keeping up a happy, pleasant conversation. But woe to the man who came back empty handed. No matter if he was rich or poor, his wife or wives took one look at his empty packhorses and then went to visit their parents or other friends. The unsuccessful hunter had to care for his horses, dry his clothing, and fix himself supper. Flathead wives who lived in the western part of Montana were reportedly more compassionate. Whether a Flathead woman's husband came back with game or not, she rushed to care for him on his return, merely happy that he had returned and that the Blackfoot women weren't dancing around his bloody scalp.

When the woman had made her husband comfortable, her work began in earnest. Hornaday estimated that a whole buffalo cow yielded fifty-five pounds of pemmican and forty-five pounds of dried meat if it were economically worked up. A woman who was extremely skilled could butcher three buffalo a day, but this output was beyond the average worker. Because there was no refrigeration, the meat had to be attended to fairly soon to prevent spoilage. The hides also had to be dealt with immediately, scraped clean of adhering fat and tissue while still warm, or they became so stiff they were difficult to tan.

A woman's tanning kit contained at least four tools: a scraper, which was a sharp flat oval stone used with both hands to clean the inner surface of the hide; a flesher made of elk horn and flint, which was used to plane the hide to just the right thinness; a bone to abrade the surface of the skin so it would accept the tanning chemicals; and a rope or buffalo shoulder blade, used to soften the robe.

A hide was prepared for scraping by being pegged flat to the ground or laced to a four-sided frame set up vertically. After the hide had been scraped, it could be laid aside until the tanner had time to get back to it. Next she stretched the skin out on the ground again, this time removing the hair if necessary and thinning the skin so that it would be even. She softened the hide by rubbing it with fat and a mixture of brains and liver, which was left on all night. The next morning, after soaking the skin in water, she wrung it out and smoothed it with a stone. The result was a very stiff piece of leather, which then had to be softened by repeatedly pulling it over a rope or through the hole in the buffalo shoulder blade.

At this point the hides that had been tanned with the hair on were ready to be used as bedding, while others could be fashioned into various articles of clothing. All of the lodge furniture and packing cases were also made of buffalo hide. Buffalo horns became ladles and spoons. Some women were even expert at manufacturing strong rope from buffalo hair.

When a woman noticed that her tipi was beginning to wear out, she started to save up hides to manufacture a new one. A small lodge required eleven buffalo-cow hides, a larger dwelling took as many as twenty-two. A Cheyenne woman did all the work on the lodge skins until the point where they had to be softened, and then she invited her friends and relatives to help her, as she would help them in a similar situation. The tipi maker prepared a big feast for the women, who each took home a hide to soften. When they had all prepared the hides, they gathered again for another feast and an all-day sewing bee. Generally a woman who was an expert tipi designer directed the work of cutting the hides and fitting them together with the least amount of waste. Some tipi makers were highly skilled in the specialized tasks of fitting the top or designing the smoke-hole wings. The experts usually received no fee for their advice, at most they were given a small gift by the hostess; they were usually content with the admiration they received from the other women. There was no doubt also a certain feeling of status and importance to be gained from being able to direct the rest of the helpers.

With such an intense reliance on the products that were provided by the buffalo, it is no wonder that many myths grew up portraying them as having supernatural powers. The accompanying Comanche story tells how a buffalo cow became a lovely woman for a time.

✿◇✿◇✿◇✿◇✿◇✿◇✿◇

The Buffalo Woman

(COMANCHE)

*Once a handsome young Comanche boy of well-to-do parents ac-
companied a party of hunters who went out to look for buffalo. The boy
selected an attractive young buffalo calf for his prey. He struck the calf
with two arrows, but she did not fall.*

*It was very unusual for an animal shot in this way not to die, but the
young buffalo had fallen in love with the boy and had supernaturally
retained her life. The young buffalo cow rejoined her herd and in time
gave birth to a calf which had been fathered by the two arrows of the
Comanche boy. The calf saw all the other calves standing around with
both mothers and fathers, and when he asked his mother about his father
she explained that he was "one of those who eats us." The bull-calf then
insisted on seeing his father even though his mother warned him of the
danger they would face.*

*So the two set off on a long journey toward the Comanche village.
When they came in sight of the circle of tipis, the mother buffalo began
to roll around on the ground and told her calf to do likewise. When she
stood up she had become a woman dressed in a buffalo robe. Her son
became a handsome boy, wrapped in a beautiful yellow calf robe.*

*Following his mother's instructions, the boy went into the village,
found his father, and told him his story. The Comanche boy, now grown
to manhood, remembered the day he had shot the buffalo calf who refused to die. He took both his son and the buffalo woman to live in his
lodge. The woman had saved the young man's arrows and she returned
them to him, telling him that she could help him and his people but he
must promise never to drink out of any stream unless she had given him
permission.*

*During the time she lived with the Comanches, Buffalo Woman
helped the tribe many times. Once when they were all starving, she gave
just a small piece of dried meat and fat to the man with whom she lived,
he ate his fill and passed it to the next family, who also satisfied their
appetites and passed the remainder on to others. The little piece of meat
went from family to family without ever being entirely consumed. Another time, when the tribe was out of food, the Buffalo Woman instructed each family to pack a parfleche [buffalo hide packing case] as if
it were full of jerky. In the morning every parfleche was full of dried*

115

meat. Later she led the hunters to a herd of buffalo where they were able to take enough animals so that everyone had plenty of meat to eat and to store.

One day the father of the buffalo calf was riding across a dusty prairie and became very thirsty. He remembered being warned not to drink from any stream, but thought he would just rinse out his mouth. As soon as he touched the water, the woman and boy were instantly transformed back to their old forms, and as a buffalo cow and calf they ran from the camp. Everyone was very sad, for they had grown to love the radiant buffalo woman and the calf-boy.[6]

Once a Plains woman had made a tipi, it was her responsibility and her property. The Sioux even thought of the dwelling as female, naming the various parts of the tipi after parts of a woman's body. When the tribe was on the move following the migrations of the buffalo, it was the woman's job to take down the tipi and pitch it again in a new location. The skin tent was so well-adapted to the nomadic life-style that a tipi could be struck and loaded, along with its furnishings and contents, in less than fifteen minutes. When a new camp had been decided on, two experienced women could raise a tipi and be ready for housekeeping in about an hour. Through continual practice a woman could estimate rather accurately just where she should pitch her tipi in the camp circle in relationship to the other tents. When the dwellings were too far apart there was danger from attack; when they were too close together the women didn't have enough room to work. Men never helped to set up camp. In fact, if one Assiniboine man saw another helping a woman with any of her tasks concerning the lodge he might remark, "Since when has he become a woman? Hereafter leave him out at gatherings of the men for he may start teaching us to make women's dresses."[7]

In other Plains groups the rules separating men's and women's tasks were not so rigidly enforced. Although Omaha women were generally expected to keep the lodge supplied with wood, it was not unknown for a warrior of that tribe to help his wife carry wood home on days when he knew it was difficult for her to complete her task alone.

The Pawnee were also a Plains people, living in the general area of Kansas and Nebraska, but their unusual household makeup, their reliance on agriculture for some of their food needs, and the fact that they dwelt for part of the year in permanent villages of sod houses set them apart from most other Plains tribes.

Dr. Gene Weltfish, a woman anthropologist who studied the Pawnee life-style in depth, repeatedly comments on the beautiful organization of the daily routine in a Pawnee camp. Apparently the women rarely got together to discuss coming events or to make plans; rather, each individual knew where she fit in the life of the household, and without orders or assignment she did those chores that were hers to do.

The Pawnee lived in villages of ten to twelve large domed earth lodges which housed up to fifty persons each. The interiors of the lodges were divided down the middle into northern and southern sectors, which alternated in performing all the functions that were necessary to keep the household running smoothly. Two meals were served every day. If one side prepared breakfast for everyone, the other side fixed dinner. There was no set routine for which side provided which meal, it all just happened according to the inclinations of the inhabitants on a particular day—like a ballet with no choreographer. It all seems somewhat astonishing if one considers that in order to serve a meal to as many as fifty people, a woman first had to raise, dry, and store all the vegetables she used and butcher and dry all the meat in addition to manufacturing each bowl, ladle, and spoon. Dr. Weltfish maintains that every Pawnee began to learn this delicately orchestrated life-style at a very early age: "In the detailed events of everyday living (she) began (her) development as a disciplined and free . . . woman who felt her dignity and her independence to be inviolate. I was often confronted with the feeling that they expected of me a kind of independence and decisiveness that was not considered becoming to a woman in our society."[8]

The household duties were distributed among the women roughly according to age. Each side of the house was divided into three stations: the central stations on each side—due south and due north—were occupied by mature women who directed the work and provided the main food stores. Immature maidens and newly married young women lived in the areas to the back of the lodge. They did some work, but their main job was to care for and please the principal male figures of the household, who provided protection and fresh meat for the entire household unit. (In the chapter on marriage we have already discussed the Pawnee custom whereby young women married capable older men and waited until they were more mature before marrying younger more handsome husbands who were less experienced in life.) The stations on both sides nearest the door were taken by the old women (symbolically on their way out) and all the children past the age of infancy. These women had the major responsibility for the little ones, freeing the young mothers for more demanding labors. In larger dwellings, several women shared the duties of each station.

Pawnee women were the horticulturists in the tribe, and they were extremely competent, raising ten pure varieties of corn, seven kinds of pumpkins and squashes, and eight different types of beans.

They planted their crops in the spring, and about the time the plants were sufficiently mature to grow on their own it was time for the women to begin packing and preparing for the annual summer movement to follow the buffalo. The large household units broke up, and smaller clusters formed around able hunters.

During the migratory hunt the women took charge of packing and unpacking the tent and household goods and tended to the meat and hides the men provided, in addition to their usual tasks of fetching water and wood, cooking, and raising the children.

By early autumn it was time for the Pawnee to return to their villages to harvest the crops that had been growing all summer. Generally the earth lodges had become so infested with fleas during the tribe's absence that the people just camped near the fields and began their harvesting chores right there until the women had a chance to get the houses cleaned out and ready for habitation. When the households re-formed, people did not necessarily join the same persons they had lived with in the spring. There were many reasons why a woman might decide to join a different household, but as each group functioned in essentially the same way, a woman who knew where she fit in one household could take up the same position anywhere she chose.

The women directed the harvesting, but everyone helped with the work—bringing the crops in from the fields, roasting the pumpkins and cutting the flesh into long spirals, winnowing the beans and separating them by color, and most important of all, roasting, husking, and drying the corn.

WOMEN AS FARMERS

A number of other Native American women also planted gardens to supplement the wild plants and animals they harvested from the forests and plains. Among these were the women of the Huron tribe and the Iroquois confederacy (Senecas, Cayugas, Mohawks, Onondagas, and Oneidas), who lived near Lake Ontario. Although the men helped with the heavy work of clearing the land, it was the women who prepared the land for planting, watched over the growing plants, and brought in the harvest.

Seneca women worked together in the fields under the direction of a field matron, generally a respected older woman whom they all elected in the spring and agreed to obey. They started work in one woman's field, labored there until the necessary tasks were completed, and then went on to another woman's field. It was the field matron's job to see that all the women worked together so there would be no complaints that some of the women had had to work harder than others. She also supervised the rest periods when the women sang, played games, and told stories. Harvesting, too, was a communal effort. Each mutual-aid society divided into three groups: the first group husked the corn and threw the ears into baskets, others carried the corn to the storage places, and the rest of the women cooked a feast for the field workers.

While it is true that these early agriculturalists spent quite a bit of time and energy securing supernatural aid for their crops, they also relied on some practical techniques to ensure success. The Huron women, for example, soaked their seed corn for several days before they planted it, in an effort to hasten germination. Late spring frosts are a danger to gardens in the Northeast, so instead of relying entirely on the protection of the gods, the women planted their squash seeds inside their longhouse dwellings in bark trays filled with powdered wood. Then when the weather had turned warm enough the seedlings were transplanted into the gardens. During the parts of the year that Huron women were not busy gardening, they ground the surplus corn into meal which was traded for meat and skins to the Algonkins who lived to the north. They also spent time sewing birch-bark bowls, weaving reed baskets, fashioning mats of corn leaves, and rolling hemp fiber into twine which the men used to make snares and fishing nets.

In the days before white contact there was a fairly even balance in the amount of food provided by the two sexes—women supplying the grains, vegetables, and fruits, and the men bringing in the meat and fish and helping with the heavy field labors. However, when the northeastern tribes were at war with one another, the men had little time for hunting. And later, after the Europeans had arrived and it was possible to barter beaver pelts for guns and ammunition, the men were again diverted from their normal activities. When the normal balance of food production was upset the women had to increase their cultivation activities to make up for the absence of the game that the men provided.

LIFE IN THE PUEBLOS

The pueblo peoples of the Southwest—the Hopi, Zuni, and the Pueblos along the Rio Grande—were also agriculturalists. But in that dry land, farming was very hard work, dependent in some villages on irrigation, in other places on special planting techniques designed to allow the plant roots to seek out the slightest bit of moisture in the soil. There was very little game, not enough to occupy the men full-time as hunters. So, although the women owned the fields, having inherited them from their mothers, the land was worked by the men of the villages. They grew corn, beans, squashes, pumpkins, and melons. The women supplemented what the men produced by gathering wild plants and by raising tiny gardens of chilis, onions, and other flavoring herbs.

The crops were considered the property and responsibility of the men while they were still growing, but as soon as the produce was harvested and entered the villages it belonged to the women. The female members of Zuni households each year welcomed the new corn into their homes with a rite called the "Meeting of the Children." When the first ears had ripened in the field, the farmer picked the most nearly perfect of them and tenderly carried them home in his arms. Arriving at the doorway of the home he called to the women: "We come!"

"Ah? How come ye?" queried the women.

"Together, happily," the farmer replied.

"Then enter ye!" called out the chorus of women's voices, one of the women beckoning him to place the ears in a decorated tray in the middle of the room. After a brief ceremony, each person present sprinkled sacred prayer meal over the tray of corn. These rites were always performed gratefully and reverently, for the Zuni held these special ears in such honor they regarded them as conscious beings.

Because corn was the favorite food of the pueblo people and their most important staple, the women had to spend many hours kneeling before the grinding stone transforming the hard kernels into meal for use in preparing various dishes. In fact, the women spent so much time at this task that the grinding stones and troughs were permanent and built-in fixtures in their homes. The stones were usually arranged along one end of a room with just enough room between the slabs and the wall for the women to kneel facing the room. The grinding slabs were such an important tool that women would constantly be on the watch for stones of the needed size and roughness.

Sometimes they might have to look for years for a perfect piece of sandstone or lava, and then after they found it spend weeks chipping and smoothing the rock into just the right shape.

Although grinding was back-breaking, grueling labor, the women did not complain; rather they took pride in their skill. They even sang while they worked to show their gratitude at being blessed with a rich harvest. Maidens sometimes had a sort of contest to see who could fill the most storage baskets

---

❀◇❀◇❀◇❀◇❀◇❀◇❀◇

Corn Grinding Song

(HOPI)

Oh, for a heart as pure as pollen on corn blossoms,
And for a life as sweet as honey gathered from the flowers,
May I do good, as Corn has done good for my people
Through all the days that were.
Until my task is done and evening falls,
Oh, Mighty Spirit, hear my grinding song.[9]

❀◇❀◇❀◇❀◇❀◇❀◇❀◇

in a week. Twenty-five pounds of cornmeal was considered a good day's work for an accomplished grinder.

Helen Sekaquaptewa wrote that when Hopi maidens helped their mothers, they didn't grind for just a little while before a meal was cooked, they ground all the daylight hours. If a maiden or a young matron went to visit her friends, she didn't play, she ground corn. And when she had ground enough corn for her own family, she kept on grinding for an aunt who had no daughters.

In her autobiography, *No Turning Back*, Hopi teacher Polingaysi Qoyawayma (Elizabeth White) remembered her return to the pueblo town of Oraibi after being away for several years at white men's school. When she complained about the difficulty of grinding corn on her knees, the centuries-old custom of pueblo women, her mother told her, "Mother Corn has fed you as she has fed all Hopi People, since the long, long ago when she was no longer than my thumb. Mother Corn is the promise of food and life. I grind with gratitude for the richness of our harvest, not with cross feelings of working too hard. As I kneel at my grinding stone, I bow my head in prayer, thanking the great forces for provision. I have received much. I am willing to give much in return, for as I have taught you, there must always be a giving back for what one receives."[10]

Skill at corn grinding was such an important attribute for a pueblo home-maker it was glorified as a virtue even for the supernatural women in legends.

❖◇❖◇❖◇❖◇❖◇❖◇❖◇

The Envious Corn Girls

(TEWA)

Long ago in a pueblo village near the Rio Grande, White Corn Girls lived with their husband Olivella Flower Boy. Blue Corn Girls, Yellow Corn Girls, and All Colors Corn Girls also lived in the village. They were jealous of White Corn Girls and wanted to take their husband away, so one day they invited White Corn Girls over to grind corn. The White Corn Girls declined graciously, saying they had their own grinding stones. The parents of the White Corn Girls suspected that the other girls were out to do some harm to their daughters and tried to warn them, but the White Corn Girls did not pay any attention.

The other girls decided they would try to get White Corn Girls to go with them for water. So they took their water jugs and went over to the White Corn Girls' house saying, "We came to invite you to go for water with us. We have been inviting you to grind with us and you would not go. Now we want you to go with us for water and be our sisters." The White Corn Girls consented to go. When they went to White Water Lake the other girls tried to get the White Corn Girls to fill their jugs first, but the White Corn Girls, knowing that the other girls would try to push them into the lake, insisted that Blue Corn Girls, Yellow Corn Girls, and All Colors Corn Girls fill their jars first. Before the girls went home they sat down to talk together. Blue Corn Girls, Yellow Corn Girls, and All Colors Corn Girls again proposed a grinding contest with White Corn Girls, saying that those who ground the best corn should be the ones to live with Olivella Flower Boy. The White Corn Girls finally consented saying, "We are the youngest of you all, and we may not be able to grind as much as you. Still we may as well say yes."

The next morning the girls all gathered with their corn, and they all started grinding at the same time. It was decided that whoever finished first and ground the finest flour would get Olivella Flower Boy. Soon the Blue Corn Girls noticed that their flour was not ground as finely as that of White Corn Girls. So at lunchtime, when all the other girls were in another room, they sneaked out to the grinding stones and exchanged some of the fine flour of White Corn Girls for flour that was not so fine. Yet when White Corn Girls returned to their grinding stones, their supernatural powers returned the fine flour they had ground back to their grinding stones. Then the other girls, unable to understand why the White Corn Girls were grinding so fine, accused the White Corn Girls of having better grinding stones. So White Corn Girls said, "If you think our stones are the best we will take your stones." So they took other stones and kept on grinding and their flour was still the finest. They also finished first.

When all the girls had finished grinding they put their flour in baskets and tied the baskets up with cloths. Then they all dressed in their finest clothing. The Blue Corn Girls were the first to take their flour to Olivella Flower Boy, sure that he would pronounce their flour the finest and marry them. But Olivella Flower Boy refused them, saying that they ground too slow. Yellow Corn Girls were the next to take their flour to Olivella Flower Boy. He refused them too, on the grounds that their flour was not fine enough. All Colors Corn Girls were also refused for their flour was too coarse. Then it was time for White Corn Girls to go to Olivella Flower Boy. They walked into his house and said, "Good morning. Here we have brought this flour. If you like it we will be your wives." They unwrapped their flour and put it in the middle of the floor. Olivella Flower Boy took a pinch of the flour and it was very fine.

"This is the kind of flour that women grind," he said. "So you will be my wives."

"When we feed you with this flour then you will go and get deer," they said.

"Yes," he replied. "You are my wives now. All that is in this house is yours."[11]

❀◇❀◇❀◇❀◇❀◇❀◇❀◇❀◇

Young Zuni women occasionally made a social event of grinding corn. Frank Cushing, who lived with the Zuni for many years around the turn of the century, was a guest at one of these "crooning feasts." As he described the event, it was one of those very special times in human existence when work and play and worship all combine into one ecstatic experience.

The party that Cushing attended began early in the morning when the young women, dressed in their best clothes, congregated at a home where there was much grinding to be done. While the young women were breakfasting together, older women bustled about, roasting corn and cleaning the grinding stones. Then about a dozen young men, elaborately dressed and painted, arrived and ceremonially greeted the maidens. Eight of the young women then went to the milling stones and knelt to work while the others provided musical accompaniment for their labors. An old grandmother began clapping her hands and singing a song celebrating the corn goddesses, an elderly man began drumming, another fellow played a cane flute, and the youths crowded around the drum, chanting. Soon the eight girls who were at the grinding stones were grinding in time to the drumming and singing, falling into the rhythm of the drum as they moved their arms and bodies back and forth, back and forth. The maiden at one end of the milling line would crush a quantity of toasted kernels, pass the coarse meal to the next girl, who ground it finer and passed it again until, after being passed down the line and growing finer at each stone, the meal came out as fine as pollen. The girls moved their grinding stones up and down in exact time and passed the meal from trough to trough in perfect unison.

Cushing continues: "Sounding drum, shrieking flute, clanging rattles, and the wailing, weird measures of the chant, nothing missed time by the fraction of a second, and although the din raised was perfectly deafening, the melody was by no means bad, the pitch excellent and the effect really inspiriting. It seemed to endow the girls at the meal trough with new life, making them absolutely one in every motion. . . . Even the women who stirred the parching pots and those who were idle patted the floor with their feet and nodded their heads in accord with the drum strokes. Finally, as if to break into all this admirable monotony, the girls yet unoccupied at the mill each grasped in either hand an ear of corn, all fell into line along the middle of the room and danced up and down, swaying and gracefully extending their bare, olive arms from side to side, thus adding beauty to the scene, yet diminishing in no way its cadence."[12]

It was so much fun that the participants kept up their activity until late in the night. Apparently there would have been more of these "crooning feasts" but the amount of meal that was produced was so copious that it was difficult to store and protect from mice.

❀◇❀◇❀◇❀◇❀◇❀◇❀◇

How Women Learned to Grind

(ZUNI)

Once, many generations ago, there lived a beautiful goddess of the ocean —the "Woman of the White Shells," younger sister of the Moon. This goddess was the special patroness of beauty and grace and she imparted an attractiveness almost equaling her own to those into whose hearts she deigned to breathe. So that she would not be defiled, she lived in a cave.

One day when some maidens were passing near the mountain, suddenly the beautiful goddess appeared to them, sitting high up in the rocks, dressed in sparkling white cotton garments. She beckoned to the maidens to approach her, reassuring them with her friendly smile.

"Sit ye down by my side," she said to them, "and I will teach you the arts of women." Then with a sharp-edged fragment of jasper, she chipped out a mealing stone of lava. Next she fashioned another stone of finer rock, long enough to reach entirely across the mealing stone. Taking white shells and white kernels of corn, the goddess ground them together between the stones, demonstrating to her pupils a grace of movement before unknown to women. Now, leaning ever so lightly on her grinding stone and glancing slyly under her waving side-locks, she talked to the watching maidens, teaching them how to tease their lovers; then dashing the hair from her eyes, she turned back to the mealing trough and began to grind, singing meanwhile, in time with her labors, the songs that ever since young women have loved to sing, young men loved yet more to listen to.

She stopped then and picked some long stems of grass which she made into a brush and used to sweep together the flour she had been grinding. Of this she gave to each of the maidens an equal measure.

"Take it," she said, "and remember how I have made it that ye may be blessed with children and make more for them and they for theirs. With it men and women shall cast their prayers to the Beloved and maidens shall beautify their persons." Then she took a little of the flour between her palms and applied it lightly to her face and bosom until her countenance appeared almost as white as her mantle and as smooth as dressed doeskin. And ever since that time women have won the most lingering of lovers with the wiles of the mealstone.[13]

❀◇❀◇❀◇❀◇❀◇❀◇❀◇

Although grinding occupied much of the pueblo homemaker's time and energy there were myriad other household tasks to which she had to give attention, not the least of which was cooking. There was usually plenty of food in a year when the rains had been regular, but Hopi women were well aware that at any time and for any reason the gods might decide to withhold the prayed-for thunder clouds and force famine to visit those on earth. For this reason women often put a tiny pinch of sand into the food they were cooking. Polingaysi Qoyawayma (Elizabeth White) wrote that when she returned home to the Hopi town of Oraibi after being away, she was horrified to see her mother throwing dirt into the corn dumplings she was preparing. Her mother explained, "A small portion of food is being prepared for many hungry people. To it we add sand as a prayer for abundance. Sand, whose grains are without number, has in it this essence. What is more plentiful than the sand of Mother Earth in its endlessness? We remember that as we mix our food in its lack of muchness. Now as you knead this dough in your warm hands, bear good thoughts in your heart, that there be no stain of evil in the food. Ask that it may have in it the power and greatness of Mother Earth; then those who eat it will be nourished in spirit as well as in body."[14]

Because of the unpredictability of the rains, Hopi homemakers were very thrifty and tried to store up a year's supply of corn in case a crop should fail. Each house had an underground room where the women saved everything that might be edible. Peach pits, melon and squash seeds, and bits of uneaten corn all were thrown into this lower chamber along with ashes to keep away the bugs. Hopis knew that in times of acute scarcity they would be happy to eat what had been considered garbage, so they took care to conserve every scrap that might some day save their children from death.

Hopi villages were small and very close-knit. People relied on each other, particularly their relatives, for help. There was an ongoing exchange of wares and goods between the women; Hopi housewives even arranged their own version of today's "swap meet," when they all congregated in the central plaza, bringing their surplus corn, beans, or peaches to trade for whatever they needed. One Hopi woman remembered that her younger brother, who was a very fussy eater, cried one day when his mother set a big stack of flour tortillas down on the table. The little boy didn't like anything made of wheat, so his mother merely picked up the basket of tortillas, went to the plaza, and asked the crier to call out notice of a trade. It wasn't long before the mother returned with some piki (blue corn wafer bread), and her little son ate heartily.

After a Hopi woman had taken care of the grinding and cooking or traded for what she needed, she had to supply the household with water. With the invasion of the fierce Athapascan tribes from the north (who later became the Navajos and Apaches) the Hopis moved their towns up onto the mesas and located their dwellings right on the edges of the steep rocky cliffs as a means of protection. This was a fine way to live, with a beautiful view of the surrounding countryside, but unfortunately the springs were still at the bottom of the mesas. This meant that several times a day the women had to make their way down the steep and perilous trail to the only water source, carrying on their backs large water jugs which held from two to five gallons. In summer, when the spring ran very slowly, the task of water fetching went on day and night. The women stretched big blankets over the rocks so they could have shade in which to sit and sew, darn, or gossip while the water slowly dribbled into their jugs. When a woman's jar was filled she hoisted her burden onto her back and slowly climbed the steep path to the village. Once home she emptied the water into a larger storage vessel and returned to the well to get in line again. At night the women waited for each other so two or more of them could ascend the path together.

Hopi women were also the home builders in their society. When a maiden married and took her husband home with her in the traditional fashion or when a family had so many children that they needed more room, the women of the household organized a building party, inviting all of their female relatives. The assistance of the men of the family was needed to fetch and raise the large beams and to cut the sandstone building blocks, but the women supervised the building, mixed all the mortar and applied it, plastered the walls, and built the corner fireplace. The Hopi woman's world revolved around her home—she was born, lived, gave birth, and died all in the same dwelling—no wonder she took special care to do the best work she could when she added a room to her house, the center of her universe.

THE NAVAJO WAY

Among the Navajos, who were neighbors but not relatives of the Hopi, the woman also ruled the home, but her influence did not stop there. She not only did all the cooking, cared for the house and children, managed the herds of sheep, butchered the domestic animals, made all the clothing, entertained all the guests, and wove rugs in her spare time, but she also had a voice in all the family affairs. There was no activity that was off limits to the Navajo woman if she was able enough to handle it. Restrictions on achievement were never made on the basis of sex, only on the basis of ability.

The high prestige enjoyed by the Navajo woman was no doubt linked to her economic independence, mainly derived from her ownership and management of livestock. The Navajos began raising sheep and goats soon after these animals were introduced in their area by the Spanish explorers who drove flocks along to furnish themselves with fresh meat on their journey. The animals that came into the hands of the Navajos through gift, purchase, or theft soon multiplied into great flocks. Although some Navajo men owned sheep, the livestock was primarily the property of the women—perhaps because they used the wool for weaving, perhaps because they could guard the sheep near home while the men were off hunting and fighting.

Sheepherding is not an easy job, and the Navajo woman who was successful had to express an abiding concern and an intense identification with her flocks. While a woman might send a child to take a flock out to graze on an ordinary day, when it was time for lambing she strove to provide each laboring ewe and each tiny lamb with her individual attention. No matter if the sheep all began dropping their lambs in the middle of an unseasonal blizzard, the Navajo woman was right there with them in the middle of the snow and sleet, even sleeping in the corral so that she could be close enough to assist with difficult births. The Navajo woman knew most of the sheep in her flock as individuals from the moment of their birth, through each lambing season, through each shearing, when she gathered their wool for the rugs she would weave, until the day she butchered them and they ended up in her cooking pot.

The Navajo woman had and still has complete control over the management and disposal of any of her property and livestock, and some women accumulated more wealth than their husbands. Theoretically it would have been possible for a woman who was a good livestock manager to become very rich. Yet the Navajo woman, as an integral part of her social structure, would not consider retaining any of her wealth for her exclusive use. Wealth is not reckoned according to the status of an individual but by the position of the whole extended family, so a Navajo who has acquired a greater than average share of material goods experiences heavy social pressure to share her bounty with all her relatives. Any Navajo who allowed her relatives to suffer while she enjoyed economic privileges beyond their reach was considered a very low person, indeed.

Because Navajos figured their descent through their mothers, Navajo women were always accorded a dignified role in the home, but after they gained some economic stature through their ownership of livestock, they took control of the family purse strings and gained a little clout in the decision-making process. Each extended family, comprised of perhaps several sisters and their common husband or separate husbands, their daughters and their husbands, and the daughters' children, was headed by a matriarch, whom all the other family members recognized as having the final word in all family affairs. There was no formal decision as to who would occupy this position— one of the mature women who displayed the wisdom, intelligence, experience, and necessary leadership qualities simply assumed the role upon the death or encroaching infirmity of her mother or aunt. Although the mother-in-law taboos prevented her from talking directly to her sons-in-law, the work of the young men was indirectly controlled by the matriarch, who made all the economic decisions.

WOMEN OF THE NORTHWEST COAST

Like the Pueblo and Navajo wives and mothers, the women of the northwest coast tribes also enjoyed fairly high status. But because food was more plentiful along the rich coasts than in the dry deserts, the women of the Northwest did not have to labor quite as endlessly as did their sisters to the south. Although it was necessary for everyone to work and contribute to the labor pool, the wealthier women were able to assign the heavier, less desirable, tasks to their slaves.

The Tlingit, who lived along the southern coast of Alaska, resided in large wooden plank houses housing from two to eight families each. A fire was kept going in the middle of the house all day long, filling it with scorching heat and thick smoke, for there was no chimney.

The house was owned by men who were generally brothers or very close relatives, and it was usually more harmonious if the wives were either sisters or otherwise closely related to each other. A typical household would include a house chief, his wife, unmarried daughters, sons below eight or ten years old, and one or more sisters' sons above that age, several brothers of the house chief, their wives, unmarried daughters, small sons and older nephews, the wives and small children of the nephews, aged persons belonging to that house, and slaves.

Each Tlingit household worked together as an economic unit, the women cooperating to collect shellfish and to preserve and store the men's fish catch during the summers and to gather berries and other plant materials during the autumn. Each member of the family was expected to be industrious, not out of any feeling that it was particularly sinful to be idle, but simply as a necessity for survival. The women worked hard, yet they saw no reason to hurry and bustle about; they worked at their tasks at a slow and steady pace, showing great patience and endurance. Once food was brought into the home by either the men or the women, every household member had equal access to it. Even a lazy person would not be denied food, although a man or a woman who remained indolent for very long could expect to be upbraided by the house chief.

☘◇☘◇☘◇☘◇☘◇☘◇☘◇

The Lazy Women

(TLINGIT)

Once there lived a mother and a daughter who were both rather lazy. Neither of them was a bad woman, but they always felt that if they could get someone else to do their work for them, so much the better. It came to pass that the daughter married and according to the custom moved to live near her husband's family. All summer long she had a gay time and did not work at drying fish. When people asked her why she wasn't preparing for winter she replied, "Oh, mother always dries fish for me." The mother likewise was not working at preserving any fish, for she assumed her daughter was drying fish for both of them. When winter came it was a year of famine. These two women were the first to die.[15]

☘◇☘◇☘◇☘◇☘◇☘◇☘◇

Because there was usually an abundance of food on the northwest coast, women there had the leisure to devote some of their creative energy toward their cookery. The usual methods used in cooking were boiling, broiling, roasting, and steaming. Around 1900 a Kwakiutl woman was able to relate about 150 recipes off the top of her head without even exhausting her mental cookbook. But the cooking chores did not entirely rest on the women. It was not uncommon or humiliating for the men to help with the cooking, serving, and cleaning up, especially on ceremonial occasions. Men of the Lower Chinook tribe always prepared and served the great feasts.

The women of the northwest coast groups not only had freedom from a great deal of household drudgery, they also had definite political rights. Vancouver, an early visitor to the Tlingit, reported that some women were held in such high esteem in the villages he visited that it was they who were the real leaders whose judgment the men willingly followed. Among the Eyak, who lived just north of the Tlingit, no bargain could be made without the approval of the women of the household, and the women's opinion was consulted on every decision of more than passing interest.

OPPRESSED WOMEN

But what of Native American women who lived in tribes where their status was not high? The Chipewyans, who lived in the northern subarctic areas of Saskatchewan and Manitoba, represented a people among whom the women were oppressed. Each family was a self-sufficient unit, and there was little feeling of community even when a number of families happened to be camping together. Chipewyan women were often treated cruelly by their husbands and fathers. The women prepared the meals, but the men ate first, leaving whatever they didn't want for the women, which at times amounted to almost nothing. If a woman didn't please her husband in any small way, she could expect a beating, and though it was an odious crime for a Chipewyan male to kill another man, no one thought too much about it when a woman died from a beating delivered by her husband. It is no wonder that female infants were often allowed to die of exposure immediately after birth. Chipewyan women considered this practice kind in the long run and were often heard to say that they wished their mothers had done the same for them.

The Yurok, of northern California, were another group which held women in low regard, considering them dark, inferior, and even contaminating. Men didn't even live at home with their wives and children for the greater part of the year, congregating instead in all-male sweathouses. Erik Erikson, who did a psychological study of the Yurok, seemed to feel that the Yurok women were actually very accepting of their formal role—they didn't question their position or act dejected about it. They managed to exert a power over the daily affairs of the home and children that was denied to them with regard to the more "important" aspects of life.

Erikson writes of the Yurok woman: "She doesn't seem to take the laws too literally or too seriously in a personal sense, not questioning the fact that it is the man's job both to create and uphold the taboos and hers to encourage her children to adhere to them; and she seems to derive a feeling of belongingness from them as if she had long forgotten what they really mean—if, indeed, all the avoidance does not flatter her feeling of being dangerously attractive. Maybe she can act this way because in turn her powerful position in everyday life is not questioned by the men and does not seem less convincing to them because so much of it evades verbalization and rationalization—the only criteria we seem to accept as denoting cultural importance."[16]

WOMEN WHO DIDN'T CONFORM

Not every Native American woman conformed to the standards her tribe set up for the ideal wife and mother. Of course a woman who was not satisfied with her traditional role found it very difficult to find an alternate method of expressing herself, and the pressure on her to conform to what was "right" was tremendous. Men's ability to do women's work, if they wanted to, was never questioned; however, women were often excluded from traditional men's work on the basis that they lacked strength, coordination, or intelligence. Except in cases where extraordinary strength was required, evidence of such innate incapabilities is lacking. The sexual division of labor was almost totally rooted in custom and tradition, although the separation of tasks was usually attributed to the physical differences between the sexes and thus given a biological rationale.

An Indian woman who wanted to step out of her role challenged the entire social system of her tribe. Yet there were some women who were strong and individualistic enough to risk condemnation for their independence. It is interesting that once a rare woman made the break and established herself as a person who was strong enough to hold her own in the male sphere, she earned a high reputation. Since men's work was usually thought of as superior, a woman who could do men's work was considered superior to other women.

Ruth Landes, who studed both the Eastern Sioux and the Ojibwa, noticed that the isolation of the Ojibwa family for much of the year compelled both sexes to develop self-reliance in all spheres, so there were many instances where Ojibwa women took on the skills of men. But among the Eastern Sioux, the dense village life made for considerable sex-specialization of work.

Actually most Ojibwa women who performed men's tasks, such as hunting large game, did so because of the death, desertion, or illness of a male figure. Many widows who preferred not to remarry became capable of supporting their children well, and other women whose husbands were sick or just lazy were able to take up the full support of the family by performing both men's and women's tasks. Some women learned to hunt by going out with their fathers when they were girls, particularly if there were no sons in the family, but as for other traditionally men's tasks, such as house or canoe building, the women were self-taught. Yet no matter how frequently a particular male-associated job had to be performed by the women, and no matter how skilled they were at doing it, that job remained classified as a male job. Interestingly, Landes reports that Ojibwa men were often more accepting of an unconventional woman than women were. A woman would look on another woman who was doing men's work as somewhat unusual or extraordinary. Men, on the other hand, would regard such a woman in light of the occupation she followed; to them a woman who qualified as a trapper was considered a trapper, not a weird woman. No matter how unusual a woman's behavior might be in terms of the work she chose to do, no institutional obstacles were placed in the way of an Ojibwa woman who wished to assume a masculine role; the only sanction requisite for her occupational irrregularities was her own desire.

It was easy for Ojibwa widows to remarry and gain a male partner who would share the household tasks, so women who lived alone obviously preferred the solitude and self-reliance their singleness allowed them. Many women who lost their husbands prolonged their widowhood for quite some time until a man came along for whom they were willing to give up their independence. One of these women was Gaybay. Her mother, Keeshka, was widowed when Gaybay was a girl of about ten or twelve, and the older woman chose to remain single, living alone with her daughter. She taught Gaybay how to manufacture mats, rabbit-skin robes, and birch-bark roof coverings. The two women kept up with all the seasonal occupations, making maple sugar and maple syrup in the spring, gathering rice and berries in the summer, and catching fish and killing large and small game in the fall, drying it for winter use. They never associated with other people, always living by themselves on an island. Eventually Gaybay did marry, but she was soon widowed and returned to live with her mother. The two took up their economic pursuits as before. Keeshka never did remarry, but Gaybay had five husbands. During the periods when Gaybay was a wife, she performed only the conventional women's tasks of taking care of the home and helping her husband on a hunt at his request. But during her intervals of widowhood, which were much more lengthy, she found no difficulty in adjusting to the occupational life of a man.[17]

Although among the Eastern Sioux it was more uncommon for women to do men's work, there were still women who participated in the hunt and rode in war parties where they stalked, scalped, and mutilated the enemy. Any woman who wished to pursue buffalo on horseback with the men during communal hunts was considered somewhat brash, but she was not forcibly deterred if she followed the rules designed to protect all the hunters. Apparently it was a desire for glory and adventure that led a Sioux woman to become a hunter; except in unusual cases a woman did not need to hunt to provide food for herself, for in Sioux society all of the food was shared. A woman who was successful at hunting was accorded the same honors as a man, except that she was never allowed to go so far as to lead a hunt.

The North Piegan or Blackfoot Indians, of southern Alberta, recognized that there were a certain number of particularly strong-minded women and called them "manly hearted" women. The appellation arose because the Blackfoot culture was a male-oriented society, and any woman who achieved distinction did so in terms of men's values.

A manly hearted woman was usually a wealthy mature widow or the chief wife of an important man. Whereas a typical "good" Blackfoot wife was shy, meek, and docile, the manly hearted woman was aggressive, independent, and bold, not afraid to speak out in public or to seek sexual satisfaction. She was also incredibly efficient, being able to accomplish more in a day than an average woman did in a whole week. She was able to trade the surplus goods she produced for horses, the capital of the Blackfoot economy, and thus add even more to her accumulated property. The usual Blackfoot wife would refer to any horses she owned as "my husband's horses," while a manly hearted woman called both her own and her husband's horses "my horses." Because she was well-off financially, the manly hearted woman was always dressed in beautifully decorated, well-tanned skin clothing which emphasized her sexual attractiveness.

The key to what differentiated a manly hearted woman from a woman who was considered merely an aggressive upstart was wealth and status. Poorer women of less distinguished families who exhibited the personality traits of a manly hearted woman were regarded with contempt.

There are several documented cases of Indian women who did not choose to do men's tasks but who rose to the occasion of supporting themselves when they found themselves entirely alone. An early explorer named Samuel Hearne was in Canada in January of 1771 when he came across a strange snowshoe track while out hunting with his native guides. They followed the track and came to a little hut where they discovered a young woman sitting alone. It seems she was a Dog Rib Indian who had been taken prisoner by another tribe. In the summer of 1770, after a year of captivity, she had escaped from her captors with the intention of returning to her own country, but the turnings and windings of the rivers and lakes were so numerous that she got confused and lost her way. So with the beginning of fall she built herself a hut and determined to survive the winter. By the time the explorers found her she had not seen another human for nearly seven months.

During all those months she had supported herself very well by snaring partridges, rabbits, and squirrels. When she had used up the few deer sinews she had taken with her, she began to use the sinews of rabbit legs and feet for making snares and sewing clothing. She also fashioned herself an outfit of rabbit fur. During her spare time the woman had made several hundred yards of twine from the inner bark of willows, planning on using it to construct a fishing net when spring came.

Despite the Dog Rib woman's obvious courage, inventiveness, and resourcefulness, Hearne's Chipewyan guides still could not relate to her as an independent individual, capable of directing her own life and making her own choices. Treated as simply a remarkable piece of property, she was won and lost at wrestling by more than six different men in one evening.[18]

Another such incident took place on an island off the shore of southern California. According to reports from the early 1500s, the Santa Barbara Islands—Anacapa, Santa Rosa, San Miguel, Santa Cruz, Santa Catalina, San Clemente, Santa Barbara, and San Nicolas—were inhabited by an intelligent and handsome people who lived well off the rich flora and fauna of the island. Somewhere around the late 1700s or very early 1800s a Boston trading company landed some male Kodiak Indians from Alaska on San Nicolas for the purpose of otter hunting. A feud developed between the Kodiaks and the native inhabitants, with the result that the visitors killed off all the adult male islanders and took the women as wives. Apparently this was not a satisfactory arrangement, for by 1830 fewer than forty inhabitants remained on the once populous island.

The Franciscan missionaries, who were converting the coastland inhabitants to Christianity and had brought the inhabitants of other islands to the mainland, in 1835 sent a ship to "rescue" the last few survivors on San Nicolas. Before the ship reached the island, a sudden gale came up, whipping the water furiously. A landing was made with difficulty, and the ship was in danger. Wishing to leave the bad weather as soon as possible, the captain loaded the islanders onto the ship in a great hurry and set off. As soon as the ship was under weigh, a woman realized that in all the excitement and confusion her child had been left behind. The captain tried to tell the agitated mother that he could not return to the island under the present weather conditions but that he would return the next day to fetch the child. The woman, a widow between the ages of twenty and thirty, could be neither calmed nor restrained, and she jumped overboard and struck out through the kelpy waters for shore. She was soon lost to the view of the other passengers.

The captain truly intended to return for the woman and child, but before he could make arrangements to return to the island his ship was wrecked and there were no other suitable vessels on the lower coast. After a few years had passed, even those persons who had been most concerned about the fate of the Indian woman and her child assumed that the two had probably died since they had last been seen.

But in 1850, one of the mission fathers, still remembering the incident, sent another ship to look for the lost woman. The captain who had been commissioned to make the search made three voyages to San Nicolas before he located her. Near the end of the third search attempt the captain came across a house made of whale ribs skillfully interlaced and a rush basket containing bone needles, sinew thread, shell fishhooks, and ornaments. Convinced that the woman was hidden somewhere on the island, he organized a thorough search and looked until he finally found her in a brush enclosure surrounded by a pack of wild dogs who apparently were quite devoted to her. They growled at the captain's approach, but the woman quieted them with a word, and they scattered. This female Crusoe, dressed in a beautiful robe of green cormorant feathers, was initially frightened of her rescuers, but after an adjustment period of just a few minutes, she set to fixing them a meal of roots she had gathered. After fifteen years of solitude, the healthy, attractive woman was eager to leave the island, and she quickly gathered together her belongings and made ready to depart. She was anxious to rejoin friends and relatives from whom she had so hastily departed fifteen years before.

The captain of the rescue ship took the woman home with him and put her in the charge of his Spanish wife. None of the Indians from the little San Nicolas band could be located, nor could anyone be found who spoke the woman's language. The woman managed to communicate through sign language that when she had returned to the island alone she had not been able to find her child and eventually assumed that it had been eaten by the wild dogs.

She had been so upset when she could not find the child that she wept until she became ill and then lay prostrate for days until she was finally able to revive herself by crawling to a spring.

Eventually the abandoned woman was able to kindle a fire by rapidly rubbing a pointed stick along the groove of a flat stick until a spark was struck. She lived during her captivity on fish, seal blubber, roots, and shellfish. With great foresight she had even stored dried food in crevices against the time she might be ill.

Juana Maria, as the Indian woman was eventually baptized, indicated that she had at various times seen ships pass her island, but none came to rescue her. Every time one sailed by she watched it until it passed out of sight and then threw herself on the ground and cried until she regained her composure and was able to face her lonely life with a light heart once more. She had also seen people on the beach several times but was so afraid that she hid until they had gone. Then after they left she wept, disappointed that she had not made herself known.

In a few short weeks after her rescue, the robustly healthy Indian woman began to droop and was soon too weak even to walk. Death followed quickly, and she was buried in the walled cemetery next to the Santa Barbara Mission.[19]

A Maricopa woman from Central Arizona displaying the
individuality of a non-traditional hairdo. *(By permission Sharlott
Hall Historical Museum of Arizona)*

Women of Power

LEADERS, DOCTORS, AND WITCHES

The descendants of the Anglo-Saxon invaders of North America have traditionally viewed Native American women as powerless drudges, subservient
to the chiefs and braves who ostensibly dominated tribal life. While it is true
that in many Indian societies women had little opportunity to hold office or sit
on the council, this does not mean that they had no chance to exercise power
and authority outside of their homes.

Just as not every man was a chief, not every woman sought a position of
influence, but in most tribes those women who were natural leaders had some
accepted outlet by which to express their talents. Where the structure of their
society allowed, some women became political leaders. Other Indian women
sought power by becoming medicine women or witches.

LEADERS

The feminist movement has brought to the fore much discussion of
matriarchies—that is, societies ruled by women. While there has never been a
true matriarchy in ancient or modern times, the Iroquois did come as close to
it as any other society. The Iroquois were a woodland culture and inhabited
the area that is now New York.

Women in that society had the upper hand economically because they
owned the fields, crops, and houses. Descent was traced through the women

and all titles, rights, and property passed through the female line. While this still left power in the hands of men, it gave the women a great deal of control over the exercise of that power.

Although Iroquois women did not actually hold the position of chief (called a sachem in that tribe), it was they who not only chose the leaders but also decided if the men they selected were doing a creditable job. Each clan was divided into lineages, and at the head of each lineage was an older woman—the matron—who derived her position from her age and her qualities of leadership and diplomacy. One of her duties was the coordination of the economic activities of the female clan members—not only their work in the fields, but also their contributions of food for charity and public festivals.

When one of the sachems died, it was up to the matron of his lineage, in consultation with her female relatives, to select his successor. If the new sachem's conduct was not satisfactory, the matron would warn him three times, giving him a chance to improve. After that the matron would ask the council to depose him. Because of her position, it was necessary for the matron to always conduct herself with great decorum, so that when she had to admonish an erring chief her warnings were respected.

Women leaders were not unusual among the early northeastern Indians, according to reports from some of the first English settlers. There were, of course, no trained anthropologists among these early travelers—there were no anthropologists at all then—and the surviving accounts of these powerful women are frustrating in their brevity.

As far back as 1584, English explorers encountered on the shores of what is now Virginia a woman whom they termed a queen because she was married to a man they considered to hold the rank of king. She was stately and beautifully dressed, wearing a long leather cloak lined with fur, a headband of white coral, and waist-length earrings made of pearls the size of peas. When this woman visited the strange invaders she was always accompanied by forty or fifty ladies-in-waiting.

As for women who were rulers in their own right, some of the earliest information deals with a woman called by the Pilgrims the "Massachusetts Queen," a widow who on her husband's death had taken over his position as leader of a confederation of various Indian tribes in Massachusetts. The tribes eventually began to war with each other, and by 1620 the queen was left with only the remnants of one tribe, called the Nipnets or Nipmucks. In 1643, this woman and four other prominent chiefs made a covenant with the settlers agreeing to subject themselves to British rule if they would be offered protection from other tribes.

Two female chiefs were instrumental in aiding King Phillip, a sachem of the Wampanoag, in his unsuccessful war against the English from 1675 to 1676. One of these brave leaders and fighters was Wetamoo, also known as the Squaw Sachem of Pocasset, who joined Phillip in his attempts to form a confederation of East Coast Indian tribes to stop the English colonization of their lands. The Squaw Sachem brought three hundred warriors and provisions to aid in the struggle, during which the Native Americans attacked fifty-two of the ninety existing English towns, completely destroying twelve of them. It is possible that these forces might have succeeded in routing all the colonists from the land, but treachery in the Indian ranks turned the tide, and by late summer of 1676 Wetamoo's twenty-six remaining warriors were surprised and imprisoned. Wetamoo alone escaped capture, and she was later drowned while attempting to cross a river. When the English found her body, they cut her head off and set it on a pole within sight of the last of her warriors, who expressed their grief by loud wailings and lamentations.

Apprently Wetamoo did not see her civil and military duties as detracting from her femininity. Mary Rowlandson, who spent some time as a prisoner among Wetamoo's people, wrote that the woman leader usually dressed beautifully. At a dance "she had a kersey [woolen] coat covered with girdles of wampum from the loins upward. Her arms from her elbows to hands were covered with bracelets. There were handfuls of necklaces about her neck and several sorts of jewels in her ears. She had fine red stockings and white shoes, her hair powdered and her face painted red."[1]

Another squaw sachem who helped Phillip for a short time was Awashonks, who ruled a point of land now in Rhode Island. In 1671 she had entered into articles of agreement with the court of Plymouth, saying she, and as many of her warriors as she could persuade, would give up their arms and cease their long-standing war against the English. However, four years later, in the tide of Phillip's successes, she was induced to join him for a while. She and her warriors aided the cause for about a year, then Awashonks met with an Englishman friend of hers and agreed to return to peace if he were to guarantee that she and all her people would be spared. We read that unlike Wetamoo, Awashonks was noted for her masculine qualities.

Predating the English accounts of prominent Indian women were reports from de Soto and the Spaniards accompanying him. Early in May in 1540 after having lost their way and spent some days wandering about the wastes of what is now southeast Georgia, Fernando de Soto and his advance guard came across three Indians who told the Spaniards that in the town ahead, named Cutifachique, there was a woman ruler who already had news of their imminent arrival and was awaiting them. When the party came to the banks of the river which separated them from the town, four canoes appeared carrying a kinswoman of the ruler and many gifts, including shawls and beautifully tanned skins. The woman welcomed the visitors, explaining that the chieftess herself had not come because she thought she could be most helpful by remaining behind in the village to arrange to receive her guests. She then took from her own neck a fine string of pearls and placed them over de Soto's head in a symbol of friendship.

Canoes soon arrived to take the entire group to Cutifachique. The chieftess greeted the Spaniards most cordially, offering them great quantities of food and many lovely pearls. After a week of such treatment the soldiers wanted to settle there, but de Soto was not content with what he found and wished to continue his search for gold. He wanted the chieftess to escort his party to assure their welcome in other towns, but by this time she had had enough of the crude behavior of the white-skinned explorers and just wanted them to leave her town. In return for the hospitality the gracious ruler had extended to him, de Soto had her placed under guard and forced her and some of her female slaves to accompany him. In every town the inhabitants were quick to obey the orders given by their ruler, and even the poorest hamlets contributed something to the strange men. After about two weeks, the chieftess managed to escape her captors and fled to her home with several of her slaves.

Much later, in 1767, another Spaniard named Solis visited what is now the southeastern United States. Reporting on his stay in a Caddo town he wrote, "In this village there is an Indian woman of great authority and following whom they call . . . 'great lady.' Her house is very large and has many rooms. The rest of the nation brings presents and gifts to her. She has many Indian men and women in her service and these are like priests and captains among them. She is married to five Indian men. She is like a queen among them."[2]

Being the descendants of some of the early southern peoples, the Cherokees continued to accord women some say in the government of their towns. Although women did not normally speak during the daily council meetings, they did vote with the men in selecting their leaders. Also, the women in each Cherokee town elected delegates to the Women's Council, which was presided over by the "Beloved Woman." This matriarch and her council did not

142

hesitate to challenge the authority of the chiefs when they thought that the welfare of the tribe demanded it.

One of these beloved women was White Rose, whom the English called Nancy Ward. In this position White Rose had the right to request the freedom of captives, and she once rescued a Mrs. William Bean, who had already been bound to a stake and was about to be burned. She was a great friend to white men and often alerted them to a coming raid. After the American Revolution she gave a speech to a commission set up by George Washington in which she pledged her hand to maintain peace between her tribe and the white settlers. Yet she was always true to her people, and to her last days she urged the Cherokees to hold on to their ancestral lands and not sell them.

Women also played a very important role among the Natchez, who lived along the lower Mississippi River and had an unusual system of government. The society was divided into several classes, with the Suns being the chiefs, followed by Nobles and Honored People, who were also considered aristocracy. The rest of the people were called Stinkards.

The principal leader, or Great Sun, was always a male; because nobility was transferred only through the female line, this ruler was succeeded not by one of his sons but by the son of the woman most closely related to him. This woman was also considered a Sun, or White Woman. While the women Suns generally did not meddle in governmental affairs, they did command great respect from the rest of the populace, who were expected to supply them with the best products of their farming, hunting, or fishing endeavors. These aristocrats also had the power of life and death over their subjects; if anyone displeased them they had only to command, "Rid me of that dog," and they were instantly obeyed by their guards.

The Suns, both men and women, were not allowed to intermarry and were required to take mates from the Stinkard class. Husbands of White Women functioned more as servants than partners—they were not allowed to eat with their wives, they were required to stand at attention when in their wives' presence, they even had to salute in the same manner as the rest of the servants. Their only privileges were freedom from labor and a chance to exercise authority over the other servants. A White Woman was allowed as many lovers as she pleased, but if her husband were unfaithful, he could fully expect to have his head bashed in. His reward for a life of faithful servitude, should he outlive her, was to be strangled at her grave so he could accompany her to the afterlife.

In some of the tribes on the western side of the continent we also find women in leadership roles. Among the Sinkaietk, a Salish tribe that lived along the lower Columbia River in southeast Washington, as well as in some of the neighboring groups, there were women who served as chieftess of their bands. Although it was required that the woman who held this office be related to the chief, the holder of the position was officially elected and formally installed by the council. The extent of the power she exercised varied from group to group. In one band from which we have a report the chief was the group manager, and the chieftess was a consulting adviser only in cases of murder, revenge, or emergencies. If her decision differed from that of the chief, the people were free to follow either.

This recognition by the Sinkaietk of the equality of sexes is not unexpected. An early traveler to the area observed that along the lower Columbia, where the women's root digging contributed substantially to the support of the tribe, they seemed to assume an air of liberty and independence unknown among the neighboring tribes. Older women were particularly respected and were consulted in all matters of importance.

In northern California, the Nisenan sometimes had a woman at their head. The chieftainship was primarily hereditary, and, if on the death of a chief, there was no male relative competent to fill the position, the deceased's widow, daughter, or niece might be chosen to succeed him. A woman in this office had no actual power, although she was always consulted by the leading men; the measure of strength she held depended on the degree of support she had from the populace. Besides advising the council, her duties included planning community activities and food gathering, arbitrating disputes, acting as official hostess, and arranging "big times" or celebrations.

In the southwestern groups, where women often have high status and command considerable respect, we find several tribes in which there were specific positions of leadership filled by women. In the pueblo societies, men generally ran the governments and controlled the ceremonies, but women had an important place in religion and, owing to their control of the households, they had more say in civil matters than appeared on the surface. The men had to go home at night after discussing policy all day with the other men, and if a man had an opinion that was unacceptable to his wife or mother-in-law, it might become somewhat uncomfortable for him.

The leader of a Hopi town was usually assisted in his duties by a woman relative, who was called "Keeper of the Fire." She was chosen for this honor on the basis of her wisdom, intelligence, and interest in religious ceremony. The male head priest or chief kept his office in this woman's home and consulted her on many decisions, drawing on her experience and knowledge of precedents.

Every clan in a Hopi village was also headed by a matriarch, or clan mother, who enjoyed certain privileges as a result of her seniority. The clan mother was always consulted by her male relatives on any matter which fell within her realm of competence or sphere of influence, for example, family quarrels or other such disputes. The matriarch of the leading clan did not necessarily hold the position of Keeper of the Fire—sometimes a younger woman was felt to be more suited to the job.

The Western Apache recognized some of the stronger and more influential women as "women chiefs." Almost invariably these leaders were wives of chiefs or subchiefs; however, even though a headman's wife was accorded some respect, not every woman whose husband was a chief was considered a woman chief.

The typical woman chief did not inherit her status, nor was she formally chosen—she simply evolved into her role and gained recognition because she displayed wisdom and strength and was a shining example of Apache woman-hood. She was never idle, and through her industry accumulated wealth, another prerequisite for women chiefs. She was expected to be most generous in sharing her food and other material goods with those who were less fortunate.

Sometimes an Apache woman leader might speak in council or at a war dance in an effort to inspire the men, but usually her functions involved organizing other women into wild food gathering parties, encouraging them to contribute food for community feasts and ceremonials, and urging them to gather sufficient food supplies for the winter. She also gave advice on child care and family living. To fill her moccasins today would require a social worker, a family counselor, a pediatrician, a home extension agent, a business adviser, a minister's wife, a volunteer, and a favorite aunt. Apache women usually contributed the most in terms of leadership and influence between the ages of forty and sixty, when they were considered to be in their mental prime.

Although the identities of most of the Indian women leaders are forever lost in time, the stories of a few have survived, usually because they were in some way associated with white men who preserved details of the women's lives in notes and journals. One of the most famous of all early Indian women was Sacajawea, who served as a guide to the Lewis and Clark expedition. Sacajawea was only about twenty years old when she led the explorers all the way from North Dakota to the Pacific, carrying her baby on her back the whole way. Many people do not know that Sacajawea lived another eighty years—dying in her sleep when she was one hundred years old. She was unusually respected among her people, the Shoshone, and they called her Porivo, or chief. During negotiations for the Great Treaty of 1868, which proposed establishing a reservation for the Indians, Sacajawea was allowed to speak in the council meetings, an unthinkable situation for a woman under normal circumstances. But Sacajawea's people respected her advice, and the whites valued her understanding and influence.

Another leader, not so well known, was Rosana Chouteau, who was elected second chief of the Osage Beaver band in 1875. The council had met to select a successor to Rosana's uncle, who had died. From a field of three men and one woman, a council decided on Rosana, who was extremely reluctant to accept the job. Yet later, when she had become accustomed to her position, she expressed some pride in the work she was doing, as she told a United States official, "I am the first one [woman chief] and I expect to be the last one. I think my band obeys me better than they would a man."[3]

MEDICINE WOMEN

Practicing medicine was a way for many Native American women to gain prestige, power, and even wealth.

Early Native Americans perceived essentially two different types of illnesses: those that resulted from natural causes and could be cured by natural means such as herbs, and those physical and mental problems that were precipitated by supernatural causes and thus called for supernatural cures. Some early medicine women specialized only in natural curing; others used both natural and supernatural means to cure patients who came to them.

The knowledge of herbal medicine was not confined exclusively to the women in the early tribes, but generally women seemed to be more familiar with various herbal potions and brews. Women who practiced medicine were usually middle-aged or older—partly because by this age a woman was no longer busy caring for small children, and partly because older women were free of the taboos associated with menstruation. Among the Delaware and in many other tribes it was believed that a woman herbalist lost her power to cure while she was menstruating, and she was not allowed to prepare remedies during that time.

Any woman who had a gift for curing was in constant demand by patients.

There were no pharmacies in those days, so medicine women spent much time wandering around the wild areas surrounding their villages seeking out the elusive herbs and lichens, gathering leaves and bark, and grubbing for days in search of particularly efficacious roots. Ruth Landes writes that the native pharmacopoeia of the Ojibwa was remarkably extensive, including, besides numerous herbs, such animal products as bear gall and skunk secretions. Some women were so dedicated to their art that they traded herbs with medicine women in other tribes to expand their skills with plants not indigenous to their area. Modern medicine has shown that many of these herbs were effective remedies. Some of the old-time natural potions are still in use today or have become ingredients in more sophisticated medicines.

Kwakiutl women, on the coast of British Columbia, prayed to the medicinal plants as they gathered them, asking the herbs to take pity on the patient, saying, "I have come, Supernatural-Ones, you Long-Life-Makers, that I may take you for that is the reason why you have come, brought by your creator, that you may come and satisfy me."[4]

The Reverend John Heckewelder wrote in the 1800s that wives of the white missionaries ministering to the Iroquois often appealed to the native women for help for what were then termed "female complaints." Apparently the white women experienced relief from whatever it was the Iroquois medicine women prescribed. Heckewelder also gives a story of his own cure: "I once for two days and two nights suffered the most excruciating pain from a felon or whitlow [tissue inflammation] on one of my fingers which deprived me entirely of sleep. I had recourse to an Indian woman who in less than half an hour relieved me entirely by the simple application of a poultice made of the root of the common blue violet."[5]

In some Native American groups the wife of a medicine man was able to learn the secrets of doctoring by assisting her husband. A Cheyenne man who possessed supernatural powers enabling him to cure illness could not practice by himself; he needed a female assistant, and if his wife wouldn't help him, he had to find another woman who would.

The wives of Comanche medicine men often helped their husbands in their work; persons needing medical assistance initially approached the wives rather than going to the medicine men directly. It was impossible for a single Comanche woman to become a doctor—the only way a woman in that tribe could acquire healing power was through her husband. She was not allowed to practice by herself until after his death, and then only if she was past menopause.

Among the Nisenan, in northern California, women who wished to become doctors spent six or seven months under the tutelage of a medicine man. During their rigorous training the women were initiated into all the secrets of medicine except those which dealt with the use of poisons. It was feared that if women had this knowledge they might become mentally unbalanced at some time and kill everyone, "women being very weak headed."

That women were more responsible than men when they held such power —at least among the Ojibwa—was demonstrated by the behavior of the shamans in that northeastern tribe. The Ojibwa society considered the practice of medicine essentially a male profession, but a woman who was interested in medicine could learn or inherit medical skills from her husband. Some women were even able to gain power and knowledge of medicine on their own. From all accounts these women made very good doctors and were highly respected by the other villagers. But the interesting thing was the attitude of medicine women toward their profession. Traditionally male Ojibwa doctors were sullen, suspicious, quick tempered, violent, and, of course, greatly feared by the other people. They demanded constant reassurance of their own importance, and anyone who did not express proper deference to these powerful men risked being the victims of sorcery. Women doctors didn't seem to behave like such prima donnas. Not having been trained as children to feel violent pride or shame, most medicine women just concentrated on their doctoring work and did not give much energy to suspicion or arrogance.

In other tribes, women who doctored with herbs and other natural agents learned the art from their mothers or grandmothers and added to their repertoire of medicines by trial and error. Sometimes a supernatural, in the form of a human, an animal, or perhaps just a voice, would appear to a woman in a dream and instruct her to use a certain root or herb to cure a specific disease.

Even if a woman inherited the right to practice medicine from her mother, father, or other close relative, her powers usually had to be personally validated by a dream in which a guardian spirit appeared to her and gave her specific knowledge. Sometimes after a woman dreamed the proper dreams, she had to wait until an elderly woman doctor chose her as successor and shared with her the special songs and formulas that had miraculous power to bring good weather or to cure disease. Then when the old doctor died the younger woman took over her position, using the songs she inherited in addition to the new ones she dreamt from time to time.

A Cocopah woman whose mother was a medicine woman was likely to follow her mother's profession if she had the proper dreams. The dreams told her what powers she would have: for example, if she dreamed of a fox or coyote she would be able to cure gun and arrow wounds, or if a roadrunner appeared to her in her sleep she would have the power to cure snakebites. Cocopah women also treated difficult childbirths, children's diseases, eye and stomach trouble, diarrhea, bone fractures, bruises, and other injuries. Any woman who wanted to have dreams giving her curing powers had to forego dances and fiestas, for the Cocopahs believed that the nature deities or spirits appeared only to those persons who did not indulge in such frivolity.

In other tribes, women who sought medicine power had to do more than just remain quietly at home awaiting the appearance of spirits—it was necessary for a power seeker to actively petition the spirits by fasting and suffering. Mandan women wishing to have a vision fasted in their gardens or on the corn-drying scaffolds. They believed that the supernatural powers one received were in direct proportion to one's suffering.

Alfred Bowers, in his study of the Mandan, recounts the tale of a young woman named Stays Yellow who fasted in the woods in quest of a vision. She stayed awake all night and just before dawn she fell asleep and dreamed she saw two old people doctoring a woman who was experiencing a difficult childbirth. Stays Yellow saw that the old people, a man and a woman, were using black roots which they dug up in the forest, and she listened to the song they were singing. While the two people were doctoring the laboring woman, they were also administering to several dead watersnakes. The old woman chewed up black roots and blew the masticated mass over the snakes. Every time she did this, a snake came alive and slithered away. The last of the snakes was slow to revive for it was pregnant. Each time the old woman blew chewed root on the female snake, it gave birth to one of its young. The old people then told Stays Yellow that henceforth she would have the power to doctor women who had difficulty in childbirth.

Stays Yellow didn't begin to use her skills until she was quite an old woman. One day she learned that there was a woman in her village who was about to die in childbirth, for the other doctors had given up on her. When Stays Yellow arrived, the poor woman was scarcely alive, but she was still conscious and could talk. The old woman confessed that she had no great powers but promised to try what she had learned in her dream. She chewed the black root and blew it over the sick woman and sang her medicine song. Then she requested a stiff feather. Putting her knee on the patient's belly and lifting her head, she opened the sick woman's mouth and pushed the feather down her throat. The patient strained as if to vomit, involuntarily contracting her abdominal muscles. The fourth time the feather was put down her throat the laboring woman delivered a fine, healthy baby. Stays Yellow then boiled some of the black root and gave the woman the resulting tea. She received a good horse, ten blankets, and many yards of calico as payment from the woman's grateful family.

When R. L. Olson was investigating the Quinault, along the coast of Washington, he was told the story of a young woman who had decided to become a medicine woman. She went into the mountains alone and fasted for ten days. Every day she worked at gathering tree limbs and branches until she had collected a huge pile of wood. On the tenth night she set fire to the wood and sat down to wait. As the leaping flames began to engulf more and more of the logs and give off intense heat, the young woman heard a mournful howl which came from a nearby mountain. When she looked toward the peak it seemed to sway. The cry came closer and the fire grew hotter. When she moved away from the burning wood a huge animal something like a wildcat appeared to her. The animal had a sharp nose, and its face was so long that it dragged on the ground. Approaching the fire, the animal raised its head and howled. The young woman was afraid and told the animal, "I don't want that kind (of power). I don't want you for a guardian spirit." The strange animal retreated, but soon the water of the nearby lake began hissing and boiling up, and many kinds of animals came swimming toward her. She was so frightened that she lost consciousness and had a vision in which the animals brought her five kinds of spirits to choose from. She grabbed at the spirit which could bring back lost souls.

Curing illness by means of recapture of the soul was a common and spectacular treatment among the Quinault. When a person's illness was not a simple pain or an obvious physical injury, it was believed that the patient was suffering from loss of his or her soul. Souls reportedly traveled along the road to the dead at different speeds, those of severely ill persons traveling faster than those of people who were less sick. To find and bring back a soul on the road to the land of the dead, a medicine woman had to have a spirit who was familiar with the road.

When a medicine woman was attempting a cure she lay down on a mat spread on the floor and sang a song she had learned in her vision until the spirit entered her body and she went into a trance. The young woman in the story above had been given some crystals in her vision, so whenever she entered a trance she clutched a crystal in each hand. When she spoke it was the spirit speaking through her. As she and the spirit progressed along the road toward the land of the dead, searching for the lost soul, the spirit voice described the various places they were passing, including any evidence of the soul's having passed that way. Sometimes a search might last two days and two nights, depending on how far the soul had gone.

If the soul had gone beyond the reach of the medicine woman and her guide, she reported failure, but if she managed to overtake the lost soul, she captured it in her cupped hands. When she had made the return journey and recovered sufficiently from her trance, she poured the soul back into the patient through the top of the head. The pouring motions were repeated several times and were sometimes accompanied by gentle massage.

All the doctors among the Yurok, of northern California, were women, which is surprising since Yurok women were banned from most other religious or supernatural activities. The profession was highly paid, and a good Yurok doctor could expect to become wealthy. One might assume that in view of the material rewards and the prestige to be gained every woman would wish to become a medicine woman, but actually not many women relished the thought of sucking out and later swallowing "pains" from a sick person's body. The pains were described as being slimy and bloody and looking like a pollywog.

Each Yurok woman who became a doctor went through a fixed series of events before she received her full power. First she had to dream of a dead person who had been a doctor while alive. During the dream this person put "pain" into her body.

A Yurok medicine woman described how she had received the requisite vision when she was young even though she did not wish to become a doctor and had actually run away from home to spend the night with a girl friend in order to escape her mother's nagging about the subject.

She related, "There I dreamt a woman is coming, her hair is long, she has grass skirt and small basket. She say to me, 'Come with me in there.' I say, 'All right,' and she holds a basket. She say, 'You look in there.' I look, mist closes sky, water dropping out of sky, white, yellow, black bloody, nasty." (Erik Erikson, the researcher to whom she told her story, interprets this as meaning, "Through the mist I saw the sky come together. Out of the cleft I saw water dropping, white, yellow, and black. It looked bloody and nasty.")

She continued, "She hold little basket out so water dropped in it; she turn around, I see stuff in basket, I kind of afraid, I turn around. She say, 'You stay there.' I go, I look back; she throw basket on me, it hit me on mouth; I swallow stuff, I no sense any more, I wake up with noise. Nancy [her girl friend] wake me up. 'You crazy,' she says. I never tell I dreaming that night; not sleep again.'"[6]

The mother and the grandmother of the young woman who had the dream were doctors, and apparently the social pressure was so strong for her to become one too that she submitted to the will of the community through her dream. The morning after the dream the young woman was sick, and from her symptoms the people of the community realized she was on her way to becoming a medicine woman.

She then had to undergo a lengthy training program, during which time she learned to control her stomach and esophagus so that she could swallow a pain and then regurgitate it without throwing up food with it.

Apparently once a Yurok woman had a dream about the pains she was almost compelled to continue with the training. Erikson was told about a woman who ran away after she had the dream, refusing the rest of the teachings which would allow her to become a practicing doctor. She became a neurotic person with chronic indigestion, vomiting whenever she saw traditional Indian food. She even passed on her symptoms to one of her daughters.

It was not unusual for Indian women who had supernatural dreams to refuse to accept the power that was offered to them. Coming Daylight, a Gros Ventre woman, told anthropologist Regina Flannery that she had rejected such power, explaining, "Even before I was married, I had a particular kind of dream which indicated power to extract illness from the body of a patient. This dream occurred four nights in succession. Each morning I would tell my grandmother about it. The old woman got angry each time and told me not to talk about it, to keep it to myself so that I would become a great doctor. But I had already made up my mind that I did not want such power, the immediate reason for my refusal being that I had seen doctors who swallowed what they had sucked from the weak spot in patients whom they cured and I just couldn't bring myself to have to do likewise."[7]

❀◇❀◇❀◇❀◇❀◇❀◇❀◇❀◇

How the Owls Gave Hunting Medicine

(MENOMINEE)

Long ago some Menominee people were moving about the countryside during their fall hunt. There was one little girl who was always crying and fretting because she was lonely and had no brothers and sisters to

152

play with. The little girl's mother tried to hush her by threatening to throw her to the owls.

When the Great Birds Above heard what the mother was saying they asked the Owl, "Why don't you take the child? She has been offered to you many times."

The Owl replied, "I heard all that, but it was only said to the child to scare it because I look so ugly. That's why I don't go and take it, for all parents say that to children to frighten them."

But the little girl did not stop crying so her mother said, "Child, I will throw you outdoors for owls to come and take you away." Then she picked the little girl up and put her out of the house, saying, "Now Owl, come and get her, she is yours."

The child was heard crying for a while but then all was quiet. The mother went outside to see what had happened but the little girl was gone. The distraught mother looked in every wigwam in the village but the little girl had vanished.

At the very time the mother was looking for her child, the little girl was enroute to the owls' den in the wilderness, for Owl had finally come to take her away. One of the owls, who was the little girl's grandmother, put her in a fancy wigwam and kept her there warm and comfy all winter. Every once in awhile the grandmother owl would promise the little girl to take her home to her parents, saying, "I will give you some of my medicine and I will take you back where I got you. The medicine I shall give you is called Spotted Fawn Medicine and it is intended to charm deer and other game so that they may be killed. Medicine of this kind must be kept wrapped in a spotted fawn skin and is named on that account. It is very powerful, this medicine I shall give you, grandchild, for you and your parents and great-grandparents to use in the future among all your people as long as the world shall last."

As it drew near spring, the parents of the lost girl went out to the woods to make maple sugar. At that time the grandmother owl told her grandchild that it was time for her to return home, and she would take her to the edge of her parents' sugar camp. "Stand there silently until your mother comes and finds you," the grandmother owl instructed. "Don't allow her to touch you at all for four days. Then you must tell her to go and prepare a tiny wigwam for you to remain in for four days. This must be away from the sugar camp in a clean place where no one has done any trampling on the ground and you shall remain there, silent."

The mother had given her child up for lost and was very happy to see her. She wanted to embrace the little girl, but the child warned her, "Do not grasp me, for I am forbidden to allow you to touch me for four days."

153

Then she told her mother to build her a tiny wigwam and also asked that her father come to visit her frequently during her four-day stay there, so that she could instruct him how to use the medicine given to her by the owl grandmother.

The medicine should always be prepared by a pure young girl. It is made up when a number of hunters wish to use it. The girl who has the medicine builds a small wigwam and the men who wish to hunt come to the wigwam and take a steam bath together. While the steam saturates each hunter, songs are sung, and the sacred power of the owl is invoked. The other sacred powers hear it too and send aid to the hunters. All wild animals are called by the spell and approach the wigwam. The hunters meet the game coming to them. The medicine must always be kept and guarded by a pure young girl.[8]

The Huron recognized a classification of illness in addition to those brought on by natural causes and those precipitated by supernatural means. These were the desires of the soul, and they could be cured by fulfilling those desires. The patient usually dreamed his or her own cure, and the rest of the community cooperated by acting out whatever it was the sick person had dreamed, an early form of psychodrama. One Huron woman dreamed that she would be cured if all the young men and women of the village assembled and danced naked in front of her. She also requested that one of the young men urinate in her mouth. The entire ritual was performed as she requested, and apparently it worked.

A Huron woman who was suffering from a nervous disorder claimed that when she went out of her house one night the moon had appeared to her as a stately, beautiful woman and ordered that all the surrounding tribes should bring to the patient the distinctive products of their nation. The moon also directed that ceremonies should be held in the woman's honor and that during the rites she should be dressed in red to resemble the moon and look as if she were made of fire.

After the woman's vision she became giddy and suffered from muscle spasms so severe that she could not move. The other villagers put her in a large basket and carried her to the center of the community. There she named twenty-two presents she wanted, and the people all hastened to collect the articles she had named. The chiefs instructed everyone to keep large, bright fires burning all night. When it was dark, the woman's muscles began to relax so that she could walk if assisted by a person on each side of her. She walked down the middle of every house in the village, going right through the cooking fires, all the while claiming to feel no warmth. Later all the people painted their bodies and faces and ran through the village wreaking havoc, breaking pots, throwing furniture around, and kicking the dogs. This was typical behavior when the villagers were helping someone satisfy a soul desire, and it was assumed that the more noise everyone made the more they would help the patient.

Apparently many Huron women sought relief through dreaming cures for their soul desires. There really wasn't much room for self-expression in their daily work, so a strong woman who needed to demonstrate her individuality tended to rely on what was one of the few socially acceptable ways for her to assert herself and stand out from the mass.

SHAMANS AND PROPHETS

Some Native American women who acquired supernatural power became shamans and used their talents to control the weather, foretell the future, and ferret out witches. Women were well-represented in this profession in many of the early tribes.

Copper Eskimo women had a chance to earn great respect in their communities by becoming shamans. To enjoy the privileges of being a shaman, a woman had to make certain sacrifices, usually observing a food taboo. D. Jenness, who explored the Canadian Arctic in the very early part of this century, was told of two shamans, a man and a woman, who began to hold a seance but in the middle of it decided to drink a little deer blood, which had been prohibited to them by the spirits who had given them their power. The man's familiar spirit immediately left him, and he lost all his shamanistic powers. The woman, whose name was Mittik, got up and walked away from the village toward the sun. As she was walking up the side of a ridge she suddenly disappeared into the ground, and a moment afterward a dog sprang out of the spot where she had vanished. The next minute the dog disappeared, and Mittik was back again. This change happened three or four times in front of the astonished Eskimos. Finally Mittik walked back to the camp, but her faculties were impaired. The other shamans in the village laid their hands on her and with the help of their familiar spirits were able to restore her to her senses.

Jenness was also able to take part in a seance while among the Copper

Eskimos in the Northwest Territory. He and his party were considering an excursion, so a woman shaman named Higilak gave a seance to discover if Jenness could make the journey he wished and return by sled before the snow melted. The seance was held about midnight, but it was not dark, for the time was May, when the sun never sets below the horizon that far north. Higilak sat in the back of the tent in a corner, and her husband Ikpakhuak was slightly in front of her. All the other adults in the community also crowded into the tent. Jenness wrote:

Higilak began by delivering a long speech setting forth the whole question at issue. Suddenly she uttered cries of pain and covered her face in her hands. Dead silence followed for a few minutes, a silence that was only broken by an occasional remark uttered in a low tone by someone in the audience. Presently Higilak began to howl and growl like a wolf, then as suddenly ceased and raised her head, when, behold, two canine teeth, evidently a wolf's, were protruding one from each corner of her mouth. She leaned over to Avranna [another man] and pretended to gnaw his head, then began to utter broken remarks which her audience caught up and discussed, though very little of them could be interpreted. Every now and then she had to put her hand up to her mouth to keep the teeth from falling out, and once she slyly pushed them right inside out of sight, pushing them out again a few minutes later. After about a quarter of an hour spent in this manner she suddenly broke out into cries of pain again and concealed her face in her hands behind Ikpakhuak's back. Then I saw her carefully drop one hand towards her long boot, into which she apparently slipped the teeth, for a moment later her face reappeared without them. This was the critical moment, the moment when the wolf's spirit inside her body gave its answer to the question at issue. A few broken words issued from her, uttered in a feeble falsetto voice that was almost inaudible. Her audience was bending eagerly forward, drinking in every syllable. In about two minutes it was all over and Higilak, after a few more cries of pain (the familiar was leaving her) followed by two or three gasps, resumed her normal bearing. The seance was now concluded but some of the natives lingered for a few minutes to discuss the oracle that had been delivered to them. Higilak herself professed to be ignorant of it, for a shaman should not be conscious of utterances given under the inspiration of a familiar; accordingly she had to question some of the bystanders to find out what she had said. In speaking of this seance some time afterwards, the natives stated as an incontestable fact that Higilak had been transformed into a wolf."[9]

Southeast Salish women, who lived in the area of the Washington-Idaho border, also were able to claim considerable power and privilege by becoming shamans. Among the services performed by shamans for the public good was

156

control of the weather. Part of the technique of weather control was for a shaman to let blood from a cut on her head fall on the snow. One winter the weather was so severe that all the livestock were dying of the cold. The snow was so deep that they could not find any grass to eat. So the people sought the aid of an old woman who had power over the weather. She sang her power song and then asked her petitioners to cut a gash in her head. As soon as her blood had fallen on the snow, a south wind began to gather force and soon blew in rain clouds. Rain soon fell and washed away the snow. All the people who owned livestock were grateful to the shaman for saving their stock, and they all contributed to pay her fee.

Some Southeast Salish shamans had power over the fish their people relied on so heavily. Once a young Salish man constructed a salmon weir, but he didn't seem to be catching any salmon. His grandmother, who was named Sikuntaluqs, decided to help him. She took a walk by the weir and lay down on the opposite bank of the river. Not long after dark a kingfisher flew by, and then the old woman slept. During the night the weir began to fill up with salmon, and by dawn it was overflowing. The old woman called to the people, and the fishermen ran down and were able to gather more than two hundred fish. Then the weir broke.

After the fishermen had all the salmon out of the trap, Sikuntaluqs took off her moccasins and went swimming in the creek. It was generally forbidden for a woman to come within half a mile of a salmon weir, and many of the people began to chastise Sikuntaluqs for her actions and remind her of the taboo. But the powerful old woman paid no heed to the chattering of the people on the bank, shouting to them, "I was the one who made the salmon come. It's all right if I take a swim."[10]

Women with strong shamanistic power were sometimes feared and resented even if they used their power in a benevolent manner. The story is told of a Mohawk medicine woman named Sky-Sifter who lived in the early 1800s. Just how much of the story is legendary and how much is true is unclear, but it is said that she was the daughter of a chief and was very well-known for her medicine power. Sky-Sifter was an imposing woman who stood almost six feet tall and had flashing black eyes and hair that touched the floor when she was seated. People tended to stay out of her way when she was disturbed about something. Some believed that her medicine was so strong that nothing could be hidden from her.

Sky-Sifter owned a lavishly decorated canoe which no one was allowed to touch, and she kept it near her private tipi where she lived alone when she was not with her family in their longhouse. The other people became so afraid of this powerful medicine woman that they began to make plans to kill her. But Sky-Sifter had spies who informed her of the secret plans. One night the other villagers arrived to burn her alive when she was in her tipi, and when the ashes cooled a body was found in the burnt ruins. The husband of the medicine woman buried the remains of his wife in the traditional way and erected a monument over her grave. Only Sky-Sifter's closest friends knew that she had been able to escape at the last minute through an underground passageway.

WITCHES

Native American women who earned the dread appellation "witch" had much the same type of power as those women called shamans. The difference was that witches used their supernatural power malevolently to perpetrate evil and to bring harm to their fellows. Whether the witches really could command this power or not is in some ways immaterial to any discussion, for most early Americans believed that some members of their communities had control over evil forces and moderated their own behavior accordingly.

Creeks believed that witches could take the form of owls and fly about at night—during the day they returned home in their normal forms as old women (or men). Anyone suspected of being a witch was greatly feared, for the Creeks believed the evildoers could cripple people by shooting blood into their legs with a reed and that they caused the deaths of normally healthy citizens by slyly taking out their heart and spirit. Because only elderly people became witches, Creek children were frequently warned not to loiter around groups of old persons. When enough suspicion became attached to an old woman and several people accused her of evil deeds, the suspect was struck on the head and dumped in the water. She wasn't killed for being a witch but for killing other people.

The Iroquois tribes also had a deep-seated fear of witches, believing that any person could become possessed of an evil spirit and be transformed into a witch. To execute her nefarious crimes, an Iroquois witch could transform herself into any animal, bird, or reptile, then she could go back to her human form, or if she had an immediate need to escape detection, she could hide in the shape of some inanimate object.

Everyone knew that witches held periodic meetings in the dark of the night during which they initiated new members into their order. For the neophyte the initiation fee was the life of her nearest and dearest friend, whom she had to kill with an unseen poison. With such strong beliefs, it is no wonder that an Iroquois who suspected a person of witchcraft immediately became that person's judge, jury, and executioner.

On the other side of the continent from the Iroquois, on the coast of southern Alaska, the Tlingit did not talk much about witchcraft, but everybody feared it and knew that there were people living in each village who possessed these wicked powers. When a Tlingit witch wanted to harm someone she tried to obtain something from that person—a few hairs, some spittle, a morsel of food—which she then took to a graveyard and cached, with the proper maledictions, on a newly dead body or in the ashes of a cremated body. When the body decayed the bewitched person would become ill.

Sick people who thought that they had been bewitched sent for a shaman to perform a ceremony to exorcise the evil power. At a certain point in the rites the shaman got up and went to the home of a relative of the patient whom he accused of witchcraft. The suspected witch was seized and thrown into an empty hut where she was kept without food or water until she confessed or died as a result of other tortures. It was believed that Tlingit witches could fly, and it was not unexpected for an incarcerated witch to escape from a hut by flying through the smoke hole. But if the suspected witch did not escape and eventually confessed, she was expected to retrieve the objects she had hidden in the graveyard and take them to the beach to purify them in the seawater. After that the sick person usually recovered.

The Tlingit expected the relatives of an accused witch to kill the indicted woman in order to rid their kin group of such a hated individual. Sometimes even her children were killed lest they pass on the stigma. There is the story of a shaman who accused a young woman of witchcraft because she had refused him in marriage. After the accusation the woman's brother leaped on her with a dagger and wounded her before some visiting Russian sailors managed to rescue her from further punishment. Eventually the reason for the shaman's accusation came out, and he was forced to leave the area.

Tlingits believed that a witch had eight "covers," like skins, inside her body. If a person wished to give up her evil ways, she had to find a stronger sorcerer to open up the covers and cure her. Once there was a widow living in Sitka who worked black magic. She claimed that she wanted to stop her sorcery but said she couldn't help herself—she had been bewitched by someone else.

The old woman requested that Christian prayers be said for her, so some of

159

her friends took her to a Reverend Austin, a Presbyterian missionary in the area. The man was admittedly skeptical of the woman's powers and decided to test her by putting some peanuts in a bowl in the kitchen and asking her to make some of the nuts fly into her hand. Reportedly the witch handed the astonished preacher four peanuts. The woman's friends then sent for a woman who was reputed to be a very powerful sorcerer. She worked over the widow for an hour but could not open her covers—her explanation of her failure was that a more powerful witch was working against her. A few days later the old woman, in utter despair over her insane compulsion to kill by sorcery, hanged herself.

Lummi women, living on the northwestern Washington coast, sometimes resorted to witchcraft or magic when they felt neglected by their husbands. A woman who really hated her husband might cause his death by taking one of his hairs and wrapping it into the gills of a salt water trout which was migrating up a freshwater river to spawn. The woman would incant a few special words and then send the trout on its way up the river. The lure of the fish would make the bewitched person lonely and downcast, and in his desperation he might rush to the water where he would be completely overcome and drown.

Lummis who were very skilled in the black arts were restrained from misuse of their power by a secret society whose members acted as vigilantes, executing those persons considered harmful to the tribe. When the secret society determined that a person was too dangerous to remain in the tribe, they heated a long green stick and forced it up their victim's rectum all the way to her throat, forcing blood and flesh out of the witch's mouth. She was then sent groaning into the square—her gruesome death serving as a reminder of what happened to people who misused their power.

In the Southwest the ancient Zunis considered witchcraft the most serious of all offenses, and it was the only crime besides cowardice in battle that carried the death sentence.

In more recent times the punishment for this crime, although still very harsh, usually stopped short of death. Once a suspected witch had been apprehended it was necessary for her to confess to her crime, no matter how much torture had to be applied to elicit this confession.

There was one case of a Zuni woman and her grandson who were caught "witching around" in 1890. They were first discovered when a wealthy Zuni family found them peeping through their windows. These people took them inside their house and questioned the two as to why they were spying. After about two hours of questioning the old woman and the boy confessed that they were jealous of the family because of their wealth and they had planned to bring sickness and death to them all. Then the witches tried to convince the family to let them go saying, "Since you have caught us, we are unlucky and we shall die instead of you." They meant that although they had come with all their power they had been caught, and in Zuni belief a witch who is found out can expect automatic retribution.

The family didn't think it was a good idea to let the pair go, fearing they would return with even greater power, so they turned them over to the war chief, who, along with several other members of the war society, questioned the old woman and the boy. At daybreak the two were hung head down with their hands tied behind them. The war chief asked them how many people they had killed, but they did not confess, although they were repeatedly clubbed. Finally, after many hours they admitted to several deaths and offered to show their accusers the clothing and beads of the dead people if they were released. The witches produced the expected goods and also a powder they had used to paint their bodies, which they said was compounded of human flesh, bones, and earth taken from a graveyard.

Then the two were hung up and clubbed again until they confessed to the deaths of two people of the wealthy family that had accosted them. Eventually they were released with the warning that if they were ever caught again they would be killed. The boy died that night, and within a short time the accused woman and every member of her family had died. There remained, however, the suspicion that their deaths were not unaided by one of the Zuni secret societies.[11]

Navajos and Apaches have also had very strong feelings about witchcraft. Among the Navajos, aged, childless women were often suspected of witchcraft, especially those who were very rich (having obtained wealth through their power) or those who were very poor (seeking relief from their poverty in this way). When one or more Navajos decided through some sort of divination or by witnessing suspicious acts that a woman was a witch, she was summoned to a meeting and urged to confess, for it was believed that a confession would produce a cure in the bewitched person if the victim wasn't already too far gone. If the suspected witch was reluctant to admit to any evildoing, she was tied down and not allowed to eat, drink, or relieve herself until she had changed her mind and given a full confession. Once this was done the victim was expected to begin to improve slowly and the witch to die within the year from the same symptoms afflicting her victim. A person who would not confess was killed after four days; in some cases she was allowed to live, if she left the community immediately and permanently.

Apaches, like Navajos, never actually saw anyone practicing witchcraft; they just saw the results of what they interpreted as witchcraft. Someone suddenly became ill, a person inexplicably died after having had words with someone who had been acting strangely—these are the types of occurrences that prompted accusations of witchcraft. A plausible accusation by one person backed up by a few other disgruntled citizens was usually sufficient to "prove" the guilt of an Apache witch. A confession given under pain of torture was accepted as full proof of evildoing. An accused witch could attempt to defend herself against the charges and would be successful if she could prove that she had no supernatural powers and that it was highly unlikely she would wish to harm the victim. If a witch was unsuccessful in her defense, she would be hung by her wrists from a tree so that her feet just cleared the ground. Then a fire would be built under her and she would be slowly burned to death. "Witches do not burn up quickly; they keep on living a long time," one Apache stated.

Most of the available information about sorcery in North American tribes tends to support the fact that the belief in witchcraft was much more extensive than the practice of witchcraft. Many social scientists have attempted to analyze what functions these beliefs played in the early societies.

Most early Native American cultures were organized into small groups of related individuals who lived and worked closely with each other all their lives. So that relations would be smooth and daily life would be harmonious, many hostilities had to be repressed. But hostilities cannot be repressed for-forever—feelings of tension and anger have a way of insisting on expression, whether they are directed toward the original object of frustration or else-where.

Belief in witchcraft provided a channel for the expression of hostile feelings; it was a form of hating that was socially approved and justified. It wasn't only other people who aroused the ire of these early Americans—there were many conditions that could cause anger and frustration in a group that had little control over its environment. When the expected rains didn't come and the crops shriveled and died in the unrelenting sun, when a family froze to death in the snow, or when a hunter arrived home consistently empty handed, it was comforting to have some place to turn, somewhere to lay the blame for the terrible misfortunes. "He was bewitched," and "They all had a spell on them," helped to explain what was essentially not understandable.

Belief in witchcraft also provided a reassuring answer to why usually powerful medicine men and women were sometimes unable to cure a patient. If it was assumed that witches had power to induce illness that could resist the strongest of conventional treatments, then it was possible for patients and doctors to continue to believe in the efficacy of traditional methods even when they didn't work. "She was bewitched," was the answer.

Belief in witchcraft was very powerful as a method of social control. If a woman knew that any actions that were in some way different from the normal, narrow range of activities she was expected to perform would cause suspicion in someone who might be watching, she would no doubt think very carefully before departing from her usual behavior. In this way, fear of sorcery was also a powerful stabilizing influence on society. Anybody who was a rabble-rouser, iconoclast, or even too liberal was immediately branded a witch and burned or otherwise killed for her misdeeds. It was a most effective method of putting a quick stop to any revolutionary thoughts.

As far as the victims were concerned, the state of being bewitched sometimes offered a chance for a little attention. Clyde Kluckholn, in his treatment of Navajo witchcraft, explains that many of those who have gone into a trance or suddenly fainted at ceremonials or other large gatherings were often persons who were somewhat neglected or of low status. Wealthier people tended to have their problems diagnosed in the privacy of their homes. Attributing one's problems to being bewitched was a way of getting sympathy when nothing else seemed to work and was also an acceptable way of explaining why one's life was not all that one desired it to be.[12]

Another less profound but no less plausible theory for the continued belief in witchcraft is that which ascribes to it some entertainment value. The whole cycle of activities which surrounded a witchcraft accusation offered relief from dull routine and provided emotional release and diversion for the members of the society.

A Mohave Indian woman, with tattoos similar to those given to
war captives. *(Courtesy of Arizona Historical Society)*

Women and War

HELPERS, FIGHTERS, VICTORS, AND VANQUISHED

War occupied much of the time and energy of the early Native Americans. Wars were fought to protect territory, food supply, and ultimately the continuance of the tribe; wars were fought for revenge against previous injuries; wars were fought as a means of gaining prestige by the valiant warriors; and wars were fought for the sheer hell of it.

Although fighting battles with the enemy was usually the duty of the men, women could not help but be involved in martial activities. Most Indian women limited their participation to helping outfit their brothers and husbands for their expeditions, but other, stronger willed and more individualistic women became warriors in their own right. Some more unfortunate women became part of the spoils of war, dragged from their homes, the captives of enemy warriors.

When a war party was getting ready to go out on a raid, the camp or village was always full of activity. Women were hurrying to complete extra pairs of moccasins for the men and getting together foods that could be packed and taken along. Women who had lost sons and husbands or other relatives in previous battles were apt to visit the lodge of a distinguished warrior and urge him to wipe away their tears with enemy blood.

In a Comanche camp, if the war party was a popular one, young maidens serenaded the lodges of renowned warriors whom they wanted to join the party. The young women chanted songs recalling the victories of ancestors and the

165

valor of warriors still living—rather like a football pep rally. Any woman, young or old, who promoted a successful raiding party expected to be rewarded with a horse or other captured object when the warriors returned home.

What the women did after they had waved the men off, wishing them luck and hoping for their safe return, varied from tribe to tribe. Mandan maidens fasted while their brothers were away on war expeditions in the hope that their sacrifice would bring the young men success in striking the enemy or capturing horses. When a war party was out, the girls or young women would go separately each day at dawn to a low hill or a scaffold in the garden where they would cry for their brothers' success, addressing their prayers to all holy things. They remained prayerful all day, but they usually took along some quill work or other task to occupy them in their lonely vigil.

In northern British Columbia when Kaska men went off to war the wives who remained in camp constructed a number of humanlike dummies using robes and skins stuffed with brush. Each morning the women attacked the dummies with ceremonial wooden knives in the belief that the ritual would give additional strength to the warriors. Every married woman whose husband was gone on a raid girdled herself with a fancy outer belt which she wore the entire time the war party was out. Any woman who untied her belt would be considered responsible for any ill luck which befell the fighters. The belts were apparently a symbol of a woman's chastity in her husband's absence, and they may have indirectly had some survival value for the men, as a warrior whose wife was properly belted didn't have to waste time on jealous thoughts but could focus on the business of war.

The Apaches spent much of their energy on raiding and warfare, and women contributed to the war efforts in a variety of ways. When a family or clan decided to sponsor a war party, one of the members went around to all the camps to solicit women to participate in the dance that always preceded the departure of the war party. The messenger said something like, "Loan me your wife tonight. She can dance with a man but she will return to you just as she left you. She can dance all night; even if she is dancing with another man and talking with him it means nothing. The same way with girls. They will come back in the morning."[1] For the sexually straightlaced Apaches, it was necessary that the invitation include the assurance that the women would be expected to dance only and wouldn't be coerced into any hanky-panky.

When the Apache warriors rode out of camp, the wives they left behind were supposed to pray for their husbands every morning for four days; every time they pulled a pot of meat off the fire, they prayed that their husbands would get what they wanted. Not all the women stayed behind in camp—some wives left their children with grandmothers and followed their warrior husbands into battle where they prepared food, dressed wounds, and when necessary bravely fought beside the men.

WARRIOR WOMEN

The entire Sioux society revolved around war. Sioux women were formally barred from participating in any of the war games, but many women went along on war parties, making their preparations quietly and then sneaking behind the men as they rode out of the village. Usually these heroics were confined to just one episode, and then the women went back to being conventional homemakers—even if they had performed so gloriously in battle that they earned the male accolade of "brave."

Sometimes a Sioux woman might have a dream that would urge her to join a certain campaign, but most often a Sioux woman took to the warpath to seek revenge against the death of someone dear to her, perhaps a brother. Sometimes old women in mourning begged to be taken on a war party so that they could mutilate the enemy corpses. One Sioux matron earned her war honors accidentally; an Ojibwa had been lurking in the woods near a Sioux camp, and the woman killed him when she threw a large deer bone into the brush, striking the skull of the unlucky warrior.

There survives the story, possibly based on truth, of a young Warm Springs Apache maiden named Lozen who became a powerful and respected warrior. Lozen was the sister of Victorio, a famous chief; she took advantage of all the opportunities offered to Apache women, and when they weren't enough for her, she took more.

When very young she became expert at riding and roping, and she was always able to bring home enemy horses when she went on a trip. She developed this skill to the point where she was better at stealing horses and stampeding a herd than any man in her tribe. The legend assures us that Lozen was truly dedicated to helping her people, not merely gaining glory for herself. One time she found herself alone in enemy territory with a young mother and her baby. It would have been easy for Lozen to have escaped by herself, but instead she spent several grueling months leading the young woman and her child to safety.

As this valorous Apache woman matured, she began to develop the uncanny power to determine the location of the enemy, and many times she was invited to sit around the council fire when the leaders were planning war strategy. Throughout her life she dedicated her life to helping her people at the side of her famous brother.[2]

Another outstanding warrior woman was Ehyophsta (Yellow Haired Woman), a Cheyenne who made a direct stand in an important battle between her people and the Shoshonis in 1869. The Shoshonis thought that they were attacking a weak camp of only seven lodges, and they were expecting to go in and capture all the Cheyenne women and children. They didn't know that the tiny Cheyenne camp was reinforced by many of their allies secretly hiding in the tipis. During the battle, two braves, one Shoshoni and one Cheyenne, were clinched in a one-to-one battle to the death. Ehyophsta was in the thick of the battle when she rode up to the struggling pair. She dismounted, drew her butcher knife, and stabbed the Shoshoni twice. After the intruders had retreated, the villagers were searching the area looking for wounded people and came across some of the enemy hiding in the clefts of rocks. Most of these unfortunates were discovered and immediately shot. One young Shoshoni warrior was dragged out of hiding, and someone suggested that it might be wise to question him. Ehyophsta spoke up and, asking the others to step aside, indicated that she would do the questioning. She stepped forward, lifted up the young man's arm, and thrust her knife into his armpit. Then she scalped him. This deed made her eligible to join the small society of Cheyenne women who had been to war with their husbands. It was said that this exclusive group held secret meetings which no one else was allowed to attend.

Warrior Girl

(TEWA)

Once there lived a girl of the Cottonwood clan who would not mind her mother or father or uncle. They were always telling her to be a good girl but she got angry very quickly. Finally these people got tired of telling her to be good so they just ignored her. Once when she was grinding corn many enemies began to come close to the village. Her uncle came to her and grabbed her arm and said, "Take your bow and arrows and go and fight with the enemies who are coming. You would not mind us and behaved like a boy. Now it is time for you to go and fight and be brave."

The girl laughed "Ha! Ha!" and said, "I am very anxious to go and fight the enemies. I am not afraid. I will do all I can."

Her uncle handed her a bow and arrows. Then she looked around and there was a rattle hanging on the wall. She stepped up and got it. Then she started to sing. As soon as she stopped singing, she laughed "Ha! Ha!" She sang four times in the room and then she went outside and sang four times. Every time she paused in the singing she laughed "Ha! Ha!" because she was not afraid to fight.

Then she started off toward the enemy. Some of the villagers laughed at her but she just went on, singing and laughing, happy that she was going to fight. Before she met the enemies, she pulled her dress up four times to show the enemies that she was a girl. Then she fought, and she killed all the enemies in one day. When she turned back after the fighting was done, the men saw that she had on a mask—one side was blue and one side was yellow and it had long teeth. The men were afraid of her, but they followed her back to the town as she sang and laughed. The battle earned the girl the name "Pohaha"—Po, meaning wet, for it is said that she was wet between her legs while she was fighting, and haha for the laughing that she did.

That night Pohaha's uncles came to her house and told her that they had been thinking she must be a man and had decided to put her in as war chief. Even if she was a girl, she was a man. As war chief she would have to lead her people against enemies, protect them from sickness, and treat them as her children. After that she became a good woman.

When she died she left her mask and said that it would represent her even if she was dead. "I will be with you all the time," she said, "the mask is me." That is why the Cottonwood people keep the mask.[3]

❀◇❀◇❀◇❀◇❀◇❀◇❀◇

There are many stories of Ojibwa women who sought the warpath. Some of them went as maidens on campaigns organized by their fathers and served as the reward for the best young warriors, who were allowed to take them as wives. Other women were prompted by desperation and thoughts of suicide, while yet others fought in a frantic attempt at self-preservation when they or their children were cornered. But one Ojibwa, named Chief Earth Woman, fought for the glory of war—one of the few Native American women to seek the enemy on the warpath like a man.

Chief Earth Woman's first military enterprise was inspired by her love for a young warrior, who unfortunately was already married and the father of two children. But Chief Earth Woman still flirted with the handsome young brave, and when he and other men made plans to attack the Sioux, she decided she wanted to go along. Whenever the men started off on a trip, the women usually paddled along beside them in canoes for some distance. But when the other women turned back this time, they noticed that Chief Earth Woman was not with them.

The spunky maiden was able to convince the leader of the war party to allow her to continue by confiding to him that she had had a dream that gave her special supernatural powers. Indeed she was able to predict the movements of the Sioux and so aided her party to better overtake the enemy. When the Ojibwas surprised the Sioux, Chief Earth Woman's lover was the first to kill one of the enemy, and she ran up to the victim as soon as he fell and took his scalp off.

When the war party returned to their camp, Chief Earth Woman joined the other new warriors in singing, "So that's how the Sioux heads look," and she was given the traditional honors just like her male companions.

One young Ojibwa woman who accompanied her father on a campaign took not only the scalps of two of the enemy warriors but also the genitals of one of them. This maiden's mother had always been a very jealous woman and was often fighting and scuffling with other women whom she considered her romantic rivals. During the victory dance her daughter threw the enemy's severed genitals at her crying, "Here, take this. This is the kind of thing for which you used to fight and quarrel. You used to cut women's faces and pull their hair over it. Keep it! I brought it for you!"[4]

❀◇❀◇❀◇❀◇❀◇❀◇❀◇❀◇

Hé-é-e, the Warrior Girl

(HOPI)

Many years ago some Hopis were living outside the main village. In one household the mother was occupied in putting up her daughter's hair in the butterfly whorls customarily worn by Hopi maidens. The mother had finished only one side of the hair whorls, the hair on the other side still hanging loosely, when they saw enemies sneaking toward the village.

The maiden snatched up a bow, quiver, and arrows from the wall of her home and raced toward the village to warn the other people. Then she led the defense until the men in the fields returned and routed the enemy. She has been personified ever since as a kachina and always appears with her hair partially up on one side and hanging down on the other side.[5]

❀◇❀◇❀◇❀◇❀◇❀◇❀◇❀◇

Not all Indian women who engaged in fighting actually chose to do so—sometimes they just had to join the battle to save themselves and their children.

Such was the case with an old Pawnee woman named for her exploit Old-Lady-Grieves-the-Enemy. One time the Poncas, perhaps aided by some Sioux, were preparing to attack the Pawnee village of the old lady, who was then about fifty years old. The enemy was creeping up toward the village, their pockets full of hay so that they could burn the houses to the ground. The men of the tribe felt they were so heavily outnumbered it was useless to fight, and they remained cowering in the houses. The old lady could not resign herself to such cowardly action, so she decided to do whatever she could. Stripping off her clothing she donned a loincloth, twisted her hair into a knot on her forehead, rubbed soot from the fireplace across her eyes (signifying defiance of any danger, particularly fire), and took off after the invaders with a war club. This roused the men to action, shaming them into attempting a defense.

Old-Lady-Grieves-the-Enemy killed one Ponca right outside her house, and eventually the Pawnees were able to repulse the attackers. Years later when members of the two tribes were reviewing the battle, the Poncas recalled that when the old man came out he seemed so brave that that was what held them back. Then the Pawnees told their former enemies that the old warrior was a woman.

The feisty old Pawnee woman didn't let the rest of the village forget that it was she who had inspired them to battle. When she noticed a jealous husband beating his wife, she'd chastise him, saying in her deep full voice, "Fine brave men you are! Your place is out beating up the Poncas. They came here to burn up our whole village. We women do you no harm. It's the Poncas you should be out fighting with."[6]

There is also the tale of a Cherokee woman who by her spontaneous fury inspired her people in a battle. A hostile war party had attacked a Cherokee town, killing the chief. His wife, who was named Cuhtahlatah (Wild Hemp), was so grieved when she saw her husband fall that she snatched up his tomahawk and shouting, "Kill, kill," rushed on the enemy. At that point her people were in retreat, but when they saw their fallen chief's wife brandishing her weapon they rallied and with renewed courage continued their resistance with such energy that they gained complete victory.

Cherokee women sometimes joined their men in fighting off the colonists who were threatening to take over their lands. The report survives of a campaign made by a General Griffith Rutherford against the Cherokee in 1776. The white men lost nineteen men to the Indian warriors but eventually managed to drive their opponents back. After the main body of Indians had retreated, the soldiers noticed a lone warrior looking out from behind a tree and immediately shot and killed the hapless soul. When they examined the body, they discovered that it was a woman, painted and stripped like a warrior and armed with a bow and arrows. She had already been shot through the thigh and had been unable to flee with her comrades.

Had this female warrior survived she would undoubtedly have become a member of a Cherokee sorority of sacred persons who were called "Pretty Women." To belong to this assemblage was considered a high honor, and only women who had performed a heroic deed or who were the mothers of warriors were eligible. The Pretty Women joined the men of their tribe at every war council and were expected to counsel the war chief on such matters as strategy and time of attack. They also decided the fate of any prisoners or captives taken in battle.

Usually, however, when women joined the fighting they played a more passive role than these legendary warrior women. During one battle when Custer and his men were trying to attack a group of Cheyennes, the women and children were trying to flee while the warriors were attempting to hold off the white attackers. A mother named Buffalo Woman finally became so exhausted from trying to carry and drag her three children to safety that she stopped and sat down for a moment. She and her children were immediately taken prisoner by one of the white soldiers, who began to march them back to the army compound. As they were going along, Buffalo Woman noticed a number of Indian warriors coming in from the south. She gave no outward sign of what she knew but began to beg the soldiers to wait for a moment because she wanted to wrap her children's feet in rags to protect them from the freezing snow. The soldiers didn't understand her words, of course, but apparently they understood what she wanted when she began to tear pieces of cloth from her dress and bind up the feet of the little ones. While Buffalo Woman was cleverly delaying her captors, the party of Indians was able to get between her and the rest of the command. The Indian warriors recognized their kinswoman, charged her captors, and led Buffalo Woman and her children to safety.

This story is similar to that of some early Natchez women living near the present town of Natchez, Mississippi, who played a central role in helping their men deviously overcome the intruding French. These southern Indians were opposed to the presence of the Frenchmen from the first, but they bided their time until they had a plan. Meanwhile, the Frenchmen, who were having a fine time with the Natchez women, became lax and unguarded because of the seeming goodwill of the men of the town. The white men visited the Indian town at night in an unsuspicious way and freely admitted the Indian women into their own garrison.

The Natchez warriors worked out a plan with their women, telling those who had French lovers to arrange to meet their paramours inside the fortress on the same night. The women complied and set up the usual appointments. But when the evening arrived, it wasn't the women who entered the fort but Natchez warriors in disguise. The Indian men were finally able to release their pent-up hostilities, and they exterminated the French. All the Frenchmen except one, that is. His Natchez wife really loved him, and she double-crossed her own people by warning her lover of the coming attack. This lucky soldier escaped quietly down the Mississippi River, carrying news of the disaster to other Frenchmen.

The Natchez had all moved into the fort and were having a fine time when they were surprised by another contingent of Frenchmen, who took them all into custody, moved them from their homeland, and resettled them in another area. One can't help but wonder at the reaction of the lovestruck young Natchez woman when she realized the far-reaching effects of her betrayal.

VICTORY CELEBRATIONS

These stories of Indian women warriors depict truly exceptional individuals. Few Native American women were so daring and aggressive as to go out on their own to kill, scalp, and plunder. The typical wife and mother waited at home while the war party was out—praying for the safety of the expedition, caring for the children and the gardens, and keeping up the normal routine of camp life in the absence of her man. But all the while she was quietly performing her daily duties, she knew that if the warriors returned home victorious and with many enemy scalps, she would have her chance to taunt and debase the enemy, for it would be her privilege to dance with the scalps during the victory celebration.

The women's scalp dance apparently served a profound purpose in Native American societies, for it was remarkably widespread, with just the details of the celebration varying from tribe to tribe. The gory war trophies were usually suspended from the ends of poles or sticks, and the women waved the scalps about like flags as they danced and sang themselves into a frenzy, giving vent to rage, hostility, and fury. It might at first glance seem unusual for women, who spent their lives in nurturing, to take such an orgiastic role in the victory dances, gloating over the misfortunes of other poor creatures much like themselves. But it is unrealistic to expect women not to have a need to release their pent-up anger and hostility. They had been conditioned to the war psychology since they were children, just as the men had been, and they took part in the prewar rituals, working themselves into a high state of anger and resentfulness. It was they who felt the economic loss when a brother or husband was killed, and they who were condemned to years of widowhood when their men were killed. It is no wonder they were angry at the enemy. Yet most women were denied the excitement or the release that the men found in combat. The women had to wait until the men returned from battle with scalps or captives, for the victory celebration was the proper time and place for the average Indian woman to release her tensions.

And release them she did. Cree and Assiniboine women blackened their faces when they danced with the scalps; Natchez and Osage dancers dressed like warriors and painted themselves above the waist; and Menominee women "bought" scalps from their brothers, paying them gifts "to wash the blood from their hands." The Apache victory celebration was a time of rare sexual license for mature, widowed, or divorced women, who danced naked and beautifully painted. Warriors enjoyed watching the women dance, and it was considered a fine way for a woman to thank the warriors for revenging the death of one of her relatives. If an Apache war party had gone out to avenge the death of a particular warrior, any male captives taken would be turned over to the female relative closest to the dead man. The woman would first torture the prisoner, helped by some of the other women of her camp, and then kill him.

If a Papago woman's husband returned from a war expedition against the Apache with an enemy scalp, neither she nor he was allowed to participate in the victory dance. Instead, they went separately into seclusion, living in little brush shelters. The victorious warrior was attended by his godfather, and the godfather's wife took care of the warrior's woman. It would have been very dangerous for a killer to have returned to his family before his period of ritual purification. The Papagos believed that an enemy's death let power loose and that power had to be tamed before it could be used. So for sixteen days the warrior and his wife remained in exile while every night in the village the rest of the people celebrated. Young girls danced with the bows, arrows, clubs, and shields of the warriors, and old women past the age of menopause danced with the powerful Apache scalps.

Victory Song

(PAPAGO)

Here I stand, singing for my prisoner
Come and see, oh, women!
I dreamed that I saw light
At the tips of the warriors' feathers.[7]

Some Papago women did not want to submit to the long purification rites, so they asked their husbands not to be killers during the expedition. Other women were more devious: because a man could not go on the warpath when his wife was menstruating (because he had less power at that time), some women simply took off for the Little House when an expedition was being organized, either in an effort to avoid the longer, postwar seclusion or in fear for their husbands' lives. In *Autobiography of a Papago Woman*, Chona relates the story of one woman who told her husband she was menstruating because she didn't want him to go to war. According to the local gossip, the woman was punished for her lie, for she never menstruated again.

CAPTORS AND CAPTIVES

Whether an Indian girl or woman found herself in the position of a cruel, vengeful torturer or a quivering, frightened captive depended to a great extent on the strength and success of the warriors who protected her—her fate as a prisoner depended on the customs of her captors.

In many of the early tribes, particularly those in the East and Southeast, as soon as victorious war parties returned home they turned their captured enemies over to the women, who decided if the poor unfortunates should be killed right then, tortured, or kept as slaves.

The Gros Ventre of Montana had a saying: "Women and children do not make good charcoal"—meaning that women and children should be captured in conflicts with the enemy, but they should be neither killed nor scalped. Captive children were adopted into families who had lost their own young ones through war or illness.

The Sioux also commonly adopted their captives into the tribe, children being taken into the family of their captor and treated like the other children. A captive woman was frequently allowed to choose if she wished to marry her captor or if she wanted to be returned to her people. Sioux warriors usually took female captives only with an eye to getting an attractive new wife—otherwise it was too difficult and dangerous to bring enemy women into the tribal circles.

Yumas, who lived at the mouth of the Colorado River in southeastern Arizona, frequently captured enemy women and forced them to dance in the festivities that followed the warriors' homecoming. During the dancing the captives were ill-treated, but when life had settled back to normal, they were bartered or gambled away by their captors and often ended up as the wife of an old man whose own wife was dead or too feeble to carry on the household duties. From this point they were fairly well-treated—they performed the same tasks as the Yuma housewives, and there is no evidence that they were overworked or exploited. The majority of these women settled down permanently in the Yuma villages without attempting to escape.

Yuma children who were captured by the Cocopah were adopted by childless couples who treated the youngsters so well that they rarely, if ever, tried to escape. Every morning the adoptive parents took their children to the riverbank and bathed them with water heated in a large clay water jug. The washing had a ceremonial function and wasn't required for native-born Cocopah children. Children taken captive by the Kaska, of northern British Columbia, didn't fare so well. That tribe killed many young captives in earlier days by spiking them on sharpened stakes set up around a fire.

The Creeks were fairly kind to women and children captives and usually adopted them into the tribe. Although a former enemy never became a fully privileged Creek, the offspring of the captives were considered full-fledged members of the society. Male captives were not so lucky—they could expect nothing but the most painful torture inflicted by the wives of their captors. Each woman prepared a long bundle of dry cane or the heart of a pitch pine, and as the victims were led to the stake, the women and their children beat the prisoners with the burning ends of their torches. If a captive looked as if he was about to expire before the women were through with him, he was revived with a large splash of cold water. Early white explorers, appalled at what they witnessed, described the women as "singing with religious joy" while they conducted these rites.

Natchez customs were similar. However, if a Natchez widow who had lost her man in war saw a man she liked when the male prisoners were paraded before the village completely naked, she could claim that captive as her husband. Apparently there were times when the pace of punishment became too much even for the torturers, and a woman would step in to make a quick end to a captive's agony. French explorer Le Page Du Pratz wrote in 1758, ". . . when he suffers too long, a pitying woman lights a cane torch and when it is burning well makes him die in an instant by putting this torch to the most sensitive place and the tragic scene is in this way ended."[8]

Southeastern Indian women were no kinder when it came to dealing with female captives. There was no end to the rage, anger, and violence Caddo women unleashed on the unhappy female captives their warrior husbands brought home. Armed with sticks and sharpened skewers, the Caddo women lost no time in lighting into the quaking prisoner, one pulling out a fistful of her hair, another gouging out an eye, still another wacking off one or more of her fingers. Finally, one of the tormentors gave the captive a heavy blow on the head with a club while others buried their skewers many times in her body. When the poor woman had finally expired, they cut her body into many pieces, which they divided among themselves. Slaves that had previously been captured by the Caddo were then forced to eat the flesh of their former tribe mates, an extreme humiliation.

The Iroquois, who got along so well among themselves, were able to let out most of their tensions when it came time to deal with war captives from other tribes. When victorious Iroquois warriors returned to the village with prisoners, each captive was assigned to a family and led to the door of that family's home. The chief matron came out and looked the prisoner over. She might decide that the man or woman who stood before her should be adopted into the family to replace someone who had died or been killed or that the captive might make a good slave to help the women with their chores. If the matron refused to accept the prisoner—"threw him [or her] into the fire" it was called—there was no chance for the captive, who was soon burned to death.

At this point male captives who had been singled out for possible adoption still had to prove their valor to the powerful Iroquois women. At an appointed time, usually three or four days after the return of the war party, the women and children of the village armed themselves with whips and arranged themselves in two parallel rows. Each captive was forced to run down the long avenue of whips. Those who fell from exhaustion were immediately condemned as unworthy to be saved and were led away to torture, but those who managed to endure this test were received with open arms and immediately entered into all privileges and assumed all the obligations of the deceased person they were to replace.

The Iroquois' treatment of prisoners was often harsh, but there was some justice in the fact that they usually didn't fare any better when they were taken prisoner. When Huron warriors were successful in a raid against the Iroquois, they immediately tortured and killed any Iroquois women or children they had captured; men captives were taken back to the Huron villages where they were first turned over to a prominent family to replace one of their own dead and later tortured to death in a grisly rite which might last as long as seven days.

After the prisoner had died, his belly was cut open, and all of the children were given a part of the intestines attached to the end of the stick so that they could carry the trophies around the village as a sign of victory. The body was then cut up, roasted, and consumed by the celebrants.

The Yavapai of central Arizona also sometimes ate their captives, not because human flesh was relished but to vent spite against the enemy in as vicious and terrible a fashion as possible. One of the last incidents of this custom occurred between 1830 and 1850 when a small party of Halchidhoma Indians was surrounded by a party of Yavapai. All the Halchidhoma were killed except a woman and her small daughter. The Yavapai dug a long pit and built a fire in the trench using many large logs. When they had a deep bed of coals they threw a deer carcass in the pit to roast, and then they grabbed the little girl and held her down on the coals until she died. Each Yavapai then ate a piece of venison and a piece of human flesh. The mother later escaped and made her way back to her own people to report the terrible death of her daughter and other companions.

Native American warriors did not generally sexually assault their female captives. The Iroquois would not hesitate to kill any captive who was not able to keep up with a fast-moving war party, but they never raped the women. Because Creek warriors were ritually forbidden to have sexual intercourse until three days after a raid, their female captives usually were not violated. The Cocopahs considered it ceremonially unclean to assault a woman prisoner, fearing insanity if they did so. Their captives were sometimes given to old men for wives, but this was of a somewhat different order from violent rape. Elderly men were thought to have lost most of their powers anyway, so they were less vulnerable to the ill effects of a foreign woman. The one notable exception to this rule was the Flathead tribe where the rape of an enemy woman was part of the institutionalized war complex.

PAWNEE CEREMONIAL CAPTIVES

The Pawnees, farmers and hunters of the central Great Plains, had a special use for young women prisoners. Every year the Pawnee warriors organized a special expedition to bring back a captive enemy girl to play the starring role in one of their most important ceremonials. In the Pawnee creation myth, fruitfulness and light had come into the world through the mating of the Morning Star and his realm of light with the Evening Star and her realm of darkness. The first human being—a girl—was conceived of that union, and Morning Star regularly demanded a girl in return.

After the young maiden, about thirteen years of age, was brought back to the Pawnee camp, she was extremely well treated and not told of her eventual fate. The day before the ceremony, the maiden was dressed in special clothing and her body was painted red on the right side, to symbolize day, the time of the Morning Star, and black on the left to represent night, the time of the Evening Star.

A scaffold was built, but every effort was made to keep the young captive from suspecting what was coming. Before dawn on the appointed day her hands were tied with special braided elk-hide ropes, and she was led to the scaffold. By this time the girl was looking around wondering just what was happening. It was considered lucky if, in her innocence, the girl mounted the rungs of the scaffold without resistance. By the time she was tied down, the poor maiden had probably realized that the end of her life was very close. Just as the Morning Star rose, one of the priests shot the girl through the heart while another struck her over the head with a club. Then every male in the tribe shot an arrow into her body, older relatives performing the act for little boys too young to draw a bow. When the priests buried her body, they consecrated her death to the fertility of their soil and the success of the crops, singing, "The whole earth she shall turn into; the whole earth shall receive her blood." In the village there was general rejoicing and a period of sexual looseness as a ceremonial celebration of fertility.

In 1816 the Pawnees captured a young Comanche girl and were preparing to sacrifice her in the spring rites in 1817. A young warrior of the tribe, named Man Chief, had several years before accompanied the chief of the tribe, who was his father or uncle, to talk to William Clark in St. Louis. While the two Indian men were with Clark, the former explorer tried to talk them into abandoning the Morning Star ceremonial. The two agreed that the practice should cease, but they could not convince their compatriots. When it became apparent to Man Chief that his people were really intending to sacrifice the young Comanche girl, he intervened just at the moment they were tying her to the scaffold. Riding up in front of the assembled throng, he announced to the waiting crowd that he had come for the girl, whereupon he cut her free, threw her on his horse, and galloped off with her, later sending her south to rejoin her people. The last known Pawnee sacrifice was of an Oglala Sioux girl on April 22, 1838.

SLAVES

Not all captives ended up adopted into the enemy tribe or cruelly tortured to death. Some prisoners were taken with the thought that they would serve as slaves for their captors. Many of the northwest coast tribes kept slaves, and there was even an intertribal slave market near the Dalles in Oregon. Nearly all of the people who ended up in the unenviable position of merchandise at this market had been war captives, but some of them were children or grandchildren of persons who had been forced into slavery.

The Flathead Indians, of Montana, found it almost more trouble to keep a male slave than his labor was worth, but female slaves were another matter, for they could be put to household chores around camp where they could be constantly watched. For a Flathead to capture an enemy woman was almost as honorable as capturing a horse. A female prisoner was typically shamed by having all her hair cut off, her face smeared with charcoal, and her clothing daubed with red paint.

The treatment of a Flathead slave depended to a great extent on the household where she lived. She usually served as the drudge for the mistress of the household and as the prized sex partner of her master. If the wife was jealous, the slave was in constant terror of being killed; on the other hand, if she failed to please the man of the house, her chances of survival were also small. There was, no doubt, an occasional Flathead wife who accommodated herself to the presence of slaves, happy to have her own labors lightened and proud to have a captive around as a sign of her husband's wealth.

One Flathead woman remembered that when she was a child, news reached camp that her father was coming home, bringing with him two beautiful Shoshoni women whom he had captured when he came on their lodge in the wilderness. Her mother flew into a rage, and deciding that no beautiful young Shoshoni maidens were coming into her household, she took an axe and went to wait for the party beside the trail. When her husband appeared he was leading the enemy horses but no beautiful maidens. Fortunately for the Shoshoni girls, the Flathead warrior had met a white trader on the trail who had bought them for some blankets and a little flour.

The Lower Chinook on the Washington coast held more slaves per capita than any of the surrounding tribes—an average upper-class family owning two or three slaves. While a slave was useful she was fairly well treated, living in the same quarters as the family and sharing their food. However, if a slave got sick or when she became old and feeble, she was neglected until she starved to death and then her body was unceremoniously thrown in the hollow of a dead tree. If a slave had been purchased as a companion for a child, she was almost certainly killed if the child died.

The Tlingit of southern Alaska also had a large slave population, most of whom were taken captive in raids on nearby non-Tlingit towns or from non-related Tlingit towns. A woman taken in a raid wasn't actually considered a slave until her clan had been given a chance to ransom her—the price being based on the social rank of the captive. Yet no matter how much a woman's family paid to get her back, there remained a definite smirch on her reputation which might be brought up any time she happened to be in a quarrel. An insult of this type was usually oblique, one woman saying aloud, "I wonder if she knows about herself?"

A woman who for some reason was so unlucky that she was not ransomed faced a toilsome and probably short life as a Tlingit slave. Slaves had to perform the more difficult labors, and they were the complete property of their masters. Whenever a chief decided to build a new house he strangled a slave to saturate the building with blood. If a chief wanted to emphasize his importance over another chief, he would kill a number of slaves. In retaliation the other chief would kill as many or more of his own slaves, and so it would go until all of the prisoners had been sacrificed for the aggrandizement of their masters.

Another story of captive slaves and what happened if they attempted to escape comes to us through Olive Oatman, a white girl who, with her sister, was captured by Apaches as the Oatman family made their way across the Arizona desert on a journey to California. After her release, Miss Oatman (whose sister died in captivity) wrote of her adventures.

Olive Oatman recalled that after she and her sister were taken they were marched over 250 miles during the next three days. After they arrived at the Apache village they found their lives very difficult, since the women who directed their labors gave them much work to do but fed them very poorly. The two white girls were allowed only the leftover food, and they had to compete with the dogs for even those scraps. Olive attributed their survival to the fact that they prayed a lot and were able to dig a few edible roots. After the girls had been in this miserable condition for a while, a delegation of Mohaves arrived in the Apache camp. One of the members of the party, the daughter of the chief, was a beautiful, mild, and sympathizing woman. She spoke with the white girls in Apache, which they had learned by that time, telling them that the Mohaves were going to buy them. The transaction was completed, and the Mohaves and their charges started on a 350-mile journey that took ten days of walking. When the girls reached the Mohave camp, they found that their lot was going to be worse, if possible, than their existence among the Apaches. They found themselves in the role of slaves, not only to the adults but also to the children. Although the girls pleaded not to be tattooed like all the Mohave women, they received the customary markings anyway—not those of regular Mohave women, but those of captives so that they could be recognized if they escaped to another tribe.

During a time of very low food supply the younger sister, Mary Ann, got very weak and eventually died, perhaps of starvation. Olive had constant thoughts of escape, but she put these thoughts aside after she saw what happened to a young Cocopah woman who shared her state of captivity among the Mohaves.

The Cocopah captive was a tall, handsome young woman of about twenty-five. Miss Oatman writes, ". . . I saw upon her countenance and in her eyes the traces of an awful grief. The rest of the captives appeared well and indifferent about themselves. This woman called herself Nowereha. The other captives were girls from 12 to 16 years old, and while they seemed to wear a 'don't care' appearance, this Nowereha was perfectly bowed down with grief.

I observed she tasted but little food. She kept up a constant moaning and wailing except when checked by the threats of her boastful captors."[9]

Miss Oatman learned that the Cocopah woman's town had been attacked in the night by Mohave warriors. The Cocopahs started running, hotly pursued by their enemies. Nowereha had a small baby, but after she ran with the child a short distance, her husband came up to her, grasped the child, and ran on. The husband and baby escaped; Nowereha was captured.

After a week of wandering around the village, "the perfect image of desperation and despair," Nowereha disappeared. The village and the nearby trails were searched, and when the grieving mother was not located it was decided that she had killed herself. Several days later a Yuma Indian came into the camp driving the poor disheveled Nowereha before him. She had managed to travel 130 miles by going up river, traveling at night, swimming, and stepping on rocks.

The next morning the Mohaves planted a heavy post firmly in the ground and attached a crossbeam to it. The unlucky Nowereha was fixed to this cross with wood spikes driven through her hands and ankles. Olive and the other Cocopah captives were led in front of the cross and told to keep their eyes on the suffering woman until she died, as an example of what would happen to them if they tried to escape.

Then the Mohaves started running around the crucified captive in what white people imagine as the classic war dance, shouting, stamping their feet, and taunting their prisoner.

Miss Oatman concluded: "After a little while several of them supplied themselves with bows and arrows and at every circlet would hurl one of these poisoned instruments of death into her quivering flesh. Occasionally she would cry aloud, and in the most pitiful manner. This awakened from that mocking, heartless crowd the most deafening yells. She hung in this dreadful condition for over two hours ere I was certain she was dead, all the while bleeding and sighing, her body mangled in the most shocking manner. When she would cry aloud they would stuff rags in her mouth and thus silence her. When they were quite sure she was dead, and that they could no longer inflict pain on her, they took her body to a funeral pile and burned it."[10]

WOMEN AS PEACEKEEPERS

Despite the excitement the military campaigns brought and the possibility of acquiring slaves to help with the work, some Indian women decried the wartime efforts and begged their men to stay at home. Olive Oatman, the white girl captured by Apaches and sold to the Mohaves, later described the attitude of the women when the Mohaves were making plans for war against another tribe. She writes: "Great preparations were also made by the squaws, although with much reluctance as most of them were opposed to the expedition as they had been also in the past to kindred ones. Those of them who had husbands and brothers enlisted in the expedition tried every expedient in their power to dissuade them from it. They accused them of folly and a mere lust of war and prayed them not thus to expose their own lives and the lives of dependent ones."[11]

The Shawnee, who lived in what is now Kentucky, built a war restraint right into their society. The mother or another close female relative of the principal Shawnee chief was always appointed as the peace woman. Her duty was to prevent by her entreaties and remonstrances the unnecessary spilling of blood. If the war chief was bent upon some campaign that was not popular with the rest of the people, the councilmen would appeal to the peace woman. She would then go before the war chief and remind him what torture it was for the mothers in the tribe to watch their sons march off to death. She also pleaded for the innocent women and children of the enemy tribe, reminding him that they had done nothing to deserve the misfortune which would fall on them if the tribe entered a full-scale war. It is said that the peace woman seldom failed to win her point.

Among the Iroquois the powerful women of the tribe played a similar role in regard to unpopular war plans. Very eloquently they would lament the sorrows of bereaved mothers and widowed wives and recount with great feeling the losses suffered on both sides. The warriors, who were afraid of being thought cowardly if they did not fight to the entire extermination of both sides, no doubt welcomed the sane intervention of the women. Though pledged by their manhood to continue fighting to the death, they knew as well as anyone what grief was caused, for there was not one of them who had not lost a father, a brother, a son, or a close comrade in armed conflict.

WHEN DEATH WON OUT

While no Native American women could have been more devoted to peace than those calm and placid souls who lived in the southwestern pueblos, there came a terrible time in the history of Acoma Pueblo when the women chose to kill themselves and their children rather than submit to despicable tyranny.

184

When the Acoma noticed the first Spaniards ride into their land on their strange large creatures, the pueblo people were curious, but they accepted their visitors politely, since they came in small parties and did not stay long. However, the Native Americans did not feel so peacefully inclined when, in 1598, Don Juan de Onate, who was appointed governor of the region by the Spanish crown, began to make the rounds of the pueblos, requiring the submission of the inhabitants. The Acoma felt very powerful, perched as they were on a four-hundred-foot-high rock, and provisioned with stores of corn and water in their reservoirs—powerful enough to risk falling on a group of Spaniards who were strutting about on the edge of the cliff, frightening some of them so they jumped off the cliff, hitting the others with clubs.

The Spanish did not take this attack lightly, and they planned and executed a revenge that drew rivers of blood from both sides. Though the Europeans were winning the battle, the Indians, desperate to save their homes, gave them no rest nor any chance to eat, sleep, or sit down. When the Spaniards called on their adversaries to surrender, promising them justice, the Acoma replied they would rather die at their own hands than submit. What happened next is recounted in blank verse by one of the Spanish soldiers named Villegra:

> And not the braves alone, but women also.
> Some slew themselves, like Dido, and the fire
> Consumed their bodies, while their Spartan children
> Sought like their mothers, a grim death, while others
> Threw themselves in the raging flames. Some mothers
> Clasping their children, leaped from the high summit.
> . . . .
> Many, in different ways, found death.[12]

A young Pima woman carrying one of the tribe's exceptional
baskets which she has decorated with a family design. (*Courtesy of
Arizona Historical Society*)

8

Time for Fun

CRAFTS AND RECREATION

Up to this point we have discussed the Native American woman largely in terms of her work—and while it is true that her household labors were constant and often taxing, there was also room in her life for pleasure.

Indian women sought relaxation in widely different ways—some found release in intense games of chance, gambling away their very clothing; others preferred physical sports; while still other women found it possible to get away from the mundane immediacies of life while working at their crafts.

CRAFTS AS EXPRESSION

Life in an early Indian village did not offer a woman a great deal of opportunity for self-expression. She was expected to build and furnish her house just like all the other women; she cooked whatever food she was lucky enough to have on hand; her dresses were almost identical to the dresses of all the other women in her village. The production of handicrafts was one of the few outlets a Native American woman had for expressing her artistic talents and creativity.

It is quite obvious that the Indian woman enjoyed having beautiful equipment for domestic use. Her products often exhibited technical and esthetic standards far above the requirements of mere utility. A comparison of a "primitive" Indian woman's intricately decorated pottery and finely woven baskets with the modern housewife's drab plastic dishware makes today's utensils seem utterly insipid. But the early Indian woman wasn't inspired merely by the desire for lovely pots and baskets to use for gathering foods and serving meals; she also garnered a great deal of joy in the acts of conceiving new patterns and implementing her inspirations. The most rewarding aspects of handicrafts were often more psychological than material, yet because these early people had no time for "art for art's sake," such as paintings and sculpture, her talents had to be confined to the manufacture or decoration of useful items.

A woman's talent for fine craftsmanship was usually rewarded by the respect she received from the other women—the real connoisseurs of handicrafts. While the finer details in the perfection of a skill might be scarcely apparent to an untutored eye, another craftswoman could see and appreciate ingenuity and true virtuosity.

BASKETRY

Basket making was the primary mode of artistic expression for many early American women. Basketry is one of the most ancient of crafts; simple baskets were being made on this continent as early as 7000 B.C. In all tribes the making of baskets was considered women's work.

The making of a fine basket is laborious, slow, and exasperating work—even a very simple basket requires many hours of painstakingly close attention. By the time a woman sat down to do the actual weaving of her basket, she had already spent hours and days gathering, preparing, sorting, and storing her materials. Practically every basket maker preferred to lay in her own supplies, believing that the materials she would choose for her own work were superior to any that she might buy from someone else. Small children to care for, physical disability, or extreme old age were the only legitimate reasons for a woman's not going after available basket materials herself.

Indian women typically began learning to make baskets when they were very young, imitating their mothers and grandmothers as they watched the older more experienced women at their work. Practically every little girl played at basket making; those who persisted in this pastime attracted the attention of their elders, who then began to teach them the skills they would need to produce an acceptable basket. When older weavers got together to chat they often told stories about how they had secretly pilfered prepared basket supplies from mothers or aunts, confident that good materials would necessarily produce better baskets and immediately dispel their awkwardness and lack of skill.

The Atsugewi, of northern California, attributed the skill of basket makers to the possession of a guardian spirit. This guardian spirit could be passed from one woman to another, and a woman who was a good weaver might rub the hands of her daughter or granddaughter and so transfer her power. The guardian animal of basketry was the lizard. If a girl was interested in perfecting her art and had no one from whom to inherit a guardian spirit, she would ask someone to draw a live lizard across her palm and up her forearm. If the lizard remained calm during the process it was thought that the maiden would get the power, but if it kicked and squirmed, the lizard obviously didn't like her, and she would not receive the power she sought.

Some of the best basket makers, including the Atsugewi, lived in California, where baskets of various shapes and sizes served for nearly every household need. Baskets were used for storing and wood carrying, as pans and plates, cradles, dippers, cooking pots, sifters, water containers, ceremonial items, and even as women's hats. Months might be devoted to the manufacture of magnificent baskets destined as funeral offerings to be burned with the dead. Pomo Indian women went further than most and played with their art, including features that not only had nothing to do with necessity but actually reduced the utility of their product. The outstanding example of this is the magnificent feather-mosaic baskets produced by the Pomos, in which the exteriors of the baskets are completely covered with brilliant plumage, each little feather held in place by a stitch of the coiling. Favorite materials were the iridescent green feathers of the mallard drake's neck, the lemon yellow feathers of the meadowlark's breast, and the scarlet feathers of the woodpecker's scalp.

Those baskets expected to hold liquid had to be woven very carefully and very tightly; in some of the finest coiled baskets of California there are seventy stitches to the inch. Native American housewives were able to cook in baskets by heating rocks in hot coals and then lifting the rocks with sticks into the basket full of soup or mush.

Although these early California women had to acquire a great deal of technical skill to construct a basket that would hold water and withstand such rigorous treatment, their real chance for artistry came when they made basket hats for themselves. A good cap was an achievement and the technical eminence to which a weaver aspired. Practically every woman could weave a basket, but only a few could make a wearable cap. The maker not only had to obtain the best materials and display the finest workmanship, she also had to know how to measure someone's head so that the hat would fit well. The shape and proportion of a cap were very important—the most uncomplimentary comment that could be made of a cap was that it "looked like a soup basket." Design was also an important factor in cap making. New or particularly nice caps were usually displayed at the community dances. Karok basket makers, who lived in northwest California, often went to dances simply to check out the appearance of unusual basketry designs or old ones given an individual twist.

Apparently the pleasure women found in basket making overshadowed the tedium, for one Karok weaver told anthropologist Lila M. O'Neale that she forgot to eat when she was weaving, while another confided that she never tired of basket making, even after making them for sale for over forty years. Another woman reminded O'Neale that the price of baskets didn't really cover all the work, that it was hard to keep at weaving all day long, and that it was tiresome to spend so much time gathering and preparing materials; yet all the while she was talking this woman could hardly stop her work on a basket in progress in her eagerness to complete a pattern motif.[1]

The peoples of the Southwest were also very skilled in basket making. The Apache, the Hopi, the Paiute, the Navajo, and especially the Pima and Papago all wove serviceable and decorative baskets.

The Pima and Papago of southern Arizona were renowned for their fine baskets in earlier times and even today make decorative coiled baskets, primarily for sale to whites.

One type of basket, which was once the prized and necessary possession of every woman in these desert groups, was the carrying net, a sort of basket which was loosely woven in a lacy pattern that looks like crochet. The net was shaped like a shallow cone. It was supported by a lightweight frame made of three or four willow sticks or saguaro cactus ribs and held open at the top by a wooden hoop about two feet in diameter. The sticks of the frame protruded beneath the basket and functioned like a tripod when the apparatus was sitting on the ground.

When the women went for water, wood, or wild foods, they carried everything in the net on their backs. The carriers were held in position by a strap which went across the women's foreheads.

These burden baskets were usually made by the old women, for it took a lifetime of skill to make them well. Young women took great pains to see that their carriers were gaily decorated and that one of the sticks had a deerskin fringe which fluttered near their faces at every step. Because industry was considered a great virtue for these women, it was said that a girl never looked so pretty as with a red woven strap across her forehead and a full net on her back.

❖◇❖◇❖◇❖◇❖◇❖◇❖◇❖◇

Burden Basket Becomes a Mountain

(PIMA AND PAPAGO)

One day Coyote climbed a hill and sat down to watch the world go by. Suddenly a lovely girl came walking by and he knew this was the girl he wanted to marry.

Strangely, the girl wasn't carrying her burden basket on her back, it was walking along by itself after her. Yet a basket never walks around on its own. It seems that this girl's father was a powerful medicine man and had made this basket especially for his daughter.

The lovely girl was gathering firewood, which she loaded into the basket. She gathered a great deal of wood, and when she was finished she turned to go home, and the basket followed her.

Coyote was thinking of getting that basket and showing people how smart he was so he said, "Hahaha. So the burden basket walks around." The basket just stopped where it was and became a mountain which the people now call Quijo Toa—Burden-Basket Mountain.²

❖◇❖◇❖◇❖◇❖◇❖◇❖◇❖◇

Some of the designs used by the early basket makers were traditional patterns that characterized the work of a tribe. These designs had to be carefully learned and exactly rendered. At other times the basket maker departed from the designs of her mother and found inspiration in nature and in tribal tales and myths. New patterns arose from her soul, her memory, and her imagination. One Papago basket maker told Ruth Underhill, "When I am making baskets I hear a voice speaking to me, 'Put a cactus here. Put a turtle there. There, put a Gila monster.' "³

CERAMICS

The making and decoration of pottery have also been a woman's art, and they are a particularly fine example of how women have carried over an industry into the realm of the esthetic. The craft of ceramics was most highly developed in the Mississippi Valley, the Southeast, and the Pueblo groups of the Southwest—areas where agriculture led to permanent homes. Nomadic tribes, who moved often in search of wild plants or animals for their food, had little use for fragile pots, while sedentary peoples found them well-suited to their needs.

Pottery making was not among the earliest arts practiced by the Native Americans, but there is evidence that rudimentary ceramics were being fashioned in the Southwest as early as 300 B.C., and the Hohokam Indians were producing very fine pots by 200 B.C. The earliest pots show by the imprint on their bases that they were made by pressing moist clay mixed with shredded cedar bark into shallow baskets.

Native American women fashioned all their ceramics entirely by hand, they never used a potter's wheel. At first small objects were molded from one lump of clay; later, women learned to build larger pots by building up the sides of the jars coil upon coil. Compared to the slow and often exasperating art of basketry, pottery making was quick and satisfying, the motions smooth and uncramped. The new art was also more immediately satisfying; a skillful potter could make several pieces a day, set them to dry, and fire them the next day.

Large clay jars, or ollas, filled a real need in the Southwest, where water had to be brought to the home from a distance and stored there for the needs of the family. The finer a woman made her pot, the less heavy it was for her to carry. Early Indian women learned to construct jars of several gallon capacity with walls that were eggshell thin and so fine and smooth as to be unsmeared by the careless touch of even one finger. As women's technical skill at ceramics began to increase, they started to decorate their creations until the embellishment of the water jar, food bowl, or cooking pot became an important factor in its making. The women potters of the Southwest have developed this particular type of artwork through the centuries until it has become recognized as one of the outstanding craft arts in the world.

For generation after generation, Hopi women have viewed pottery "bees" as a common feature of their social life. If a woman sat down to decorate a pot, she was soon joined by a relative or neighbor who also had pots to decorate and would bring her work along. Pottery making was much different for the Zuni women, who maintained a reverent and respectful silence through the entire process. The women always went alone when they went out to collect their clay; no men were allowed near the clay beds. There was

no laughter, no singing, and no conversation on these pilgrimages. Zuni potters believed that if they remained respectful of the clay and pure of heart, the
traditional gathering pits would never become exhausted and the material
would appear to them. Later, when the potter was fashioning each lump of
clay into a cup or a bowl, she continued her silence, conversing only in faint
whispers or by signs, for she feared that her voice would enter the vessel and
later would escape with a loud noise during the firing, shattering the ware.

The Apaches were not generally known as potters, but the Jicarilla
Apaches, an eastern band, picked up the art from their Pueblo neighbors in
New Mexico. Jicarilla Apache women made both smoking pipes and cooking
pots from clay. Before making a journey to gather clay at a special spot,
which had the status of a holy shrine, those who were going on the trip prayed
and smoked a ceremonial clay pipe. The ritual smoking was necessary, they
believed, or they might miss the clay bed entirely and return from their trip
empty handed. The women were accompanied by men who helped them with
the heavy loads on the return trip, but the men were not allowed to take
weapons or articles made of flint near the holy spot, for flint, representing
male undertakings, was thought to be incompatible with clay, symbolic of the
woman's world. If the taboo was broken, it was sure that pots made from that
clay would break in the firing.

How the Apaches Got Clay

(JICARILLA APACHE)

*In the beginning of the world there was an old man and an old woman.
They had nothing to do and they prayed to the one who made the earth
to give them something to live on. Then one day a spirit came and stood
before them.*

*First he took them to a rock and said, "That is gold. It is worth much,
but I cannot give it to you, for you do not know how to work it."*

*Then he showed them another rock, saying, "That is silver. That, too,
is valuable, but you do not know of it or what to do with it, so I cannot
give it to you. Some day people will come from across the ocean, from
the east. They will feed you, give you clothes and food. That is why I
will send them. And they will like this silver and gold."*

*Then the spirit took the old man and the old woman to the other side
of the mountain. A big hole was there. "Go over there and dig out that*

clay," the spirit told the two old people. "I will show you how to make pots and bowls with it. You will live by this means."

Then the spirit called the woman over to him and touched both her hands with his, instructing her, "Now work the clay from your own knowledge and with your own understanding."

So the old man and woman went together to dig the clay and then the woman made a clay bowl and she did very good work. She made bowls of all shapes. But she did not know what to call the different bowls or the proper use for each shape.

That night the man and woman prayed and the spirit appeared to the woman in a dream and told her how to use the pots and what to call them. The spirit also told her that she must teach all the children what she knew.[4]

✿◇✿◇✿◇✿◇✿◇✿◇✿◇✿◇

After an Apache woman got her clay home and cleaned and before she sat down to make the pots, she tied her hair up on the sides of her head in two bunches, then she went into the bushes to relieve herself, for she was not supposed to answer the call of nature once she had begun to shape a pot. During the period of time, perhaps several days, that a potter was working, she was careful to remain sexually continent or all her pots would break and her marriage "will go like that too; it will go all to pieces."

Though the Apaches borrowed the art of ceramics from the Pueblos, they never adapted the exquisite and highly expressive art of pottery decoration found so extensively among the Pueblo peoples.

This process of decoration is where the Native American woman really got a chance to express herself and exercise her creative abilities. When the Pueblo potter sat down with her bowls before her and her handmade yucca brushes and black paint, made from boiling down a certain local weed (*Cleome serrulata*), she did not casually begin covering her pots with free-hand designs, with only her instinct to guide her brush. First she carefully studied the vessel before her. The most artistic of the women usually had already conceived of a design or part of a design that she wanted to use on a pot, and she had to measure and figure just how to adapt the design to a particular vessel. Ruth Bunzel, author of *The Pueblo Potter*, compares these women to modern artists: "Most of these women display the same symptoms which are common to creative artists among more sophisticated people. They all speak of sleepless nights spent in thinking of designs for the pot to be decorated in the morning, of dreams of new patterns which on waking they try and often fail to recapture, and above all, the constant preoccupations with decorative problems even while they are engaged in other kinds of work."[5]

One Hopi woman told Dr. Bunzel, "I am always thinking about designs, even when I am doing other things, and whenever I close my eyes, I see designs in front of me. I often dream of designs and whenever I am ready to paint, I close my eyes and then the designs just come to me." A Laguna potter related, "I get all my ideas from my thoughts. I think of my thoughts as a person who tells me what to do. I dream about designs too. Sometimes before I go to bed, I am thinking about how I shall paint the next piece, and then I dream about it. I remember the designs well enough to paint in the morning. That is why my designs are better than those of other women. Some people do not think that pottery is anything, but it means a great deal to me. It is something sacred. I try to paint all my thoughts on my pottery."[6]

Although there are some traditional designs that are used over and over, every potter is readily able to recognize her own work, and very often she can distinguish among the work done by other potters. As one woman said, "If I painted my bowls like everyone else, I might lose my bowl when I take dinner to the dancers in the plaza. I am the only person who makes a checkerboard design around the rim, so I can always tell my bowl by looking at the edge. I don't have to use any mark on my bowl because I recognize the design."[7]

A Pueblo woman felt that each of her pots had a life of its own. Zuni potters deposited a bit of wafer bread in each vase before it was fired so that the spirit of the piece would be fed with the spiritual essence of the bread. The Zunis believed that if the spirit, which entered the jar during the firing, was properly feasted and addressed, it would communicate its health and life-giving influence to any food that it later contained. Any cracked or broken pot immediately lost its resident spirit—this was considered evident from the sound of the jar when it was struck: an intact vessel gives a pleasant ring, while a damaged one issues a much duller sound.

In the Hopi towns of northern Arizona, women are still making pots in much the same way their ancestors did centuries ago. Whatever modern innovations have crept in have not changed the attitude of the potters toward their work. Art, wherever it is found, is a reflection of the culture from which it comes, thus Hopi artwork is infused with the deep religious spirit that characterizes all of traditional pueblo life.

Hopi teacher and potter Polingaysi Qoyawayma explains her relationship to her art:

Did I pray when I was forming pots? Absolutely. The clay is a living being when you put it in your hand, you know. Look at it. A lump . . . a lump that says to me, "Make me as I am . . . make me beautiful." So we converse every step of the way, the clay and I.

If I can see the beauty in my hand . . . if it touches my own inner heartstrings and I can mold it into visual, harmonious beauty, then I have met the challenge.

But I have to be alone . . . alone with the clay . . . to listen slavishly to its commands, to feel the rhythm, the pulse, the life of it.

Oh, yes, I pray. One must be alone with the Creator—the Supreme Being—to capture this feeling of oneness. One with the clay. One with the Creator. One with every living thing, including the grains of sand.[8]

WEAVING

The weaving of beautiful blankets was another craft art in which Native American women found a chance for self-expression. Weaving is so ancient that its origin is unknown, but it had passed its crude beginnings long before the arrival of white men to this continent. Weaving was known in practically every tribe, but it was among the Chilkat and Tsimshian on the north Pacific coast and the Navajo of the Southwest that women took the basic techniques and turned them into a true art form.

The woven blanket was the outstanding contribution of women artists to the distinctive arts of the northwest coast. It was originally the women of the Tsimshian tribe who developed what is now called the Chilkat robe, after the group of people who adopted and perfected the art. These fantastic ceremonial dance robes were oblong shawls, heavily fringed on three edges. The earliest robes were woven of twisted cedar bark, but later mountain goat hair was added for softness.

Better known today are the fine blankets and rugs woven by the Navajo women. Although anthropologists feel almost certain that Navajos borrowed the art of weaving from their Pueblo neighbors, the weavers maintain that they were taught by Spider Woman "in the beginning," and their beliefs are well-documented in mythology.

When the Navajo woman sits down in front of her loom to start weaving a rug it is not really the beginning of a project but the final step in a year's hard work of raising sheep, shearing wool, and spinning yarn.

✿◆✿◆✿◆✿◆✿◆✿◆✿◆

Spider Woman Teaches Weaving

(N A V A J O)

Spider Woman instructed the Navajo women how to weave on a loom which Spider Man told them how to make. The crosspoles were made of sky and earth cords, the warp, sticks of sun rays, the heddles of rock crystal and sheet lightning. The batten was a sun halo; white shell made the comb. There were four spindles: one a stick of zigzag lightning with a whorl of cannel coal; one a stick of flash lightning with a whorl of turquoise; a third had a stick of sheet lightning with a whorl of abalone; a rain streamer formed the stick of the fourth and its whorl was white shell.[9]

✿◆✿◆✿◆✿◆✿◆✿◆✿◆

Before 1800, all Navajo women made their rugs from undyed yarn, creating wide stripes with the natural black and white wool, and combining the two colors to get grey. As early as 1800 they began to experiment with native dyes and to ravel and respin the brilliantly colored fibers of the commercial fabrics introduced as trade goods. By 1890 they were using all commercial yarn, and with an upsurge of interest from undiscriminating eastern buyers the art began to degenerate, and the Navajos literally wove fast and loose. Finally the rugs became so bad in workmanship and design that the market fell off and the weavers began to return to the softer colors, earlier designs, and tighter weaves of the beautiful and long-wearing blankets and rugs produced by their grandmothers. With the reappearance of the traditional high quality, Navajo weavers were once more recognized worldwide as masters at their craft.

QUILLING AND BEADING

Women of the eastern and Plains tribes were able to express themselves artistically by decorating clothing and other articles with dyed porcupine quills and beads.

The art of fine quillwork demanded delicate dexterity and well-developed skill—there were at least nine different techniques, each used for a special task. Cheyenne women who were talented at quillwork belonged to an exclusive quilling society. These women taught the art and accompanying rituals to younger women and also assembled for social occasions during which they all boasted of their competence. Each woman described in great detail how she had decorated various robes, moccasins, and baby carriers. This formal recital of their accomplishments was similar to the way men recounted their bravery in war.

Members of the Cheyenne quilling society aspired to the quilling of thirty full buffalo robes as their ultimate goal; having accomplished that, a woman believed she had secured for herself a long life full of good fortune. Of course, some women liked quilling so much that they did not stop at thirty articles, but just continued decorating everything in their tipis.

Beadwork was found in nearly every Native American tribe, but the groups who lived near the Great Lakes and on the Plains did especially fine work. The most famous beadwork in the world was and is made by the Native Americans; no other people produces anything like it.

Indian women quickly adopted the tiny glass beads brought to them by the early traders and used them in their traditional designs, but even before contact with white men the Indians made beads out of shell, stone, deer hooves, animal teeth, bones, nuts, seeds, and shiny or brilliantly colored stones.

SPORTS AND GAMES

Native American women loved games and sports. There was little feeling among these early peoples that physical strength was "unfeminine"; the strongest woman was the best mother and homemaker. And when her tasks were completed, the Indian woman enjoyed sports that required strength and skill. Sometimes she played just for fun—often she was highly competitive.

Indian women who lived near oceans or streams became strong swimmers, learning the skill as children and continuing to enjoy water sports through young adulthood. George Catlin, a white man who traveled among the Indians in the mid-1800s, wrote of the Mandan women: "They all learn to swim well and the poorest swimmer amongst them will dash fearlessly into the boiling and eddying current of the Missouri and cross it with perfect ease. They learn to swim at an early age and women develop strong skills so they can take their children on their backs and swim across."[10]

Later in his journeys, Catlin was visiting the Gros Ventre and decided to cross the river near their village. One of the women of the chief's household took a canoe made of buffalo hide stretched on a frame of willow boughs down to the water, and, after seating Catlin and his two friends in the boat, she waded into the river, pulling the boat with her. When she got in deep water she turned her buckskin tunic over her head and threw it ashore. Then she plunged forward, drawing the boat along. In the middle of the stream the travelers were surrounded by a dozen maidens who had come out from the opposite shore. They swam in a "bold and graceful manner," and their long black hair floated on the water. The young women started teasing the white men, twirling the boat around and around. Catlin evidently enjoyed the trip, for he rewarded each of the swimmers with some bead necklaces.

Indian women also participated in such physical sports as riding and horse racing, foot racing, and snow sledding. Kutchin Indian women, who lived along the Yukon River, even challenged each other in wrestling bouts. The contests began with the little girls, the winner taking on an older girl, and so on up the ladder of age and skill with the strongest woman in the band emerging as the final victor.

Ojibwa women often participated in foot races—many of them even had dreams which they believed made them faster runners. The successful runner was allowed to be somewhat boastful of her prowess, but there was a negative side to her success. The more acclaim she received, the more she was the recipient of jealousy, which at times was very vindictive.

The games that Indian women played were relatively uncomplicated and fell into two general classes—games of chance and contests of dexterity. Games such as chess, requiring intricate rules and elaborate calculation, were entirely absent.

Kwakiutl women played a game called battledore and shuttlecocks. Each shuttlecock was made from three mallard duck wing feathers stuck into a piece of elder wood. The battledore was made of thin cedar boards tied with cedar bark to form a paddle. One woman would play at a time, trying to keep the shuttlecock going as long as possible. If a woman was playing with a shuttlecock that was not behaving properly, she would twist the feathers and blow and whistle on it "to give it life."

Many of the games involved the use of a ball, which was usually fashioned from hide stuffed with grass or animal hair. Cheyenne women played a kind of football in which they used about three hundred counter sticks and a ball about eight inches in diameter. They divided themselves equally into two teams. The first player went to the center and, balancing the ball on her instep, kicked it into the air, caught it on her foot, and kicked again. She counted how many times she was able to kick the ball before she missed and took that number of counter sticks. Then a player from the other team had a turn. When all the counter sticks were claimed, the team with the most sticks won the game.

The Creeks played a special ball game every fall when they had plenty of food and consequently more leisure time. A woman, probably someone particularly active and funloving, would make a ball and give it to a man, who had to go out and kill a deer, a bear, or some squirrels for her. After the woman had cooked the meat, she invited everyone to come to the ball ground, where they feasted, played ball, and later danced in the evenings. Men and women played against each other, the men using ball sticks and the women using their hands. A single pole, between twenty-five and thirty feet high, was erected in the middle of a circle. A mark was drawn on the pole part way up, and a horse skull or a wooden image of an animal was hung from the top. The game began when the chief tossed the ball up at the center pole. Everybody tried to gain possession of it. When one person had the ball his or her team tried to protect him so that he could throw the ball for a point. A player who threw the ball and hit the pole above the mark won a point, while a player who hit the skull or image scored more points. The game was action-packed and exciting for both players and spectators. Screams of delight and moans of disappointment filled the playing field as the team members made and blocked passes, ran into each other in their haste, even threw themselves headlong on the ground to gain control of the ball. With such rough handling the balls had a short life. But as soon as one was worn out, a woman would stitch up a replacement, and another round of feasting and game playing would commence.

In nearly every group of Native Americans, women played a game very similar to shinny or hockey. The contestants, divided into two teams of six to ten players, used sticks that were curved and flattened at one end to try to move the ball toward goal posts erected at opposite ends of the playing field. This was also a lively, noisy game, and good players developed great stamina in rushing back and forth across the playing field and brandishing their sticks, hitting one another occasionally even though aiming for the ball. The distance between the goalposts varied, ranging from two hundred to fourteen hundred yards. Another widespread game called double ball was similar to shinny. Two bags of deerskin or two short pieces of wood or other material were connected by a leather thong. Team members used curved sticks to pass the bags from player to player and advance them toward the goal. Members of the opposing team tried to knock the bags off the other team's sticks. Plains Cree women called this the testicle game, an obvious reference to the shape of the equipment.

In the Southwest, Pima and Papago women really enjoyed these ball games, and myths tell of women who traveled to any village where they heard there was to be a competition. Later on, the nuns at the Spanish missions confiscated the balls so that the women would pay more attention to their household duties and not be tempted to leave their children uncared for while seeking out hockey games.

--- ❖◆❖◆❖◆❖◆❖◆❖◆❖◆ ---

The Woman Who Loved Field Hockey

(PIMA)

Once there was a young woman who loved to play field hockey, and she was a good player. She had a little daughter. One day the woman was invited to play in a hockey game in another village. She made a hammock and placed her daughter in it. Before she left she tied some gourd dippers together and hung them by her daughter along with some lunch she had made for her. She told the little girl that when she awoke she should take the food and water and come looking for her. But she didn't tell the little girl where she was going.

When the daughter awoke she took the things her mother had left and went to see if she could find her. She walked until she came to where Eagle lived and said, "Tell me where my mother is."

Eagle said, "When you give me one of your dippers, then I'll tell you where your mother is."

So the girl gave him one, and Eagle directed her to a mountain range and told her to climb the mountains to see where her mother was.

Next the girl came to Hawk, and she asked him where she might find her mother. Hawk said he would tell her if she gave him one of her dippers. When the daughter gave him the water, he said, "She's over there, beyond the mountain range." Along the way the little girl also asked Crow and Mourning Dove for directions, and they both told her that she would find her mother just beyond the mountain range.

201

She went on and climbed the mountains and from the top she could see that there were people playing hockey. Then she saw some children and called to them to ask if her mother was there. The children told her that her mother was playing hockey, and so the little girl asked one of the children to run and tell her mother that she had come and wanted to see her.

Then one of the children ran to get the little girl's mother, and the little girl began to play. But the mother just kept playing hockey and didn't come, so the little girl decided to go find a tarantula house for herself.

When she found where a tarantula lived, she stood in the hole and sang and began to go down into the earth. She hadn't yet gone all the way in when her mother came running. Then she went all the way in. The mother told Badger, "Follow my child in and get her. She's going down into the earth."

Badger crawled into the hole and tried to reach the little girl, but he managed only to pull off an arm. He brought it back to the mother and said, "I tried to reach her but she was going down too fast. I just got hold of an arm and pulled it off," and he gave her the arm. The mother took the arm and went off and buried it.[11]

❂◇❂◇❂◇❂◇❂◇❂◇❂◇❂

There were other games played by Native American women which were much less strenuous. These games may seem simple compared with modern diversions, but we must remember that the players lived a less cerebral life than we do—they were seeking companionship and diversion in their recreation, not intellectual stimulation.

The familiar cat's-cradle string game was popular across the continent. Navajos believed that the Spider People originally taught the game to their ancestors. These early beings supposedly gave instructions on how to fashion stars, snakes, bears, and spiders, but cautioned the people to play the string game only in the winter, because then the animals they portrayed were asleep and could not see them. To play cat's cradle at any other time of year was to invite certain death from lightning, a fall from a horse, or some other mishap.

Quinault women got great pleasure from a game called "Hiding Stick Between Fingers." The group formed two lines facing each other; one team held up a blanket which concealed their hands as they passed a small bone from hand to hand down the line until someone kept it. When they were ready, they dropped the blanket, and each woman held her hands clenched under her chin, rapping her knuckles together in rhythm to a song. One of the players from the other side tried to guess who had the bone. While she was deciding who to pick, all of the women on the other side smiled and giggled to aid in the deception. If the guesser did not pick the right woman, the side that had the bone repeated the hiding.

An indoor recreation enjoyed by Assiniboine women, who lived near the border between Canada and Montana and North Dakota, was the "Odd Stick Game." Each set of two players had a bundle of forty-one peeled sticks, about twenty-four inches long. One of the players held the bundle behind her back and divided the sticks into two bunches; then she extended the sticks to the other player, who took her choice. The player who got the even number of sticks won the game. When women got together to play this game they usually spent all evening at it, stopping occasionally for refreshments served by the hostess. Men weren't even allowed to peek in at the proceedings.

Dice games were played avidly by early Indian women—they seem to have existed in some form in nearly every North American tribe. Among the Crow, only women played at dice, and when anthropologist Robert Lowie was attempting to get a Crow woman to describe the game for him, her husband became very impatient with the investigator. The old man, named Graybull, told Lowie that the women always went off by themselves to play the game, and that even he did not understand it although he had lived with Crow women all his life.

Shells, bones, sticks, or plum seeds served as dice, depending on what was available. In their dice games, Pima and Papago women used four split sticks that were blackened with charcoal on the rounded outer sides. The players, each with her own set of dice, sat in a circle, each in turn tapping her sticks on a flat stone and letting them fall. If the black sides of all four sticks were showing, the player won two points, all white was worth one point, and mixed colors gave a score of zero.

Like many women from other tribes, the Pimas and Papagos were heavy gamblers. Dice and hockey players would bet their clothing, jewelry, and even household goods on a game. There were no moral inhibitions against gambling, and they went all out in their wagers. It was not rare for a woman to be heard crying in the desert because she had lost everything she owned at gambling. It is interesting that although the bitter hardship of their desert life kept the Papagos frugal most of the time, they abandoned all caution when it came to gambling. Ruth Underhill, who spent many years with the Papagos, feels that the ceremonial aura about all of the games lent sanction to a movement of goods which otherwise might not have taken place among people with so little surplus for trade. In other tribes, such as the Comanches, generous gift giving was the custom, and gambling losses were seen only as an exchange of property between friends.

An Apache woman who has had the tip of her nose cut off,
probably as punishment for adultery. *(Courtesy of Arizona
Historical Society)*

☆
9
★

Early Sexual Patterns

A NORMAL PART OF NATURE

The glamor and guilt that frequently accompany sex in modern Western society were largely absent among Native Americans. Sex was generally regarded as a natural function to be fulfilled, just as hunger had to be satisfied, although the degree of pleasure or romance a woman associated with sex varied from tribe to tribe.

However, each Indian society did have certain traditions and taboos regulating the sex practices of its members, and the standards for acceptable sexual behavior ranged from very strict to free and unrepressed. Sexual customs were a part of the total culture of a tribe and served to strengthen group ties and prevent disruptions among the members.

Some sexual guidelines were necessary to maintain the integrity of the basic family unit, especially since this was also the basic economic unit. A married man who spent a great deal of time philandering might fail to supply his family with enough game to keep them from hunger, and a wife who passed her time in flirtation might neglect her essential duties. However, the sexual rules could not be too strict or they would be unenforceable. A society that punished the sexual infractions of its youth by death would soon have no young warriors for defense and no young mothers to perpetuate the tribe.

SEXUAL TABOOS

Although there was little of the prudishness and prurience often found in conjunction with sex in American or Western European society, there was a deep-seated feeling in many tribes that the sex act diminished certain male powers, and so a body of restrictive taboos was developed to keep men and women separated at certain times to protect the men's energies.

It was widely believed that sexual continence was a prerequisite for a successful hunt. In many societies a woman was warned to sleep apart from her husband for several days before he left for a hunting trip so as not to offend the animals he would be stalking.

The connection between sexual abstinence and a tribe's food supply is seen in activities besides hunting. Among the Apaches, sexual taboos were associated with the gathering and preparation of one of their most important plant foods—the large agave plant. After a sufficient supply had been gathered in the mountains, the succulent hearts of the agave were baked in deep pits for four days, during which time men and women were not to engage in intercourse. If when the earth ovens were opened it was found that the agave was not entirely cooked, this was attributed to the incontinence of some of the members of the gathering party.

War parties, too, believed sex inimical to their powers. Creek warriors, for example, abstained from sex not only during a campaign but also for three days before and three days after.

Other fears related to sexuality appeared in various primitive tribes in North America. Among the White Knife Shoshone, looking at a woman's genitals was very dangerous and was believed to result in blindness or illness for the viewer. Shoshone women were expected to sit always with their legs together; their skirts were cut in strips so that if a woman forgot and thoughtlessly spread her legs, the strips would cover her sex organs. It was the traditional duty of her brother or other male relative to jab a burning stick between a Shoshone woman's thighs whenever she was careless in this regard. Similarly, some Navajo groups held a strong conviction that a man who looked on the sexual parts of a woman would be struck by lightning. No wonder sexual intercourse usually took place in the dark and with little disrobing.

Menominees say that long ago there was a taboo against skin contact between men and women during love-making. Because this taboo made normal sexual relations extremely awkward and difficult, one of the gods prepared a buckskin with a single perforation to cover the woman during intercourse. In later times certain members of each band owned these robes which were kept as sacred articles to be rented out to those who might wish to use them.

INCEST

One of the most widespread taboos in Native American societies, as among peoples all over the world, concerned incest, although what constituted incest varied from group to group, as did the punishment for offenders. In the Southeast a Creek woman who was even distantly related to her sex partner could expect to be punished by "the long scratch," performed by inserting a gar's tooth or a needle into the skin at the back of the neck and making a shallow cut along the spine and then down the leg to the heel. The punishment took place in front of all the villagers and the public shame exceeded even the intense pain. If the violators were closely related the punishment was worse, perhaps even death.

❀◇❀◇❀◇❀◇❀◇❀◇❀◇❀◇

The Sun and the Moon

(CHEROKEE)

The Sun was a young woman and lived in the east while her brother the Moon lived in the west. The Sun had a lover who used to come every month in the dark of the moon to court her. He would come at night and leave before daylight, and although she talked to him she could not see his face in the dark and he would not tell her his name. The Sun was wondering all the time who her lover was.

At last she had an idea how she could discover her lover's identity. The next time he came, as they were sitting together in the dark she slyly dipped her hand into the cinders and ashes of the fireplace and rubbed her fingers over his face, saying, "Your face is cold; you must have suffered from the wind." After a while he left and went away again. The next night when the Moon came up in the sky his face was covered with spots, and then his sister knew he was the one who had been coming to see her.

He was so ashamed to have her know it that he kept as far away as he could at the other end of the sky. Ever since he has tried to keep a long way behind the Sun and when he does sometimes have to appear near her in the west he makes himself as thin as a ribbon so he can hardly be seen.[1]

❀◆❀◆❀◆❀◆❀◆❀◆❀◆

The Western Apaches believed that incest was linked with the fearsome vice of witchcraft and looked on it with great horror, referring to such behavior only in a lowered voice. Tradition forbade marriage of any persons in the same clan or related clans, no matter how remote the kinship. Occasionally a man and woman would marry and then find out they were distant relatives. When they discovered their kinship, they were required to break up the marriage and move far apart. Apaches who intentionally entered into incestuous relations were marked for the rest of their lives, if not killed. Persons suspected of incest were brought before the village and accused of the crime. If they denied any wrongdoing, which they usually did, they were strung up by their wrists from the limb of a tree for further interrogation. A woman could usually save her life by confession, for it was generally assumed that her seducer was a witch and had used supernatural powers against her, but a man was always killed.

❀◆❀◆❀◆❀◆❀◆❀◆❀◆

A Love-Death Story

(APACHE)

Once long ago there were an Apache brother and sister who had been having sex together. The other people of the village had been suspicious for a long time. The brother was aware of their suspicion and finally decided that the others knew about him and his sister. He knew that if they were caught they could expect a horrible punishment, and he did not have the courage to face the wrath of his relatives.

So the young man cut a stick about nine inches long and sharpened both ends. The next time the brother and his sister stole off together the brother took the stick along, and when they lay down he put the stick at his sister's belly. When he pushed down, the stick went through her. Because it was sharpened at both ends, it went through him, too, and they both died.

When the others missed the brother and sister they began a search and found them dead. In this case the parents were good people—not witches—and that is why the boy killed his sister and himself.[2]

Other groups went to great lengths to keep brothers and sisters apart. Cree maidens, in southern Saskatchewan, were forbidden to speak with their brothers after the boys were about ten years old. The young women expressed their continued affection for their brothers by caring for their moccasins and clothing but that was the limit of their interchange. In extreme cases a brother might speak one or two words to his sister, but she never answered. Likewise, a Comanche woman could never sit close to or touch her brother; if she violated this taboo, her brother could kill her without punishment or social disgrace.

Some tribes attempted to forestall incest by the institution of "joking" relationships among persons who might be tempted to commit this crime. For example, in Central Algonkin society, in southern Quebec, the relationship between women and their brothers-in-law and men and their sisters-in-law was characterized by intense, obligatory joking and teasing. The joking, which was sexually oriented and often obscene, was limited only by a prohibition against physical contact. Like the sexuality in certain ceremonies mentioned previously, this tradition provided an outlet for tensions before they became a problem for the family or society.

In marked contrast to incest taboos, free sexual access to certain relatives was a built-in part of some cultures and not considered incest at all. A Pawnee woman served as the sexual partner of her husband's sister's son from the time he reached puberty until he married, and a Hopi woman could openly have sex relations with her brother's son. Hopi women began to tease their nephews when the boys were quite young, calling them "sweetheart" and paying much attention to them. Sometimes during ceremonies they would catch the boys and pretend to have intercourse with them in front of the assembled crowds. When a boy reached puberty he could go to his aunt for sex whenever he wished. The aunt's daughter, who would have been the boy's cousin, was also available to him as a sex partner, but not as a marriage partner.

SEX AND CEREMONIALS

Participants in many Native American religious ceremonials were expected to remain celibate for the duration of the rituals—in some cases male dancers were not allowed to touch their wives, speak to them, or look at their faces. All participants in Hopi ceremonials were required to be continent for varying periods of time before, during, and after the rituals, supposedly because the "smell" of women was displeasing to the clouds and if the people had intercourse during the performances, no rain would fall. But even the dire consequences of the violation of this taboo—the possible starvation of the whole village—were not enough to restrain all of the people. One Hopi woman was said to have given birth to a crippled child because she had had intercourse with a man who was still wearing his kachina dancing costume.

Although the participants in many sacred rites had to curtail their own sex lives temporarily, the importance of sexuality and fertility in the normal functioning of the universe was often part of the ritual dances. The chief ceremonials were reverent prayers for abundance—of game, of wild plant foods, and of agricultural crops—and there can be no abundance without the sexual functions of nature.

Symbolic sexual intercourse was performed as a religious gesture of fertility by Hopi kachina dancers (impersonators of supernatural beings) during one of the important ceremonials. Two kachinas would appear in the plaza signifying in pantomime that they were being consumed with sexual desire. They would then rush toward a cluster of women spectators and by placing their hands on the shoulders of each of the women pretend to have intercourse with them by jumping up and down in front of them. Then the kachinas rushed over to another cluster of women and continued their pantomime until they had had "intercourse" with practically every female in the audience. Even women who were normally very shy submitted readily to these public embraces.

The explicit words, gestures, and sex motions that would have been considered offensive at other times were regarded in an entirely different light during such ceremonials, which provided a healthy and periodic release of tensions by allowing the spectators to participate vicariously in forbidden activities.

Actual sexual intercourse was included in one of the Mandan's important ceremonies. Women were the main participants in the sexual ceremonialism of the tribe's autumn buffalo-calling rites, a four-day celebration in which the old men impersonated the bison. Each night the young women, naked but wrapped in blankets, were accompanied by their husbands to the ceremonial lodge. A husband would point out an elder of his clan, and his wife would approach the old man, offering him food and inviting him to walk outside with her. The old man could accompany the young woman into the woods and have intercourse with her—an act considered tantamount to the woman's having intercourse with a buffalo. So placated, the herds would come to the prairies near the villages and the people would be successful in war and not want for food. A young woman might approach eight to ten men a night, but some say very few of the elders really accepted these sexual favors, fearing personal bad luck if they did. Usually they just went outside with the woman and offered a prayer for the success of the young couple. This ceremonial intercourse was believed to strengthen the marital bonds, for the woman who "walked with the buffalo" proved to her husband that she sought his success in hunting and warfare, which would lead to a good home, good health, and plenty of food and clothing.

The early non-Indian spectators at the Native American ceremonials did not understand the symbolism behind what they saw and were consequently shocked by some of the rites. Because of this, many of the dances were subsequently modified when non-Indians were present. Latter-day anthropologists attempting to gather traditional cultural information and legends have also encountered this Indian tendency to delete sexual references when communicating with white men. A Hopi man who had served as an informant to several early investigators was finally led to confess, "I knew the whites can see more sin than pleasure in sex, so I edited the old Hopi stories."

TYPICAL LOVE-MAKING CUSTOMS

Kissing occurred as part of love-making in many tribes. Some anthropologists maintain that kissing is a purely European phenomenon, but if this is true the practice spread rapidly throughout primitive North America once it was introduced. It is reported that Flatheads were great kissers when feeling affectionate, pressing their lips against those of their beloved and perhaps using their tongues but making no smacking sounds. Kissing also was, and is, a part of Hopi love-making. On the other hand the Apaches, who occasionally kissed small children, considered a kiss much too personal a gesture for adults to use in public and some couples were so restrained that they spent their married lives never kissing or even holding hands.

Because most Native Americans viewed sex as a natural part of life, impotence in men and frigidity in women were apparently very rare. During the sex act, most North American Indians seem to have preferred the "missionary" position. A Hopi man revealed that "any self-respecting man stays on top," and the Kaska maintained that for a woman to lie astride a man threatened his hunting ability. Navajo women believed that if sexually approached from any direction other than above, a baby conceived from that union would be born feet first after very hard labor. Navajos did not kiss during intercourse for the same reason. The less restrained Pomo reportedly enjoyed sex in many different positions, with anal sex predominating because the women were said to like it. The Mohave practiced anal intercourse to such an extent that the women sometimes developed hemorrhoids. Mohave men were never willing to let women take the superior position, and a woman could berate a drunken man this way.

Oral sex practices seem to have been limited. Pomo men and women may have exchanged oral stimulation, but among the Mohave only fellatio was practiced owing to the societal notion that a woman's sexual secretions smelled bad or "fishy." Mohave women also received very little digital stimulation, because the men did not want their hands to smell bad. A rare Kaska woman would perform fellatio, but oral contact with female genitals rarely took place because Kaska men thought a woman's sexual parts were poisonous. Although the Hopis would kiss and caress each other all over, an informant related, "It is not right to kiss the pubes."

It is hard to tell how widespread or common female orgasm was. The available literature suggests that it was fine if it happened but that the experience was generally not considered something to strive for. When Navajo women were questioned by anthropologist Flora Bailey in 1949 about the occurrence of female orgasm, their responses included unawareness that women could have orgasm, the belief that women can and should experience such a sensation, and the conviction that it was a symptom of sickness resulting from too much sex. One elderly woman told Dr. Bailey that although the man was always sure of having an orgasm, it was the woman's concern if she had one: her husband didn't know and she didn't tell him; they just didn't talk about the matter.

Sex was a seasonal activity in some tribes. In the winter, Hupa women and children slept in the xonta or family home, while the men slept in the tribal sweathouse. With the arrival of warm weather in early summer the people built brush shelters on the banks of a river, and husbands and wives lived together until the coolness of fall forced a return to more permanent dwellings.

It was love of wealth that kept Yurok men and women apart during the winter. The dentalium, or tusk shell money, of the Yurok male was evidently more important to him than sex. He believed that sex performed inside the house, which was where he kept his dentalium, would cause the shells to leave; in other words, he would become a spendthrift. It was too cold and rainy to sleep outdoors in winter in northern California, so apparently Yurok women had to wait until summer to have their conjugal desires satisfied. Among the Yurok the female orgasm was not represented among verbalized facts and did not have the connotation of an achievement. When questioned about female sexual response by a visitor, a Yurok man replied, "After all, our women were bought."

ADULTERY

Standards of sexual fidelity in marriage differed among the Native Americans. For example, the Hopi attitude toward adultery was consistent with their usual sexual frankness. A Hopi woman who had a lover was called his "private wife"; her husband probably had one or more private wives of his own who were widows, single women, or other men's wives. The spouses both knew that their mates might have sexual experiences outside of the marriage, but neither cared to know the details. Their society accepted this behavior, although individuals were expected to exercise some restraint.

Some tribes expected a certain amount of intrigue and surreptitious affairs whenever several camps got together. Prolonged ceremonials were an instance when the unusual commotion of a great gathering of people allowed the opportunity for extramarital merriment in societies where standards weren't overwhelmingly strict.

Not unlike many present-day societies, some tribes considered women the "property" of their families or husbands. In a society in which brides were purchased, a woman's virtue had a monetary value and adultery was a serious crime. Women "owned" in this way were expected to be more chaste than the men of the group. The punishment for adultery was usually more drastic and the shame more complete for the woman than for her paramour.

One of the oldest reports of the punishment of an Indian adulteress was made by two of Hernando de Soto's men who visited the ancestors of the Mobile Indians. The Spaniards were witnesses as a woman found guilty of adultery was brought before the entire village. While the villagers looked on, the woman's husband stripped her naked, shaved her (head?) with a flint razor, and then walked off with her clothing, showing that he was finished with his wife. The crowd hissed and insulted the woman in an effort to increase her shame while pelting her with clods of earth and rubbish. She was then turned over to her parents, who were instructed to take her from the area forever.

The same explorers described the corresponding practice among the predecessors of the Creeks. A husband who was informed of, or suspected, his wife's infidelity investigated. If he found her guilty, he took his wife to the forest, tied her to a tree, and shot her to death with arrows. The woman's relatives were not allowed to bury her body; it was to be devoured by beasts as an example to others.

As the years went by the punishment of a Creek adulteress gradually became the duty of the other women of the tribe, particularly if the woman's lover had a wife and children. The women armed themselves with rods as long as their arms and when they found their victim they tore off all her clothing and left her beaten and bloody. If the adulteress was married, her husband's relatives would usually gather near the uproar and rescue her if they saw that matters were going too far.

The Assiniboine adulteress was always severely punished. After her head had been closely shaved and her body thickly painted with vermilion pigment and bear grease, she was mounted on a horse daubed with vermilion whose mane and tail had been shorn. An old man led her all around the camp while announcing her infidelity and then left her with her parents, who beat her for disgracing them.

The close cropping of a woman's hair was a punishment among other groups, for many tribes considered long, lustrous hair to be a woman's chief adornment. The first time a Chickasaw woman was caught in adultery, she was severely beaten and her hair was cropped close. A woman who had had her locks shorn was embarrassed to be seen, and even in summer she would stay inside the dark, stuffy winter house, plastering her stubby tresses with bear grease until they had grown long enough to tie back. The second time a Chickasaw woman was caught transgressing she could expect the loss of her ears, her lip, or the tip of her nose. Usually these parts were removed with a knife, but it was not unknown for an enraged husband to bite off the end of his unfaithful wife's nose, knowing that no other man would want her with such a disfigurement.

216

Similar mutilation was the standard punishment for an adulteress in other tribes as well. Sioux and Apache women were among those who could expect to lose their noses for their indiscretions.

Among the Gros Ventre, in what is now Montana, a husband who had been cuckolded was forced by public opinion to take some action against his wife. He could go as far as killing her, but the alternatives included disfiguring her face, cutting her hair, or divorcing her. Reports tell of one man who cut off his wife's breasts and arms and left her to die. Another husband found his wife in the arms of the chief of his band, whereupon he immediately shot his rival.

The story is also told of a Gros Ventre man, who while visiting his brother was treated very poorly by the brother's wife. The man retaliated by warning the woman, "Some day I might hear something about you [meaning that she had a lover] and you will find out that I am as mean as you are." Not long after that someone told the man that his sister-in-law was with her lover, so he immediately got his gun and went after her. When the man came across the hapless couple he said to the woman, "So I find you aren't as mean as you pretend to be. You are generous about some things. I came to kill you." The woman replied, "Well, kill me then." Her enraged brother-in-law killed her on the spot and then told her husband what had happened. The husband then thanked his brother, saying he would have done exactly the same thing.

Apparently there were many Gros Ventre women who were suspected of infidelity, a situation attributed to the young girls' often being married off to old men they did not love. It is easy to see why a young woman paired with a man her father's age might risk punishment when a handsome and desirable young brave caught her eye.

There were two sets of circumstances where a Gros Ventre woman could expect society at large to more or less accept her infidelities, although she still had to exercise care to avoid her husband's suspicion. In the first case a woman would send a man out to accomplish some specific and spectacular war deed before she granted her favors to him. If he returned, she was supposed to accept him as her lover. In the other situation a man who wished to have sex with a woman publicly announced his intention of going against the enemy while making no effort to defend himself—virtually committing suicide.

Although it cost a Gros Ventre man status and prestige if he continued to live with a wife he knew to be unfaithful, some men were so fond of their wives that they were willing to risk adverse public opinion. Or an errant wife might get no immediate chastisement, but one day her husband might casually give her away to prove his indifference to her. In some cases if the woman's seducer paid an indemnity to the outraged husband, he would allow her to go off with her lover.

Some Native American men who found themselves cuckolded were not content to mete out the standard punishments to their wives—they preferred to inflict discipline of their own devising. An Eastern Sioux man who suspected his wife of having an affair took his gun one morning and pretended to go hunting. Instead of going off into the woods he waited nearby until his wife's lover appeared. When the wife left her paramour briefly, the husband shot and killed his rival. Then he cut a hunk of flesh from the dead lover's back and took it to his wife, suggesting that she cook the meat. After the meat was roasted the man put a gun to his wife and forced her to eat her dead lover's body, telling her that seeing she liked the man so well, she should be happy to eat his flesh. Following this scene the husband shot her.

An early traveler among the Cherokees reported an instance in which a Cherokee woman who had committed frequent infidelities received an unusual punishment from her husband and his relatives. Apparently the men decided that since this woman loved a great many men they would gratify her desire. They ambushed the wife when she was in the woods and tied her, spread-eagled, to stakes. More than fifty men lay with her that afternoon, although it is reported that they each had the decency to cover themselves with a blanket before attacking her.

Exceptionally strong-willed Cheyenne women who had flagrant extramarital affairs were subjected to the same treatment received by the Cherokee adulteress mentioned above. The outraged husband invited all the unmarried members of his military society (except his wife's relatives) to a feast on the prairie, after which each of them took a turn at raping her. The victim usually received punishment far out of proportion to her crime, as she became the target for all the frustrations that had built up in the men of this extremely restrictive society. To "put a woman on the prairie" was clearly counter to the dominant Cheyenne values of dignity and sexual restraint, and this punishment was resorted to very rarely. The men who took part were not proud of themselves; when taunted by the women in the camp for their behavior they usually didn't bother to defend themselves but hung their heads and walked away.

Sometimes even the supernatural was called on to inflict punishment on women who had been unlucky enough to be caught in extramarital affairs. In one case, a Comanche woman aptly named Looking-for-Fun almost lost her life to what she believed were supernatural powers. Her husband had suspected her of adultery and she denied it. Her husband made her swear her innocence to the sun and the earth, and although she was guilty and knew it, she went ahead and swore, "Sun, if you don't believe me, then let me perish. Mother Earth, if you don't believe me, let it be true that I won't live right upon you."

A few months later Looking-for-Fun began to have fainting spells and waste away. Frightened, she approached a medicine man for help. He told her that he thought her husband's charges were true and that she was actually being punished by the powers she had challenged. At this she owned up and told the doctor she had not confessed because she was afraid her husband would punish her severely.

When the medicine man heard the whole story he decided that the matter was beyond his powers and sent Looking-for-Fun to a specialist.

The woman, who was by now more than a little frightened, got her mother and they went to see the other doctor. Fortunately, the husband was away on the warpath and did not become suspicious. The new doctor told the two women that he would probably be able to help and gave them two choices: they would either have to sacrifice another person in the family or else provide eight horses to be killed because he could not stop the disease, he could only shift it to something else. He confessed that he would prefer to work with the horses, since he did not like to take the life of a human being.

So the women left and the medicine man performed the proper ritual. Shortly the band decided to move, and because the husband had not yet returned from the warpath, his wife got all his horses together and prepared to drive them toward the new camp. While she was driving them along one horse suddenly dropped dead, and before long another one collapsed. By the time the group reached its new camp, eight of the woman's horses had died.

The young woman was very happy, for the death of the horses proved that she would be cured. When the husband finally returned she told him how the band had broken camp and how she had lost eight horses during the move. She led him to believe that no one knew what was wrong with the horses and that was all he ever found out.[3]

Among the Crows, life was easier for unfaithful women. Virtuous women were admired, but those who departed from the ideal, even women who were positively wanton, were not ostracized by society, they merely lost prestige. The reactions of their husbands varied. Upon learning of his wife's unfaithfulness one man might not say anything, while another might go so far as to slash her face with a knife. Crow wives, on the other hand, were not jealous and realized that their men usually had a sweetheart in every camp. Some were even proud to have a husband so charming and good-looking as to attract other women, and they would prepare a feast for a visiting rival, sending her home laden with gifts. (Crow men told each other that women were like buffalo. A husband who lived too long with one wife was like a hunter who has killed the last of the herd and stays by the carcass because he lacks energy to go after others.)

An interesting and complex form of institutionalized adultery was practiced by the Crows in the 1860s and 1870s. Most of the men were grouped into two rival clubs—the Foxes and the Lumpwoods—in which a major activity was mutual wife-kidnapping. Once a year, in the spring, the clubs assembled separately and prepared to steal the wives of the members of the other club. A woman was eligible for abduction only by a man who had previously been her lover and could refuse to accompany anyone else, but sometimes men pretended to previous intimacy and carried off women by force. A woman who did not wish to be abducted might beg her kidnapper to leave her alone, or, if she were really fearful, she could hide during the kidnapping season (usually only two weeks). A woman who was trying to hide from an abductor could generally count on other women to aid in her concealment, but her husband was of no assistance at all. The gentlemen's code of honor did not permit him to resist even if his wife were seized in his presence, and any display of emotion on his part would bring pitiless mirth from the aggressor. Kidnapped women were taken to the rival camp and ostentatiously displayed. A woman was generally released by her abductor after a brief period of co-residence but she was never allowed to return to her previous husband. This system would have been of great benefit to women who wanted to leave their husbands and live with their lovers, although it is not clear whether only those women truly amenable to capture were taken.

Other less permanent types of wife-swapping were practiced among several North American tribes. In these societies a husband considered his wife adulterous only if she chose to have intercourse with someone else; it was not adultery when the man loaned his wife for sexual purposes. In California, wife-swapping was common between friendly Nisenan chiefs, and a man of this rank expected to have a woman loaned to him whenever he was visiting another village. A Nisenan husband also shared his wife with his namesake. Evidently the women were not consulted in such arrangements.

A very old report, which may have been exaggerated, told of Huron men offering their wives, if they were willing, to other men for a small gift, while village procurors had no occupation other than arranging to bring men the women they desired.

Among the Copper Eskimos the custom of exchanging wives (and husbands) resulted in an extension of the family—even the children of the two families were considered brothers and sisters and forbidden to marry. When a family was visiting a group of strangers the husband often tried to ally himself with one of the host families in a wife-swapping arrangement, so that he would cease to be a stranger and a potential enemy. Such exchanges were so frequent as to pass unnoticed in a community. There was no reason to attempt concealment.

Wife-exchange arrangements between Chipewyan males had implications more economic than sexual. Chipewyan women are said to have been guarded jealously and not allowed out of their husbands' sight if the opportunity for adultery existed. Such a wife was generally faithful even if she had to share her husband with as many as seven co-wives. When two men entered a wife-exchange arrangement, they pledged continuing friendship and mutual aid. If one of the men died, the other was pledged to take care of the surviving wife or wives and children, at least temporarily.

The severest punishment seemed to fall on women who accepted lovers from outside their own tribe. Pimas tolerated loose women among themselves, but a Pima girl caught with any man not a Pima was stoned to death. White traders who lived with the Pimas for many years were usually welcomed into all aspects of village life, but this hospitality did not allow them sexual access to the women of the tribe, and any Pima female consorting with a trader was in grave danger.

The Havasupai tell the story of a beautiful woman of their tribe who fell in love with an Apache man. The two decided to run away together. After the Apache had killed his sweetheart's husband, the lovers fled together up a steep canyon wall pursued by men from the woman's tribe. When the couple had almost reached the rim of the inner canyon, they were struck by the gods and turned into stone. There they have remained through time, it is said, as a reminder to Havasupai women of the dangers of illicit love. Apparently the warning was never taken too seriously, for Havasupai men and women commonly held brief affairs with the Navajos, Hopis, and Paiutes who came to trade. However, as late as 1900 a Havasupai woman was condemned to death by her people for unlawful cohabitation with a white man.

Of course it occasionally happened that an innocent woman was accused of adultery and punished, and then her relatives sought revenge, but the guilt of an accused woman was usually taken for granted. In some tribes, a woman could be considered adulterous without actually commiting a sexual misdeed. An adult Wishram woman was never to speak to an unrelated male, and if she accidentally met one on a trail, one of them had to move about ten feet to the side so that they would not touch each other. A married Wishram woman could accept nothing from an unmarried male—not even a drink of water. Violation of these rules constituted adultery. Any conversation between a Yurok woman and a former lover was considered suspect, as was their presence together on a trail or in a dwelling, no matter how innocent the circumstances. These crimes of "inferred adultery" were usually resolved by the offended husband's accepting some form of payment from the other man.

The leeway an Indian woman had in protesting an errant husband varied. Among the Caddo and Hidatsa it was considered indecent for either men or women to make a public display of jealousy. The correct behavior was for the injured party to speak to the adulterous spouse and suggest that he or she leave if desirous of living with his or her lover.

In other groups, two women wanting the same man fought it out physically. A jealous woman would attack her rival with a knife, or two women might go after each other with digging sticks, rock lifters, or long fingernails. It was not uncommon for two Cocopah women to wrestle and pull each other's hair to the amusement of the rest of the population. The Southern Ute recommended an unarmed scuffle between two rivals as a method of deciding one woman's right to the man. It was contended that the woman who really cared would never admit defeat and the stronger woman would make the better wife. If a Ute wife didn't want to fight and didn't particularly care about her husband, she might merely destroy some of the other woman's property and tell her to keep the man. A Shoshone wife expected her husband to stray, but she could beat the interloping woman, rip her skirt to expose her genitals, and spit on them.

❀◇❀◇❀◇❀◇❀◇❀◇❀◇

The Wife Who Killed Her Rival

(TLINGIT)

Once a man lived with his wife and little son in a cabin at the base of a mountain. While on a hunting expedition one day on the other side of the mountain the man met a woman and fell in love with her. He began to live with this woman and took her all the game he caught.

The man visited his first wife and little boy so seldom that soon they found themselves in dire need of food and skins. Once, after a long absence the man appeared, bringing only a small piece of meat. The woman gave the meat to her son saying, "That is all your father brought you."

The wife was angry so she secretly followed her husband to the cabin on the other side of the mountain. She watched him go into the dwelling and then hid herself nearby, patiently waiting for him to come out. When he finally left the cabin and headed off for the woods the wife entered the house and killed her rival with a knife. After she had taken as much of the ample food supply as she could carry, she set fire to the house and returned home with her booty.

When the husband returned to his sweetheart he found only a pile of ashes where the cabin had stood. The man was so sad that he decided to return to his wife. When he arrived at his old home his wife asked him why he was so upset, but he didn't answer her.

The wife picked up as many of her belongings as she could carry and leading the child by the hand she returned to her father. The father, who was a shaman, had seen his daughter in a dream wandering around in the prairies and had guided her footsteps homeward. The husband tried to follow his wife and son, but the shaman turned him into an elk.[4]

❖◇❖◇❖◇❖◇❖◇❖◇❖◇

Iroquois ethics were somewhat different, a woman being taught that if she found out her husband had visited other women while on ,a journey, she should not cause a commotion. As a good wife she would have a place in heaven, but her man was on the way to the house of the Wicked One. (This report may have referred to primitive custom, but it smacks heavily of European Christian input.)

Gros Ventre women, who as we have seen might expect anything from disfigurement to death for their own infidelities, were taught to say nothing when a husband returned after having been out late, perhaps with another woman. "He will always come back to you," they were told. "Just say to yourself that he is your man and will never leave you permanently." They were also enjoined not to retaliate by seeking another man.

Of course a woman could always leave an unfaithful husband, but if the man was a good hunter, she might think twice before giving up her means of support. There were some societies in which a wife would not have been punished for killing an adulterous husband, but a woman who took such drastic action usually had a hard time finding another husband.

RAPE

Rape was considered a gross sexual violation and was widely condemned among Native Americans. Because of almost universal disapproval, rape occurred only rarely, although in a few instances it was standard behavior within a limited societal situation.

The Chiricahua Apaches classified rape as stealing; attacking a single woman was considered more serious than attacking a married woman. Punishment was meted out by the woman's family rather than by the tribe, and they could go so far as killing the violator. The rapist's family sometimes offered payment in an attempt to smooth things over.

As a last-ditch measure an Apache brave might rape a woman he was unable to woo in a more conventional manner. One Western Apache man was enamored of a certain maiden and had even convinced her father to give her to him. But the young woman refused to consent to the marriage because she did not like the young man.

One day while the maiden was out gathering acorns with some women relatives the young man rode up to her on his horse and offered her a ride home to her camp. Because the maiden knew she would have to cross a rain-swollen river she accepted his offer. Instead of taking her home, the young man rode off with her into a canyon and kept her there with him all evening, forcing her into sexual relations.

When the young man finally brought the girl back he gave her the reins to his horse and told her to lead it home. Knowing he would be required to pay for his transgressions sooner or later, he decided it might as well be sooner. When the maiden returned to her camp she was still furious at the way she had been treated, and said to her mother, "My mother, kill this horse. That man has done something all over me, so you better kill the horse." So they butchered the animal and ate it.

Two months later the young woman's mother went over to the brave's camp to talk with his mother. She told the young man's mother that her daughter was pregnant so she thought it would be best if the two young people got married. The youth's parents agreed with her. That was fine with the young man because it was what he had planned from the start.

Even though sex relations among the Zuni were relatively free and uninhibited, rape was considered a grave offense. It was, however, a private transgression, rather than a crime against society. About 1880 a young married woman brought a typical rape case before the Zuni tribal council. She had gone out to pick berries and while she was bent over a bush an unmarried man of the village crept up on her silently, threw up her dress, and raped her from behind, unmindful of her cries and protestations. Afterwards the woman admonished her attacker for what he had done, saying that if he had asked her properly she probably would have consented to have sex with him. The man offered her a necklace and a dress if she wouldn't report him, but the woman was insulted and went home crying to tell her husband.

In the evening the rapist and his family were visited by the woman's husband, and the rapist admitted what he had done, again offering the necklace and dress in payment. It was decided to take the case before the council. After the story was heard by the judge, the woman said she wanted a string of beads, a necklace, a black manta, a pair of woven leggings, a tanned buckskin, a large rug, and a corn field as retribution. This was a large settlement but the defendant paid and was warned by the judge that if he ever repeated his crime he would have to pay twice as much.

Ojibwa girls feared rape by outsiders but had to watch out particularly for older men of their own tribe and even of their own households. An Ojibwa shaman being consulted in some matter might tell a girl that a young suitor would come to court her at night and then slip in under the side of the tipi himself. It was also common for a man to take his stepdaughter out duck hunting with him and then attempt to rape her while they were away from the village. When the girl got back home and told her mother what had happened, there was usually an argument between the mother and the father. Sometimes the girl and her mother left the home temporarily or permanently.

Anthropologist Ruth Landes relates the story of a youthful Ojibwa widow still bereaved by the loss of her handsome young husband. Her father-in-law told her that her late husband would come in the night to "kiss his little boy not yet conceived," but he also warned her not to build up the fire for light when her late husband's spirit appeared. Then the old lecher dressed up in a burial suit and entered the widow's tipi himself. Apparently the situation didn't seem quite right to the young woman and her suspicions were aroused, but since she had been told to remain in darkness, she couldn't see the man's face clearly. She didn't grasp what had happened until she found herself

225

pregnant. Then, outraged, she broadcast the truth throughout the village, and she and her mother moved away.

Ritualized sexual aggression was a prerogative of a special group of young men among the Southern Ute. This band of young men, most of them without families, lived together outside the main camp. Calling themselves the Dogs, they spent their time learning to be fierce warriors. Occasionally they would enter the village, whooping, hollering, and performing preposterous antics. Any woman who laughed at them, even an elderly crone, could be carried away to their camp and raped.

Flathead men considered raping the daughter of a personal foe within their band as just revenge for an injury, but such action was taken only by strong men who dared face the reprisals. It was the women of the tribe, rather than the chief or male relatives of the victim, who punished such offenders. The unsuspecting rapist would be led to some out of the way spot where he would receive the collective anger of the village women in all manner of abuse and indignity.

Some Native American women were strong enough or clever enough to defend themselves against rape. One tale, from the Comanches of the southern Plains area, concerns a man named Blow It Away who, being generally unpopular and avoided by women, tried to make up for his lack of female companionship by sneaking into tipis at night and attempting to have intercourse with whatever woman he found there. He was a chronic offender, although he never had much success. One night he picked the wrong woman —a hefty matron, strong of arm and will. When she awoke to find Blow It Away feeling her, she struggled with him and finally got him down. After ripping off his breechclout she grabbed him by the penis and started to drag him from the tipi. Her son was awakened by the commotion and begged his mother not to humiliate the poor man that way, but she was determined to teach the nuisance a lesson. Keeping a tight grip on his genitals she pulled him outside where everyone could see him. This was the first time anyone had ever taken action against the fellow, and the last time he tried to force himself on a woman.

A woman did not always need great physical strength to protect herself against rape. The methods used by two Labrador Eskimo maidens to defend themselves against attack by Canadians would work well today. The young women were spending the summer with their father camping near a lake in the line of travel of lumberjacks going back and forth from the "bush" to the nearest settlements. Their camp was located several hundred feet from shore for privacy. One day the father was away hunting and the girls were occupied with some domestic duties on the sandy beach when a canoe full of white men came into sight. These men had not even had sight of a woman for months, and there was no doubt what they were after when they began to paddle quickly toward the girls. The two sisters knew that escape was impossible so in full view of their excited pursuers, they began to throw handfuls of sand into their genitals. When they saw what the heretofore desirable young women were doing, the baffled Canadians howled with rage and turned their canoe back on its course, cursing the "dirty savages."

Although Native American women were often violated by European traders, trappers, and explorers, white women were seldom raped when taken prisoner by Indians. Apparently the widespread traditions forbidding the sexual assault of "foreigners" extended to white women also.

The wife of a white clergyman who was a captive of the Narraganset for almost three months in 1676 wrote, ". . . no one of them ever offered the least abuse or unchastity to me in word or action," and some sisters captured by the Cheyenne also did not report any sexual mistreatment. The Oatman sisters, while not particularly well-treated by the Apaches and Mohaves, nevertheless were never sexually molested.

PROSTITUTION

Prostitution probably did not exist widely among the North American Indians before European contact. Women occasionally sold their favors but did not pursue such activity full time.

A Creek woman might hire herself out to a man who was passing through her village and did not have a woman with him. No one would castigate her, for it was felt she had the right to her own body. But Creek girls kept such activity to a minimum to retain some degree of modesty.

In Southeast Salish communities, in Washington and northern Idaho, there were certain women—including some married women and others who were not able to obtain a husband—who could be had by anyone at any time. As discussed in the chapter on marriage, the Southeast Salish were a polygamous society and a woman did not always live with her husband nor was she necessarily supported by him. The typical Salish woman was very impressed by good-looking men but it is said these loose women "didn't care how a man looked." Although the rest of the community might gossip about a woman's poor taste in men, she was not publicly chastised if she remained somewhat circumspect in her behavior. Still, even women who were openly promiscuous resented being called by the term applied to a prostitute.

Life was somewhat more difficult for the Omaha woman who chose a life of sexual freedom. In 1879 there were only two or three "public women" in this rather strict Plains tribe. When such a woman's family disapproved of her behavior, it was the duty of her elder brother or maternal uncle to reproach her, which they sometimes did by shooting her with an arrow.

A Papago woman wrote in her autobiography of "wild women" who had no husbands, yet assumed the married woman's privileges of going to puberty dances and village drinking ceremonies. In those days Papago women wore no clothing above the waist, and these wild women painted ears of corn, birds, and butterflies on their breasts to attract men. So arrayed, these women would form temporary alliances with men they would meet at the social gatherings. Occasionally a woman might even go home with a man she had met in this way and settle down and become one of his wives, but usually when the party was over she left her lover for another festivity and another lover.

Between affairs she would go back to her father's house. Her parents realized that they could not control a daughter who was so inclined—they just let her have her way. If she had children, her parents cared for them. The Pimas, close cousins of the Papago, called these joyful souls "light" or "playful" women. Far from being outcasts, these women were lovingly tolerated. One informant told Ruth Underhill, "The light woman can't help it, her heart bubbles over," while another explained, "When you talk to her, she doesn't know what you say. Her heart is outside her, running ahead to the next dance."[5]

❀◇❀◇❀◇❀◇❀◇❀◇❀◇❀◇

How the Pleiades Appeared

(PAPAGO)

On Baboquivari, the sacred mountain of the Papago, there is a cave where a man lived who knew everything. He told the people many good things and sang many beautiful songs to them, intending that the people would learn the songs and sing them for a girl who reaches puberty.

At that time there was no puberty celebration. The first time they had the celebration the people liked it. But some women did only that all the time. It wrecked their homes and no one wanted them. People called them "homeless women," because they ran around and had no home. They wandered everywhere in the country and finally sent to a powerful medicine woman. When she arrived, they told her to do something to them so they would soon find rest from their homeless condition.

The woman said, "Alright, I'll do it. I'm going to put you out in plain sight of all. Every evening your relatives will see you and tell their daughters why you are called the Homeless Women. In this way women will know what a good home is. Even though a puberty ceremony is enjoyable, no one should go around just doing that."

When she had said this, she sprinkled the women with water and they turned to stone. Then she took them and threw them eastward into the sky, and they landed where they are now. They appear as seven stars and make up the constellation called the Pleiades.[6]

❀◇❀◇❀◇❀◇❀◇❀◇❀◇❀◇

LESBIANISM

The attitude of Native Americans toward homosexuals varied from solicitude and respect to outrage and disgust. Many groups, although not particularly desiring homosexual members, accepted the inevitable percentage of their number who deviated from the sexual norm and even institutionalized their role by assigning certain duties specifically to homosexuals. Lesbianism seems to have occurred less frequently than male homosexuality.

A Navajo lesbian was considered an asset by both her family and the community. In one of the tribal myths about the beginning of all things, homosexuals are described as being wealthy and as having control of all wealth. Consequently, they were usually put in charge of the household and controlled the disposal of all property.

According to a paper by anthropologist W. W. Hill, all Navajo hermaphrodites, transvestites, and homosexuals, regardless of their biological sex, were considered favored persons and were lumped into the same general grouping, which was neither male nor female. Their role encompassed the duties of both men and women and they were believed to excel in all pursuits from cooking, to sheep-raising, to the performing of certain chants and curing ceremonials. War and hunting were the only masculine activities denied this group of people and their political power was limited to that of advisor. Transvestite lesbians had sex with and married both men and women.

The Mohaves, who lived along the Colorado River, also believed that from the very beginning of the world it was intended that there should be homosexuals. They thought that sometimes a baby would dream about becoming a transvestite while still in the womb. Although the society was not offended by lesbians, families usually tried to prevent homosexual behavior in their children because such people were considered "crazy."

A Mohave lesbian, called a hwame, took a male name and wore male clothing if she needed it for riding and hunting. A hwame was accepted into all male activities but could not become a tribal head or war leader.

Generally a hwame had relatively small breasts and did not menstruate, or at least did not admit to it, but observed the taboos husbands were supposed to follow when their wives menstruated. The wife of a hwame was not considered a homosexual, but she was probably a bisexual. These women were treated well by their lesbian "husbands" who took pride in dressing them in pretty clothes and beads. One hwame even became a prostitute to the whites so that she could earn enough money to keep her wife in fashion.

Sexual activity between a hwame and her wife included clitoral and vaginal masturbation, "intercourse" with the wife on the bottom and the hwame on top, and a position called the vaginal split where the partners stretched out in opposite directions, their legs enclosing each other scissor fashion so that their vulvae touched. No oral stimulation was used because of the Mohaves' disgust at vaginal odor. Like the salacious men of the tribe, a hwame would sit around in her free time describing her wife's genitals to the assembled males.

Divorce was common among such couples and was accomplished by the wife's simply leaving, often to become the wife of a normal male. To the modern mind Mohave society appears wisely adaptive in accepting sexual ambiguity and allowing bisexuals to experiment in a homosexual role and then return to heterosexuality if they wished.[7]

Among the Kaska, in Canada, lesbianism was not only accepted but actually initiated and encouraged at times. If a family found itself with too many daughters, one of the girls was selected to be a son and was raised like a boy. When the child was five, her parents tied the dried ovaries of a bear to her inner belt. She wore them for the rest of her life as an amulet to prevent conception. Dressed in male clothing and performing the male role, these persons became outstanding hunters. Their sexual experiences were with other women, and orgasm was achieved by clitoral friction while one woman lay on top of another. If a male ever made advances to such a man-woman, he risked having his bow and arrows broken by the object of his attentions, for any sexual contact with a man was believed to ruin a lesbian's luck with game.

Looking at other scattered cases, we read that Yuma female transvestites realized their character by dreaming of weapons when they reached puberty. Secondary sex characteristics were usually underdeveloped in these women, and their status was considered different from that of a person who engaged in occasional homosexuality. The Cocopah lesbian, a neighbor to the Yumas and Mohaves, exhibited her preferences early by choosing to play with boys, make arrows and bows, and hunt. As she matured she dressed her hair and pierced her nose in a masculine fashion. She was allowed to fight in battle, marry, and establish a household. Quinault lesbians experienced no social stigma, the word for their condition meaning simply "man-acting." They dressed, acted, and worked like men, and shared sex only with their female mates.

Some Native American societies would not tolerate homosexuality. The Southern Ute actively opposed homosexuals, considering their behavior deeply disgraceful. Women could never wear men's clothing, and even children were forbidden to switch sex roles in their play.

Homosexuality was totally forbidden among the Chiricahua Apaches. Any person showing evidence of such behavior was killed as a witch. However, one story of lesbianism was often told about two married women who ran off from their husbands and made a camp together. People passing by their camp heard the two women talking. One woman was on top of the other and asked her companion if she felt something sticky. The answer was, "Yes." The fact that this story was recurrently told by the Apaches seems to indicate a natural curiosity in anything so horrid and terrible as to be utterly condemned by their society.

There was a small percentage of Apache women who were more interested in masculine duties than those generally allotted to women, but they were not looked upon as terribly unusual. Since all girls were urged to develop their strength, it was just assumed that these girls had gone a bit farther than necessary. Similarly, Ojibwa women who followed men's occupations may have been considered a bit unconventional but were not classified as inverts nor suspected of sexual irregularities.

The story is told of an Eskimo society which simply could not accept a woman in a man's role. A good-looking young Eskimo woman, who was well built and very intelligent, never associated with the young men. She said she was as strong as any of them and she could shoot and hunt big game as well as the men in addition to being able to set snares and nets. She had her own gun bought from the proceeds of her trapping. This accomplished young woman was not at all interested in the usual duties allotted to wives, but preferred male tasks. When winter came, having made a convert in a small, less athletic maiden, the woman built a house for the two of them and they lived and traded in defiance of public sentiment. One day when they were off on a deer hunt a mob of outraged townspeople reduced their winter quarters to a shapeless ruin. The next year they gave up their unconventional life-style and returned to the ways of their society.[8]

Ojibway women take part in a spirit dance.
(Courtesy of the American Museum of Natural History)

10

Religion and Spirituality

A CONSTANT REALITY

Religion was not a Sunday affair for the Native Americans. In fact, it is doubtful that an Indian woman viewed spirituality separately from the rest of her life—for her, religion was a ceaseless conversation with the creator of all things. She lived in a world of mysticism and symbolism where every part of the earth and heavens possessed a spiritual life. Everywhere she looked, the Native American woman saw the forces of creation, and this sense and understanding of her surroundings gave depth and dignity to her life.

Of course there were ceremonials, when everyone focused attention on religious matters in an attempt to prevail on the almighty forces for help and guidance. These ceremonies served to reunite the entire populace in a continuing commitment to the way of life they had chosen as a people. Through this sharing of energy, each individual was enfolded into the tribe and into the universe.

SEEKING A VISION

In the face of the great number of spirits and powerful forces with which a Native American was expected to interact, many of these early societies thought it wise for each individual to find a special guardian spirit as an intercessor. A broad analysis of North American tribes shows that most cultures considered it less important for a girl to find such a guardian than it was for a boy. Yet there were many Indian societies in which maidens were expected to seek supernatural helpers, too.

Among the Nez Percé of what is now northern Idaho, every ten-year-old child was sent into the mountains to seek a guardian spirit, this sacred vigil being considered the most important event in the life of an individual. The child was instructed to climb to one of the highest peaks, build up a heap of stones, sit down beside it, and focus attention on the purpose of the vigil. The child was not to eat or drink anything and was to try to stay awake as long as possible. After three or four days of this, the seeker usually fell into a fitful sleep, during which an animal appeared, gave the child a name, and taught it a sacred song. Thenceforth this guardian was supposed to protect the child from danger and endow it with whatever skills or physical qualities were appropriate to that particular supernatural. If for some reason the child had not received a dream visit from a guardian—whether because of inattention or homesickness—it was considered sacrilegious to pretend that a certain animal had appeared. Furthermore, if the child did lie about having received a visit from a supernatural, it could expect to arouse the enmity rather than the protection of the forged guardian.

The dream fast was the central life crisis among the Menominee, the Potowatomi, and other central Algonkin groups who lived around the area of the northern Great Lakes. When a youth or maiden reached the age of fifteen they went off alone to a secluded spot, built a tiny wigwam just big enough for one person, and fasted for eight or ten days, according to individual strength and endurance. Each day the fasters were visited by their parents. If by the eighth day the young people had not received a vision, they were given the choice of quitting or continuing. Their parents handed them two bowls; one of food and one of charcoal. It was perfectly acceptable if they chose the food; they could go on home and try again some other time. But they were exhibiting real nobility if they chose the charcoal and smeared it over their faces and presumably would be rewarded for their perseverance by the appearance of a guardian. In fact, it is very likely that anyone would begin to have visions or hallucinations after being without food and water for ten days. Those who successfully endured this test and had visions of "things on high" could expect to be rewarded by long life, happiness, and perhaps social elevation due to the protection and guidance of their guardian.

Among the Southeast Salish, maidens were sent out to find a guardian if their parents thought it a good idea for a girl to have such aid. Although ninety percent of the boys sought guardians and were rewarded with visions, only twenty to thirty percent of the young women received spirit power. The average woman, who never obtained a helper, led a satisfactory life, but those women who were fortunate enough to have visions were regarded as the equals of men.

RELIGION AND THE MATURE WOMAN

In some tribes, only those young women who were still virgins were allowed to seek spirit helpers, but in other groups a woman might be visited and promised aid by supernaturals at any time in her life.

On the northwest coast, Lummi women who had special guardians performed spirit dances at festivities and potlatches. Some women had derived their spirit helpers during times of great sorrow and suffering, and thus their religious experiences were always very intense. Women (or men) who planned on presenting their spirit dances during a particular event arrived at the celebration early and rehearsed their songs until the rest of the guests arrived. Each dancer had a chance to practice her song with the drummers, sometimes humming it several times so the drummers could pick up the beat.

When it was time for a dancer to present her song she began to groan and sob, acting as if she were having difficulty catching her breath. Experienced singers and drummers gathered close to her, giving her encouragement until she was able to rise and dance around the room, usually imitating the movements of the spirit that was animating her. Typical spirits were the sandhill crane, who enabled women to be skilled in digging clams and roots, and Old Woman, who helped those she visited become good homemakers.

Once a woman who had been chronically ill was brought to a gathering at one of the large villages, and the skilled drummers drew out her spirit song by their careful response to her strivings for expression. Amazingly, she was able to rise from her sickbed and, with what appeared to be superhuman strength, perform her spirit dance. Later, when someone scoffed at the genuineness of this experience, the woman sang a song about a snow-banked canoe. The next morning the villagers were most surprised when they awakened to find the town blanketed by deep snow. Now the disbelievers pleaded with her to make the snow go away. The woman painted her face, boldly walked into the freezing ocean, silently walked back out, and returned to her home. Almost immediately a soft rain began to fall which completely melted the snow before daylight.

Women played a definite and important role in a wide variety of Native

American ceremonies, particularly those religious rituals which dealt with prayers for a sufficient food supply, good health for the tribal members, and other facets of life to which women were closely tied.

Interestingly, the Iroquois ceremonial cycle celebrated only women's activities. At the time of the arrival of the white men to American shores, there were no festivals commemorating hunting or war, though they may have existed previously. Most of the dances and ceremonies were thanksgiving for the fertility of the earth, especially for the crops which were the women's chief concern. But, unlike our present-day solemn church rituals, these religious celebrations were great fun. Dance was considered not only a spiritual rite but a divine art as well, designed by the Great Spirit for pleasure as well as for worship. And as if that weren't enough, these sacred-social celebrations also served to arouse patriotic excitement and keep alive the spirit of the tribe. Each dance was something like our Thanksgiving, Fourth of July, and Fireman's Ball all rolled into one.

In Montana the Flathead Indians also saw the food quest as inextricably bound up with religion. Each season of the year had a major ritual and several minor ones. The beginning rite of the spring season was the First Roots Ceremony, which was always held before any woman was allowed to gather the staple roots. In this ceremony, two respected matrons led a small party of women to a field known to be fruitful. Upon their arrival the older matron raised her arms to the sun, praying for success, security, and good health and fortune for all; next she addressed the earth, pleading for the same blessings. The women then dug up a small supply of roots and took them back to camp, where they were cooked by the wives of the chief. When the meal was ready, the food, symbolic of all the food they would gather that season, was blessed again by prayers to the sun and the earth.

Just north of the Flathead Indians lived the Kutenai, who told anthropologist H. H. Turney-High of a women's religious rite in which the participants gained special supernatural powers. Long ago, so they say, the spirits told the Kutenai women to form the Crazy Owl Society to ward off epidemics, which they considered to be the result of disobeying the spirits. A supernatural might come to one of the members of the Crazy Owl Society at any time and tell her to sing one of the special songs. When the other members heard her they would go to her lodge and dance and sing with her. When the chief of the society felt it was the right time, she started a procession, first visiting every lodge in the village then going into the forest, where she struck a tree and passed right through it, followed by the other members. After the proper number of trees had been passed through, the chief started running toward the west, followed by her band. Soon they all left the ground and ran in the air for a distance. Presently everyone alighted and held a council. When the Crazy Owl members adjourned, they were hopeful that their ceremony had protected their families and loved ones from disease for a while.

Quite a different ceremony was required from Taensa women when the spirits ruling those people needed to be appeased. The Taensa, a small tribe that lived just north of the present site of the Natchez, were being visited by some French explorers in 1699 when lightning struck their large temple and burned it to the ground. The principal priest determined that the tragedy had occurred because the spirits were angry. As was the custom among those people, the women of the town were enjoined to bring their babies to be sacrificed in order to mollify the angry gods. This was regarded as one of the highest of religious sacrifices.

The visiting Frenchmen did not appreciate the significance of what appeared to them as heathen carnage, and, according to one report, stopped the sacrifice after five infants in swaddling clothes had been tossed onto the smoldering ruins of the temple. A report from another Frenchman states that the infants were strangled first and that seventeen babies had been thrown in the fire and two hundred more would have followed had the Europeans not intervened.

Timucua Indian women, in Florida, were required to undergo a similar rite; it was their custom to offer the firstborn son to the chief of the village. On the appointed day the mother took her son to a special place kept for the purpose. The chief took his place on the bench of honor, and the mother, after handing the baby over to one of her female relatives, squatted in front of a two-foot-high stump, covering her face with her hands and wailing at the loss of her child. Other women formed a circle and danced about with demonstrations of apparent joy. Eventually the sacrificing officer took the child and killed it on the wooden stump before the assemblage.

Among the Pueblo peoples in the Southwest, where many of the ancient ceremonies continue today, women have their own religious societies, and most of their explicit ceremonial participation is through these groups. The most sacred dances are usually performed by the men alone, although the women lend indispensable aid by doing such things as ritually washing their husbands' hair and taking food to the dancers at the noon rest period. During many observances, women are required to prepare special foods which must be brought to the ceremonial chambers in prescribed vessels at definite times. Wives also share in the excitement of a dance day by keeping open house for friends and relatives and dressing themselves and their children in holiday attire.

In Hopi towns, girls as well as boys under the age of ten were launched on their religious and ceremonial careers by their initiation into the kachina cult. During these special rites they learned that the beautifully dressed god-creatures that came to dance in the plaza were not supernaturals at all but their fathers and uncles costumed to represent these beings. A few years later all the young people were expected to take the next step in their religious participation by joining one or more of several secret societies. There were three exclusively women's societies, and a girl or young woman could join any or all of them.

In the late summer and fall, when men were busy with the crops, the women in these societies put on entertainments which were not only very pleasurable but also contained prayers for rain and bountiful crops.

The Hopi Basket Dance, which was also found in some of the pueblos along the Rio Grande, took its name from the food baskets which were used in the ceremony—a symbol of the food which preserved the life of the tribe. Baskets contained the seed that was planted in the ground; later they held the fruit of grains yielded by the earth in response to the efforts of the people. When the corn was ground into meal, baskets held the bounty, and when the meal was baked into crisp rolls of wafer bread, these were served in still other baskets. Yet the invocations to fertility during the Basket Dance were directed not merely to food; in a way food was only symbolic of the entire human race, which was urged to multiply and transmit the gift of life from generation to generation.

There are several instances when Pueblo women were allowed to join the men's religious fraternities and to dance in the ceremonials conducted by these groups.

At Zuni there were more than a dozen secret orders or fraternities, many of which women were allowed to join. There was one society, the Kotikili, or mythologic order, which very few women ever entered. However, that society did need a priestess, and when a woman of the order became old, she tried to find some girl who would take over the vows at her death. One of the functions of these women was to perform in the masked dances, personifying the goddesses. Because such a priestess could never marry, maidens were not invited to enter the society until they were old enough to fully understand the responsibilities and requirements of the position. Joining was never a duty but a privilege, rarely accepted.

Even though the young women who took on these responsibilities had fair warning of what the job entailed, human beings do have a tendency to change their minds, and this was occasionally the case with Kotikili priestesses. Tilly E. Cox Stevenson, who lived among the Zuni in the late 1800s, writes, "Even in Zuni where the people are so controlled by the priests and have such a superstitious dread of disobeying the commands of the gods, women have been guilty of desecrating their sacred office and marrying. A woman of the order married a Navajo. She was forever afterwards debarred from joining in the ceremonials, but was permitted to live among her people with no other punishment than their indignation."[1]

⁕◈⁕◈⁕◈⁕◈⁕◈⁕◈⁕◈⁕◈

Two Girls and the Dancers

(ZUNI)

Years ago when the supernatural beings came to earth as kachinas they danced during a feast as the villagers gathered around to watch them. The kachinas were the rain dancers and in the group there were two handsome young men who danced without masks. When all the kachinas were finished with their dance they started to file out of the plaza. Two young maidens had been watching the dances and were very taken by the dancers who performed without the shield of masks.

When the kachinas began to leave the plaza to depart for their own land, the two maidens ran up behind them. Eventually the kachinas noticed the girls and asked them if they wished to come along. Of course the girls wanted to go, so the kachinas consented to take them to their homeland.

The girls stayed with the kachinas for some time and were well cared for. But one day the kachinas approached them and told them, "Our children, we think it will be better if you return to your own land. We do not think it best for you to stay among us. You still have a long life span ahead of you."

The kachinas told the girls that they would perform all the dances for them so the girls should watch closely and memorize what they saw so

241

they could take the information back to their people. The kachinas did this because they decided they should no longer go to the villages, for more people might wish to leave with them.

The next day the kachinas took the girls to the edge of their village. The maidens were greeted by their relatives, who asked where they had been. The girls replied, "We were sent back because we have a long time before we can join our ancestors. But we were shown all of the dances, and we remember every detail. You will make replicas of the dancers we have seen, and from now on we will preserve them. The supernaturals will come by breath in the winds and join us. When the dancing stops, the spirits alone will return to the land of our ancestors, and that way the lives of our people will remain on this land until their time comes."

So it was at that time the kachinas of today were created from the detailed descriptions of the two girls. From that time on the people asked for blessings with prayer and rituals carried out by the kachina cult.[2]

❀◇❀◇❀◇❀◇❀◇❀◇❀◇❀◇

The presence of a few women in otherwise totally male ceremonials was sometimes of great importance to the ritual significance of the dance. In his book *Masked Gods*, Frank Waters, a long-time student and neighbor of the southwestern Indians, examines the symbolic meaning behind the role of the Deer Mothers in the Taos Deer Dance. This passage is a dynamic attempt at an explanation of the inner drama that lies beneath the surface of cold ethnological documentation:

Then down the aisle between them, down and back from each end, come the two Deer Mothers. Sedate, middle aged women with long experience, they are the best dancers in the pueblo. Confidently and slowly, as women dance, they come dancing . . . Tall, impervious, silent, they come dancing. Their white boots never lifting above the clinging snow, their heavy bodies moving rhythmically within the loose, supple buckskin gowns. At the turn they pause, shaking their gourd rattles, raising aloft their sprigs of spruce and eagletail feathers. Each showing behind, the glimmering sheet of iridescent color of her back. And in front an impassive face made stern by her spotted cheeks and the black streak around her jaw.

They all give way before her, down and back. The wild deer and graceful antelope, the massive buffalo, the wild coyotes, the snarling wildcats, the little mountain lions, and all the shrinking fawns and cubs. They all draw back and crouch down shudderingly, with strange low cries, from the sacred, inviolable Deer Mother.

Then each Deer Mother turns back, eyes down as if unconscious of their presence.

And led by the Deer Chiefs, each file of dancers follows her in great circles, spirals and diagonals. Follow her, dancing in the soft powdery snow, uttering their strange low cries of resentment, their snarls of defiance; but unable to resist and being led back again into a long oval.

Within it the drum keeps beating. It is the pulse beat of eternity keeping time to the alternate flow of life's bi-polar tensions. . . .

So it continues in the snowy down-trodden clearing between the adobe cliffs, high on the backbone of a continent—this ancient blood drama of the primordial forces unleashed in all its children. The leaping, clutching Black Eyes. The swift escapes foiled by the wary Deer Watchmen. And all the while the Deer Chiefs tossing up their branching antlers beside the drummer as, up and down, the sacred Deer Mothers dance softly before the animals held in bondage.

They give way before her as the male ever gives way to the female imperative. They try to break free of the magic circle only to be pulled back as the consciousness in its wild lunges for freedom of the intellect is ever drawn back by the eternal unconscious. And all the time they utter their strange low cries, the deep universal male horror at their submission. Out of them it wells in shuddering sobs of loathing and despair, as still they answer the call. On all fours, as the untamed, archaic, wild forces they represent, impelled to follow her in obedience to that cosmic duality which must exist to preserve and perpetuate even their spiritual resentment. . . .

Yes. One senses now something both of the force that holds us back and the force that pulls us forward on the road of self-fulfillment. Which by their bi-polar tensions keep us in equilibrium, enclosed within the warm flow of human life. For man in all his powerful lunges toward freedom is still bound to the opposite pole of his earth bound exstence till on a higher level of consciousness these opposites are united again as at the beginning.[3]

FEMALE DEITIES

Not all the gods that ruled and protected the Native Americans were believed to be patriarchal males or sexless ethereal spirits. On the contrary, the Earth Mother concept was an important aspect of religion in many American Indian tribes. Numerous lesser spirits were also given female names, forms, and behavior.

The Shawnee, who lived in what is now Kentucky, believed that a deity they called "Our Grandmother" was the creator of the universe and everything in it. As the supreme goddess, her creations were always beneficial to the Shawnee directly and to mankind in general. Our Grandmother, who looked like an old woman with grey hair, was mentioned in every religious

243

rite, and the large annual ceremonials were performed specifically to worship her, thereby preserving mankind and the world.

Our Grandmother took particular care to watch out for the Shawnee women. She told the winds that they were to treat Indian women as though they were the winds' own sisters, and she enjoined them not to stare at the women when they were naked. She also admonished the women to respect the winds. The goddess' words were not always followed by the women, however, who sometimes pulled their skirts up to their waists when the weather was cloudy in an effort to frighten the wind-borne clouds back in embarrassment, so that the weather would be warm and sunny.

❀◇❀◇❀◇❀◇❀◇❀◇❀◇

The Return of the Corn Person

(SHAWNEE)

A long time ago two old women lived with a man. One day the women went away and left the man home alone. After waiting all day he got hungry and went to find some roasting ears of corn. When he got to the field he began to take ears off the stalk and found an ear that had a part that looked just like a woman's vagina. He remembered hearing something about that and said to himself, "I heard that the Corn Person, our mother, is a woman. If this is true she will be embarrassed now when I have intercourse with her." Then he pulled out his penis and stuck it in the hole in the corn. Then he went back to his house.

The next day the old women arose early and went to look for corn. When they got to the field it was empty—the corn had all vanished. The Corn Person had fled to Our Grandmother who had created her.

Someone went after her and had to cross four oceans to find her. Corn Person was persuaded to return to earth only when the rescuer argued that it was Our Grandmother's intention that she should benefit the Shawnee on earth.[4]

❀◇❀◇❀◇❀◇❀◇❀◇❀◇

Many of the societies who lived on the rich land of the Great Plains credited their good fortune to female spirits. Some of the legends connected with these beneficent beings have been recounted in other chapters.

The Cheyenne attributed their usually bountiful food supply to a culture heroine who had the form of a very old woman. They say that long ago two young braves wanted to help their people, who were very hungry. They went to a nearby butte, where a waterfall was cascading down a cliff. Behind the waterfall the young men found an old woman who welcomed them, called them her grandchildren, and seated one of them on her left and one of them on her right.

After mildly admonishing them for not coming sooner, she promised to do something for their people. First she took two bowls, filled one with buffalo meat and one with cooked corn, and bade her visitors to eat their fill. When the young men had eaten all they could, the bowls were still full; they could not empty the vessels.

Next the old woman painted each man with red paint, adding symbols for the sun and the moon in yellow paint. When she was finished she pointed to her left, and when the two youths followed her gaze they saw the earth covered with buffalo. Then she pointed partly behind her, and when they looked that way they saw great fields of growing corn. When she pointed to her right they saw prairies covered with horses. At last, when the old woman pointed straight ahead of her, they saw Indians fighting, and looking closer they saw themselves, painted as they were, among the fighters. This, they were told, was an omen that they would be victorious in their battles and take many captives.

Then the old woman gave some corn and some meat to the young men and told them to take them back to their people. After that the Cheyenne had plenty of buffalo and began to plant corn.

Female spirits were not always as benevolent as this old woman. Near the Quinault, who lived on the northwest coast, there were supposedly forest devils who lived in the high hills and mountains. Usually these spirits appeared as women, but sometimes they would take the form of a man. During the night they made a mournful cry sounding like *a-ta-ta-tat*, with each syllable at a higher pitch than the preceding one. Once, so the people say, there was a woman forest devil who lived near a certain village. A white man built a cabin nearby. One night when he came home he saw her and wondered who she was. When he went to bed she climbed in beside him. He had sex with her, but at the moment of orgasm he fell dead. The spirit died too, and the villagers found them together the next day.

South along the west coast, near Capistrano in California, the Gabrielino Indians held a yearly bird feast commemorating a young girl who had gone into the mountains and been transformed into the White-Headed Eagle

Maiden. Each year the participants in the ceremony captured an eagle or a condor to symbolize the Eagle Maiden. During the dance the bird was passed from hand to hand, each celebrant exerting such pressure that it was gradually crushed. Death was administered to the suffering bird by a priest who knew how to press its heart to stillness. The body was skinned with great reverence and the feathers added to the Gabrielinos' store of ceremonial costumes. Apparently the Gabrielinos believed that the same bird figured in the ceremony year after year, being reincarnated after each of its annual deaths. This is a rare feminine figure in the predominantly male pantheon of the group of tribes to which the Gabrielino belong.

Perhaps one of the most developed mythologies concerning a female deity was found in the Southwest among the Navajo. The Navajos share with some of their Pueblo neighbors the concept of an Earth Mother, a goddess of creation through whose successive womb-worlds human beings emerged from the underworld to the surface of the earth. This goddess is continually self-renewing, an immortal woman. Like the earth she is young in the spring. She matures as she is nourished by the sun and rain, bears fruit in the summer, begins to experience the inevitable effects of age in the fall, and dies in the winter, only to be reborn again each spring. The Navajos call her "Changing Woman," or, in direct translation, a "Woman She Becomes Time and Again." It is this ageless cycle of death and rebirth that is celebrated during the Navajo girl's puberty ceremony and by their cousins, the Apaches, during their puberty rites.

The long, multiphase ceremony and accompanying chants that recount the birth, maturity, motherhood, and work of Changing Woman are called by the Navajos "Blessing Way" and encompass the entire history of their ancestors.

Dominga Chewiwi, a matriarch of the Isleta Pueblo, resting
next to her adobe baking oven. (*Courtesy New Mexico Department of Development*)

11

Completion of the Cycle

OLD WOMEN AND DEATH

Old age was equated with wisdom and learning in most Native American societies, and aged persons were treated with deference and respect. In many tribes, women gained more power as they became older; once they had passed menopause, they were relieved of the taboos associated with menstruation and so could take on some of the more sacred ceremonial duties from which they had been previously barred. As the Winnebagos put it, an elderly woman was "just like a man." Her opinions carried weight in discussions of tribal issues, and she was consulted regarding herbal medicines, sacred matters, and tribal history.

Generally a middle-aged matron was expected to be soft spoken and modest in her speech if she wished to be considered respectable and a credit to her husband and family. But in many tribes, once a woman had reached a certain age she was no longer expected to remain proper and demure at all times. By mere virtue of their years, some old women were allowed to be loud, raucous, and even bawdy.

Although as their strength failed women allowed their daughters to take over the more strenuous tasks, they performed whatever jobs they were able to do. Idleness was out of the question for a woman who had worked hard all her life, and her self-image demanded that she continue to be a productive member of the community as long as she could.

Older women commonly babysat, freeing young mothers from maternal duties so they could work in the fields or accompany their husbands on war or hunting expeditions. In nonpolygamous families, in which there were no co-wives to share family responsibilities, grandmothers watched over the children while mothers were confined to menstrual huts. Grandmothers not only provided physical care for the little ones but also instilled in them the traditional values and wisdom of the society. Among the Gros Ventres, in Montana, grandmothers were responsible for the teaching and training of their granddaughters from about the age of seven until marriage. The girls in turn made life easier for the older women by bringing wood and water and helping with some of the other more physically taxing chores.

The Papagos thought that young women simply did not have the experience necessary for thinking and planning, so the commanding positions belonged to the old. A mature woman directed all the work of her daughters-in-law, made the decisions for the household, cared for the youngsters when their mothers were otherwise occupied, and wove baskets in her spare time.

Among the Hopi and some other farming tribes, the old people spent much of their time during the growing season guarding the fields from marauding birds. Scattered around the Hopi fields at frequent intervals were brush shelters where old people too feeble to help in the hard work spent summer afternoons supposedly scaring off birds. The old people tended to doze off so often that the children were called from their play to guard the corn hills while the elders slept undisturbed through the long hot afternoons. At harvest time, Hopi families invited old women with no sons to work for them to help dry peaches and shuck corn, paying them a share of the produce in return for their work.

The Omahas, Poncas, Mandans, and Pawnees, among other farming groups who lived on the Great Plains, usually left old people behind in the villages to watch the crops while the other members of the tribes went off on the summer buffalo hunt. The old people were provided with a cool shelter among the trees, food, water, and fuel for their fires. They watched the cornfields and when their provisions gave out they could gather the new ears of corn and retrieve some of the dried pumpkins and jerky that had been buried in underground storage pits. They usually were not left for more than several months. Occasionally a few families would remain behind to care for anyone who was truly feeble. The Mandan believed that those persons who neglected the unfortunate would not live long, since the sacred beings often sent destitute people into the tribe for the sole purpose of detecting who were the selfish families.

———— ❀◇❀◇❀◇❀◇❀◇❀◇❀◇ ————

Young people who think first of themselves and forget the old will never prosper, nothing will go straight for them.

—OMAHA

If you see a helpless old person, help him if you have anything at all. If you happen to possess a home, take him there and feed him.

—WINNEBAGO

When you grow up and finally have your own home, pity the old men and pity the old women, pity the poor. If you see an old woman with a ragged dress, give her a blanket. Make moccasins for these old women. If you do that the One Above who watches and looks at you doing those things is going to reward you.

—GROS VENTRE

———— ❀◇❀◇❀◇❀◇❀◇❀◇❀◇ ————

Modern Americans have given much attention to the fact that elderly Native Americans who were so aged and infirm that they had outlived their usefulness were left to die by the others. While this did happen occasionally, it was usually a last resort practiced by poor families in nomadic groups.

Old people understood that with the infirmities of old age, death was near, and so the wish to be left behind usually came from them. Although it may seem that it would require superhuman objectivity to arrange one's own death, every old person had seen this decision made by countless other elderly people, and they accepted death as only another step in the life cycle.

———— ❀◇❀◇❀◇❀◇❀◇❀◇❀◇ ————

Iron Shell Saves a Grandmother

(S I O U X)

Once Iron Shell, a headman of the Sioux, was among the last to leave the encampment during a move to a summer village location. As he and his family were leaving the old site they came across a forlorn ancient woman sitting alone with a small supply of food and water. "What is the reason you sit here, Grandmother?" Iron Shell asked her.

"I'm old and worthless," she replied. "My son can no longer care for me, so I shall sit here to die."

251

Iron Shell did not feel that this was right, so he arranged her on a travois with her meager bundles and made her a member of his procession.

When Iron Shell's party reached the new camping site, he led the old woman on the travois to her son's lodge. This was a poor family, and they owned only one horse. Iron Shell called on the son, saying, "Here is your mother." And pointing to the horse that carried her on the travois, he said, "Here is a horse for her. Don't you ever again leave her like that."

The son was glad to see his mother, and as long as she lived, he dragged her from camp to camp with his family.[1]

In general the Native Americans were healthy long into old age and did not live long once they had begun to decline. One story survives of a Labrador Eskimo woman named Marie Louise who was thought by the whites in the area to be well into her nineties. A widow for thirty years, she had continued to operate her hunting and trapping grounds by herself. Her relatives, who lived in a settlement, were constantly urging the old woman to give up her solitary life and join them. But she staunchly maintained that her life had begun in the bush, her relatives and children had died there, and she was going to continue to live in the wilderness until she died.

She went on setting her traps and collecting her catches year after year, enjoying the hard work and extensive traveling. One spring, returning to the settlement with her handsled loaded with her winter's catch, she broke through the ice; they found her, dead, where the accident occurred.

MOURNING CUSTOMS

Women were the chief mourners in Native American tribes. Although death was looked on as inevitable, the death of any relative except a newborn infant or, in some tribes, a very old person, was ritually and sincerely mourned. Loud and protracted wailing was a manifestation of grief in most early American societies—sad as it was to hear the piteous and agonized moans of the bereaved, wailing was not considered as painful as silent sorrow.

Victor Tixier, an early visitor to the Osage on the Plains, reported that it took much practice and training for a woman to become a good wailer. According to Tixier, little girls often got together to improve their wailing and when they got worked up reached "a feverish exaltation which appears like the ecstasy of religious fanatics."[2]

The same explorer told of traveling with a procession of Osages when at one point an old woman, scrutinizing the horizon from the back of her horse, recognized a distant mound which others in the party weren't even able to see. Letting the others proceed on their journey, the woman dismounted and headed toward the grave, in which she had buried her daughter during the last hunting expedition. When the poor mother rejoined the rest of the group the next day, she said she had spent the night crying on her child's grave and had heard the bones move under the ground as if to thank her.

Mandan women conducted their mourning in two stages. When a person died in a Mandan village the body was bound in several layers of skins and placed on a scaffold near the town in an area called "the village of the dead." Here many scaffolds, each just a little higher than a hand could reach, were the resting place of the dead. The mothers, wives, children, and fathers of the dead made numerous trips to these scaffolds, where they prostrated themselves with their faces in the dirt and incessantly howled their lamentations.

When the lightweight scaffold rotted and collapsed, the nearest relations buried all the bones except the skulls. These, clean of flesh and bleached white, were placed on the prairies in circles of a hundred or more with the faces all looking toward the center. Each skull was placed on a bed of fresh sage, which was replaced when it began to decay. The bereaved made frequent visits to the circle of skulls, and held lengthy conversations with the dead. These visits were not the scene of groans and weeping, for several years had cured the anguish; rather, they were opportunities to remember good times and express affection and endearments. Sometimes a mother took her needlework with her and spent the greater part of the day sitting by the side of her child's skull, chatting with it or perhaps napping within the circle while cradling it in her arms.

Mourning ceremonies in honor of all the dead were part of the yearly religious cycle in some tribes, and women always played a prominent role in these rites. Among the Cree, in central Canada, an old woman who was in communion with the ceremonial spirits initiated the celebration. A long, narrow tent was erected, and each family that came brought a kettle of food and the family's sacred bundle. The ceremony began with a distribution of food, which was eaten in silence save for the smacking of lips and clattering of dishes. It was imperative that every scrap of food be consumed. After all had eaten, the leader began to intone a melancholy song; the participants joined in the wailing and began to dance very slowly, heads down and shrouded. When one dance was finished, another person would start a dirge, and the dancing went on until morning. It was a chance for all the participants to give vent to their accumulated grief and sadness. After this yearly catharsis, everyone was able to return to their daily lives, refreshed and relieved.

The Yumas and Cahuillas, neighbors in the southwestern desert, also held annual tribal mourning gatherings. The Cahuilla invited neighbors from other villages and staged a big feast in the ceremonial house. Families of persons who had died during the previous year made images of the deceased out of cloth stuffed with grass and topped by human hair wigs. On the last day of the week-long ceremony, female relatives of the departed brought the effigies out and led the procession. Later the effigies were burned.

The participants in these rites sometimes worked themselves into hysteria. One year, during the last night of a Yuma mourning ceremony, a woman fell down unconscious and was not revived for several hours. Afterwards, in relating what had happened to her, she described a great rumbling noise as if many horses were stampeding. Then she found herself riding on a horse behind a male relative who had been dead several years. The two of them were surrounded by many other riders, all headed toward the south. Finally they came to a large village. The people there appeared to be Yumas, and the woman recognized among them many former inhabitants of her town who had been dead for many years. These people came out to meet her and were very glad that she had joined them.

Soon a great cloud of smoke appeared in the west, and everybody started running. The woman tried to run with them, but she found that she couldn't move very fast, and when she tried to get away she stumbled over a block of wood and fell down. Just then she began to regain consciousness and found a medicine man administering to her. He was smoking a pipe as part of the treatment, and later the people realized that it was the tobacco smoke that had appeared in the spirit world and brought her soul back.

❀◆❀◆❀◆❀◆❀◆❀◆❀◆

Ceremonial Mourning Song

(DIEGUENO)

". . . things may be going well for you one day, then something happens and you are destroyed. This is the way life is. Remember, it can happen to you, too!"[3]

❀◆❀◆❀◆❀◆❀◆❀◆❀◆

THE FUNERAL—A WOMAN'S LAST CEREMONY

Early Native American women lived lives rich in ceremony and ritual so it was fitting that their deaths be commemorated with the same reverent spirituality that had permeated their lives. Occasionally women were even conscious participants in the early stages of their own funerals. In many tribes when it became apparent that an ill or elderly person was near death, she was dressed, painted, and sometimes even partially wrapped up for burial. It was no doubt a comfort to the dying woman to slip away from her earthly life already surrounded by mourners, knowing she would be missed, yet being urged to have courage in facing the unknown path ahead.

Omahas would address a dying woman with words of encouragement and assurance, saying, perhaps, "You are going to the buffalos. You are going to rejoin your ancestors. You are going to the four winds. Be strong," or, "Do not face this way again. When you go, continue walking." After the woman had died, she was quickly buried in a shallow grave on a hilltop, and a fire was kept burning on the grave for four nights so its light might cheer her as she traveled to the land of the dead.

In some of the Plains tribes, a woman's favorite horse would be killed and its tail placed on a pole near her scaffold or grave. A prayer would usually accompany the slaughter of the horse, something like, "Grandchild, your owner thought a great deal of you and now she has died. She wants to take you with her joyfully." The Comanches found that their supernaturals considered this sacrifice necessary at every funeral. Once an old person died poor and with no relatives, so someone contributed an old nag to be killed over his grave. But the old man was not allowed into paradise on the disreputable horse he had been given, and he returned to haunt the Comanches.

255

After that no Comanche was allowed to set out for the afterworld without a steed which did honor to the rider and his or her friends.

It was typical in the Plains groups, as it was in most North American tribes, to give away or destroy all of the deceased's belongings not buried with them. Once a well-to-do Eastern Sioux family who lost a beloved daughter did not follow this important tradition. When the girl died she left behind a trunkful of beautiful clothes, and her parents did not properly dispose of them.

Every night, when the family had retired, the girl came, moved her bed, and opened and shut her locked trunk. It became so disturbing that the family finally left the dwelling and moved elsewhere for a while. In their absence a group of youths who roamed the camp at night began to notice that the house was lit up every evening. But when they sneaked up to peep in, the lights mysteriously went out. Finally the girl's parents, unable to endure the upset any longer, asked some wise old men to try to discover what was causing the trouble. The elders stayed overnight in the haunted dwelling and saw the ghost of the daughter come and fondle her belongings. The next day they told the mother what they had seen and advised her to make a feast, invite her dead daughter's friends, and distribute all of her belongings. After this traditional duty was properly complied with the trouble ended; the elders explained the ghost had lost an earthly focus.

In some tribes, a family burned its home if someone died there. Because having to build a new dwelling was an inconvenience, particularly when it entailed cutting timbers with primitive tools, a dying person was sometimes moved from home just before death so that the house would not have to be destroyed. This was the case among the Papagos of southern Arizona. There was no avoidance of the dying in that society; as soon as it appeared that a person was near death, all the relatives gathered around and began a ritual wailing that lasted until the body was buried. The corpse was placed in a rocky niche or in a pit six or seven feet deep. A dead woman was arranged to look just as she had in life, sitting with her knees to the side and surrounded by her pots and baskets. The grave was not filled in with dirt but roofed over like a house. After the burial, one of the elders made a short speech addressed to the deceased, saying something like, "My daughter's child, you were dear to me. Now you are gone. I shall not see you again. Go now, my daughter's child, I beg of you and do not come back to frighten your relatives."[4]

Papagos believed that the souls of the dead dwelt in towns just as the people on earth did. The newly dead met their ancestors in these villages and learned from them all the ways of their new abode. Day-to-day happenings were similar to those on earth except that there was plenty of rain because this land was located in the east, where all the rains originated. It is not surprising that people with an uncertain existence in a dry land should construct a paradise without droughts.

It was believed that the souls of the Papago dead could leave their land at any time and fly back to earth in the form of owls. They did this whenever they felt a longing for one of their living relatives whom they wished to have as a companion in their new home. This is why mourners usually made a graveside plea to the deceased asking them not to return to earth.

Unlike the groups in which the community gathered to comfort a dying person, the Navajos greatly feared anything to do with death; when someone was very close to death, everybody except the dying person's immediate family left the area if at all possible. When the Navajos kept slaves they always arranged to have them do the burying; when they no longer kept slaves they were always grateful if they could find an outsider to perform the onerous task. When no one else was available to do the job, four of the mourners would bathe the corpse and dress it in good clothing, including whatever jewelry the deceased had worn in life. The body was secretly hidden in a crevice and piled over with stones, dirt, and sticks. When the burial attendants rejoined the rest of the family they all mourned for four days, sitting quietly, eating little, doing no work, and moving only when absolutely necessary. Then they all purified themselves with a ritual bath and returned to their normal lives. If the deceased had died inside the hogan, it was burned and the family moved to another spot. It was some time before the name of the deceased was mentioned, for the survivors did not wish to irritate the soul or in any way compel it to linger about the family.

A Navajo funeral was an event which concerned only those members of the deceased's immediate family present when the death occurred, but all the members of the dead person's extended family mourned the death. Navajos lived in small, isolated family groupings, but whenever two relatives or close friends met for the first time following a death in the family, they would cry together, holding each other and sobbing for as long as twenty minutes. It didn't matter if the death had occurred six months before, if a woman had not had a chance to express her condolences to the bereaved sister or mother, she would go immediately to her whenever they met.

The Hopis also believed that souls of dead people lived on but felt that these spirits were benevolent and brought rain to those still living. When a Hopi woman died, her hair was washed with fluffy yucca suds, a thin white cloth symbolizing clouds was put over her face, and she was sewn, in a sitting position, in her white cotton marriage blanket, which was tied with a big knotted belt. Later, it was thought, the spirit of the woman would move along through the sky as a cloud, the small raindrops falling through the loosely woven blanket, and the big raindrops falling from the fringes of the belt.

The dead woman's father, uncle, or another relative then carried her on his back for her last trip down the steep path at the edge of the mesa. She was buried in a grave dug in the side of the hill, and food, feather prayer sticks, and perhaps a favorite possession were placed on the grave. The dead ate only the soul or essence of the food that was left for them, and that was why the clouds into which the dead were transformed were light and could float in the sky.

For a look at a typical funeral in the Northeast, we have the report of Reverend John Heckewelder, who was present in 1762 at the burial of the wife of a Delaware chief. The village was immediately made aware of the woman's death by several women who ran through the streets crying, "She is no more! She is no more!" The villagers spent the rest of the day in mourning, while the dead woman's relatives arranged for a coffin to be built and laid the woman in it, dressed in new garments and heavily ornamented with silver broaches, bracelets from her shoulder to wrist, and wampum belts around her neck. The next day, Heckewelder and a white trader were recruited to carry the coffin to the graveside (an honor), assisted by two Indian women and two men. After they arrived at the site of the burial the lid was lifted from the coffin, and the mourners all sat in silence for about two hours. Only occasional sighs and sobs punctuated the stillness.

Finally several men stepped forward to put the lid on the coffin and let the body down into the grave, when suddenly three of the women mourners rushed from their seats and, forcing themselves between these men, grabbed at the corpse's arms and legs, first acting like they were caressing her but later pulling with more violence, all the while crying, "Arise, come with us. Don't abandon us."

Finally, in frantic despair the women went back to their seats, pulling their hair, plucking at their garments, and sobbing as if they did not know what they were doing.

The coffin was then lowered into the earth and covered over. Food was served to everyone, and gifts were distributed to all those present. Those who had rendered the most valuable services received the best presents; the three female mourners were well rewarded, since they had performed very strenuous duties.

In the South, the Choctaw practiced unusual burial customs. The corpse was covered with skins and bark and placed on a scaffold near the home of the survivors. The relatives went to the platform to wail and mourn, although in warm weather the stench from the rotting body became so intolerable that women sometimes fainted. After the body had reached an advanced state of decomposition, the relatives summoned the bone pickers, who were considered honored officials in the tribe. While the relatives gathered around, the bone pickers climbed up to what was left of the body and, with fingernails grown especially long for the task, cleaned the bones of putrefied flesh and passed them down to the mourners. The flesh and the scaffold were then burned, and the bones were put in a coffin, which was entombed in a bone house with others like it.

Surely the grandest and most horrible funeral customs were performed by the Natchez for deceased rulers. Some early French explorers witnessed the funeral of a female Sun and left a full report.

As soon as the chieftess had died, her husband, a commoner, was strangled by the couple's firstborn son so that he could accompany his wife to the village of the dead. Then fourteen scaffolds were prepared in the plaza, one for each of the men who had either volunteered or been ordered to die to serve the chieftess in the afterworld. These men were much respected for the sacrifice they were about to make, and each one had five servants to attend him during the four days of dancing and mourning.

At the end of this period, twelve dead children were brought forth by their parents; the oldest did not appear to be more than three years old, according to the Frenchman. Then a parade began, headed by the fathers carrying their dead children and followed by the dead woman and her strangled husband carried on stretchers. In unison the fathers let the children fall to the ground, and those who bore the dead woman passed over and went around the little bodies three times. The fathers then gathered them up, marched ten paces, and dropped the children again. This ceremony was repeated until the parade reached the temple, so that the tiny victims were in pieces when the convoy arrived. After the dead Sun was interred in the temple, the adult victims were strangled, and they and the babies were burned.

When a male Sun died, his wife was likewise killed so that she could accompany him. This was apparently accepted by the women, as the wife of a dead Sun explained to a European visitor, "He is in the country of the spirits and in two days I will go to join him. . . . Do not grieve. We will be friends for a much longer time in the country of the spirits than in this because one does not die there again. It is always fine weather, one is never hungry, because nothing is wanting to live better than this country."[5]

Life held few surprises for the typical early Native American woman. Surrounded by women at birth, she continued her life in the presence and company of women, sharing with the sisters of her tribe her learning, her working, her own labors of childbirth, and her death.

Innovations came slowly. Tribal customs regarding child rearing, court-ship, marriage, homemaking, and religion remained the same, decade after decade. The ordinary Indian woman's life was not material for a thrilling narrative, but it offered her comfort and security. She worked hard, and in her work and in tribal membership she gained a deep and satisfying sense of herself. Her days were often full of monotonous repetition, but at least she was spared the modern woman's painful quest for an identity.

Life for the Native Americans began to change with the arrival of the Europeans. The eastern tribes were affected first, and they moved to the west as the white settlers took over their farm lands. But more and more white settlers began arriving on the North American shores, and they were greedy for land. Every year they pushed farther west, asserting their dominance with guns, bullets, and new laws.

Soon there was little land left for the Indians. As tribe after tribe was herded onto reservations, the native cultures began to disintegrate. The men who were formerly hunters and warriors had nothing to hunt and no wars to fight. Utterly despondent, many of them turned their backs on life. Some found escape in alcohol.

Life did not change as drastically for the women. Even on a reservation there were still children to be raised, meals to be cooked, and housework to be done. Some women found they could make money by producing and selling their native crafts. With their strength and resolve, many Native American women held their families together through very dark times.

Today, Native American women are continuing to be a powerful force in their societies. A great number of them are participating in tribal government and many more are working for their people in modern extensions of traditional roles—as nurses, dental technicians, teachers, school principals, social workers, counselors, dancers, and artists. They have more choice in how they will spend their lives than their grandmothers did, but even the new career and educational opportunities do not overshadow the important gift left to them by their female ancestors—a legacy of dignity and purpose.

NOTES

(See Bibliography for full publication data.)

INTRODUCTION

1. Rosaldo and Lamphere, 1974:3. *See also* Bamberger, 1974.
2. Rosaldo and Lamphere, 1974:17.
3. Ortner, 1974:67.
4. Lurie, 1972:32.

CHAPTER 1: THE DAWN OF LIFE

1. Opler, 1941:149.
2. Opler, 1941:148.
3. Heckewelder, 1876:159.
4. Goddard, 1903a:275–277.
5. Stevenson, 1904:295.
6. Linderman, 1932:145–147.
7. Underhill, 1936:42.
8. Fletcher and La Flesche, 1910:115–116.
9. Shipek, 1970:44.
10. Mason, 1895:176.
11. Landes, 1938:102.
12. Flannery, 1953:129.

CHAPTER 2: THE INDIAN CHILD

1. Linderman, 1932:29.
2. Linderman, 1932:65–70.
3. Fletcher and La Flesche, 1910:333.
4. Underhill, 1939:159–161.
5. Olson, 1967:18.
6. Parsons, 1929:271.
7. Opler, 1938:369–370.

CHAPTER 3: FROM MENARCHE TO MENOPAUSE

1. Smithson, 1959:63–64.
2. Michelson, 1925:303.
3. Lurie, 1961:22.
4. Landes, 1938:6.
5. Shipek, 1970:42–43.
6. Underhill, 1936:33.
7. Underhill, 1968:139.
8. Smithson, 1959:61–62.
9. Basso, 1966:151.
10. Opler, 1941:119.
11. Bailey, 1950:10.
12. Mead, 1932:189–191.
13. Oswald, 1966:37.

Notes

CHAPTER 4: SHARING A LIFE

1. Opler, 1941:121.
2. Opler, 1941:125.
3. Fletcher and La Flesche, 1910:324–325.
4. Beaglehole, 1935:41.
5. Swanton, 1911:94.
6. Henry, 1897:384.
7. Swanton, 1911:323.
8. Fletcher and La Flesche, 1910:86.
9. Landes, 1968:135–136.
10. Lowie, 1909:162–163.
11. Smithson, 1959:86.
12. Hammond and Jablow, 1973:24.
13. Krause and Gunther, 1956:184–185.
14. Olson, 1936:110.
15. Underhill, 1936:38.
16. Goodwin, 1942:328.
17. Kennedy, 1961:75–77.
18. Erikson, 1943:287–288.
19. Shea, 1881:222.
20. Tixier, 1940:165.

CHAPTER 5: MAKING A HOME

1. Hammond and Jablow, 1973:6–8 passim.
2. Honigmann, 1954:131–132.
3. Flannery, 1953:82–85.
4. Radin, 1920:132.
5. Hornaday, 1889:436.
6. Wallace and Hoebel, 1952:200–201.
7. Kennedy, 1961:87.
8. Weltfish, 1965:8.
9. Qoyawayma, 1964:5.
10. Qoyawayma, 1964:71.
11. Parsons, 1929:289–294.
12. Cushing, 1920:386–387.
13. Cushing, 1920:306–309.
14. Qoyawayma, 1964:35.
15. Olson, 1967:11.
16. Erikson, 1943:299.
17. Landes, 1938:169.
18. Hearne, 1795:264–265.
19. Hardacre, 1880:657–664 passim.

CHAPTER 6: WOMEN OF POWER

1. Rowlandson, 1828:73.
2. Swanton, 1942:173.
3. U.S. Senate, 1875:48.
4. Codere, 1966:158.
5. Heckewelder, 1876:229.

6. Erikson, 1943:262.
7. Flannery, 1953:161–162.
8. Skinner, 1913:147–149.
9. Jenness, 1923:194.
10. Cline, 1938:160.
11. Smith and Roberts, 1954:44–45.
12. Kluckholn, 1944:49.

CHAPTER 7: WOMEN AND WAR

1. Goodwin, 1971:248.
2. Ball, 1970:9–189 passim.
3. Parsons, 1926:191–192.
4. Landes, 1938:150–151.
5. Wright, 1973:57.
6. Weltfish, 1965:54.
7. Underhill, 1936:15.
8. Swanton, 1911:132.
9. Stratton, 1935:161–162.
10. Stratton, 1935:166.
11. Stratton, 1935:157.
12. Underhill, 1946a:93–94.

CHAPTER 8: TIME FOR FUN

1. O'Neale, 1932:148.
2. Saxton and Saxton, 1973:320.
3. Underhill, 1939:172.
4. Opler, 1938:238–240.
5. Bunzel, 1972:51.
6. Bunzel, 1972:51.
7. Bunzel, 1972:65.
8. Wilson, 1974:48.
9. Reichard, 1934:frontispiece.
10. Catlin, 1866:96–97.
11. Saxton and Saxton, 1973:211–215.

CHAPTER 9: EARLY SEXUAL PATTERNS

1. Mooney, 1900:256–257.
2. Opler, 1941:250–251.
3. Hoebel, 1940:100–101.
4. Krause, 1956:191.
5. Underhill, 1939:184.
6. Saxton and Saxton, 1973:24–25.
7. Devereux, 1937:498–527 passim.
8. Mason, 1895:211.

CHAPTER 10: RELIGION AND SPIRITUALITY

1. Stevenson, 1887:555.
2. The Zuni, 1972:137–139.

Notes

3. Waters, 1950:187–189.
4. Voegelin, 1936:7.

CHAPTER 11: COMPLETION OF THE CYCLE

1. Hassrick, 1964:103.
2. Tixier, 1940:158.
3. Shipek, 1970:15.
4. Underhill, 1939:189.
5. Swanton, 1911:145.

ANNOTATED BIBLIOGRAPHY

Readers who wish to analyze the foregoing material on Native American women in terms of theories of women's status and role may find the following books and articles of help:

Boserup, Ester. *Woman's Role in Economic Development*. New York: St. Martin's Press, 1970.

> Although Boserup mainly concentrates on the economic role of women in recent times, the first two chapters of her book are particularly helpful for students of women's role in earlier stages of cultural development. In "Male and Female Farming Systems" she discusses the road to labor specialization, and in "The Economics of Polygamy" she elaborates on how polygamy relates to status and wealth.

Boulding, Elise. "Nomadism, Mobility and the Status of Women." Paper prepared for the Eighth World Congress of Sociology, Toronto, 1974. Mimeographed.

> The author discusses the status of women in nomad societies and argues that there is less gender-based role differentiation among nomads than among settled people. Because the world of the nomad woman is less structured and confining than that of the settled woman, she is allowed more participation in decision-making and is highly respected for her skills and adaptive abilities.

Govier, Trudy R. "Woman's Place." *Philosophy*. 49:303–309.

> This is a rebuttal to an article by J. R. Lucas entitled "Because You Are a Woman," which appeared in the May 1973 issue of *Philosophy*. Govier presents a well-reasoned argument refuting Lucas' contention that the denial of genetic differences between men and women leads to women being judged by male standards, and, in most individual cases, found to be inferior to their male rivals. Govier's article is useful in that she not only manages to counter Lucas' points but also presents a method of approaching the problem of genetic differences and cultural manifestations of behavior.

Hammond, Dorothy, and Jablow, Alta. *Women: Their Economic Role in Traditional Societies*. A Cummings Module in Anthropology, no. 35. Menlo Park, Calif.: Cummings Publishing Company, 1973.

Hammond, Dorothy, and Jablow, Alta. *Women: Their Familial Roles in Traditional Societies*. A Cummings Module in Anthropology, no. 57. Menlo Park, Calif.: Cummings Publishing Company, 1975.

> These two cross-cultural comparisons of the position of women emphasize that what is considered feminine and what is considered women's work in various cultures is based more on custom and tradition than on any innate biological capacity or incapacity of women. The authors point out that although throughout the world women are seen as primarily wives and mothers and are thought inferior to men, women resent their position and the male domination. There is also a discussion of matrilineality and matrilocality.

Lederer, Wolfgang, M.D. *The Fear of Women*. New York: Grune and Stratton, 1966.

> The author does not present a particularly balanced view of women but does

explore in depth the perilous oscillation between love and fear that men have felt toward women through the ages. Of particular interest are the chapters devoted to "The Greatest Mystery" (menstruation), how menstruating women became taboo, and how that taboo generalized into other aspects of life.

Martin, M. Kay, and Voorhies, Barbara. *Female of the Species*. New York: Columbia University Press, 1975.

This is an interdisciplinary and cross-cultural look at the economic roles of women and the biological and psychological aspects of sex differences. The authors, both anthropologists, analyze and challenge the androcentric view of cultural evolution—with its basic assumption of male economic dominance. They give an excellent overview of the complex interaction between genetic and environmental factors that influence sex roles and the status of women over time.

Reiter, Rayna R., editor. *Toward an Anthropology of Women*. New York: Monthly Review Press, 1975.

The eighteen essays in the volume are written by feminist anthropologists who are making an attempt to move beyond the pervasive male bias in anthropology. There are three papers that relate directly to issues of male bias in the interpretation of the biological and cultural evolutionary record, three that discuss aspects of sexual equality in groups organized primarily along lines of kinship, and two that offer theories concerning the origin of gender relations. Of particular interest to readers of the present volume is Judith Brown's ethnohistorical analysis of Iroquois women.

Rosaldo, Michelle Zimbalist, and Lamphere, Louise, editors. *Woman, Culture and Society*. Stanford, Calif.: Stanford University Press, 1974.

The authors of the seventeen papers in this landmark book believe that anthropology has suffered from a failure to develop theoretical perspectives that take account of women as social actors. The authors of the first three papers observe that woman's role as mother has led to cultural subordination and argue that this connection is not necessary. A number of the papers deal with women's strategies to gain and wield power in societies where power is nominally denied to them. Peggy Sanday's contribution is a statistical treatment of cross-cultural variations in women's status; she suggests that women's contribution to subsistence is a crucial variable in determining their status.

Yorburg, Betty. *Sexual Identity*. New York: John Wiley & Sons, 1974.

The first four chapters of this book give an excellent summary of the work done on sexual identity in the fields of biology, anthropology, psychology, sociology, and history. The author addresses herself to such questions as the classic nature versus nurture controversy and the relative importance of men's and women's differing anatomy, hormonal structure, and genetic makeup.

BIBLIOGRAPHY

ADAMS, WINONA. "An Indian Girl's Story of a Trading Expedition to the Southwest About 1841." *The Frontier* 10:4 (May), 1930.

ALLEN, T. D. *Navajos Have Five Fingers.* Norman, Okla.: University of Oklahoma Press, 1963.

BAILEY, FLORA L. "Some Sex Beliefs and Practices in a Navajo Community, with Comparative Material from Other Navajo Areas." Papers of the Peabody Museum of American Archeology and Ethnology 40:2. Cambridge, Mass.: Harvard University Press, 1950.

BALL, EVE. *In The Days of Victorio: Recollections of a Warm Springs Apache.* Narrated by James Kaywayka. Tucson, Ariz.: University of Arizona Press, 1970.

BAMBERGER, JOAN. "The Myth of Matriarchy: Why Men Rule in Primitive Societies." In *Women, Culture and Society,* edited by Michelle Zimbalist Rosaldo and Louise Lamphere. Stanford, Calif.: Stanford University Press, 1974.

BANDELIER, ADOLPH F. and HEWETT, EDGAR L. *Indians of the Rio Grande Valley.* Albuquerque, N. Mex.: University of New Mexico Press, 1937.

BARNETT, HOMER G. "The Coast Salish of British Columbia." University of Oregon Monographs no. 4 (September). Eugene, Ore.: The University Press, 1955.

BARRETT, SAMUEL ALFRED. *The Washo Indians.* Milwaukee, Wisc.: Milwaukee Public Museum, 1917.

BASSO, KEITH. "The Gift of Changing Woman." Bureau of American Ethnology Bulletin no. 196. Washington, D.C.: Smithsonian Institution, 1966.

———. "Western Apache Witchcraft." Anthropological Papers of the University of Arizona no. 15. Tucson, Ariz.: University of Arizona Press, 1969.

BEAGLEHOLE, ERNEST, and BEAGLEHOLE, PEARL. "Hopi of the Second Mesa." *American Anthropological Association Memoir* 44, 1935.

BEALS, RALPH L. "Ethnology of Nisenan." University of California Publications in American Archeology and Ethnology (March 29), 3:6. Berkeley, Calif.: University of California Press, 1933.

BEAUCHAMP, W. M. "Iroquois Women." *Journal of American Folklore,* 13:81–91, 1900.

BIRKET-SMITH, KAJ, and DE LAGUNA, FREDERICA. *The Eyak Indians of The Copper River Delta, Alaska.* Copenhagen: Levin and Munksgaard, 1938.

BOSCANA, FRAY GERONIMO. *Chinigchinich.* Translated by Alfred Robinson. Santa Ana, Calif.: Fine Arts Press, 1933.

BOURNE, EDWARD GAYLORD. *Narratives of the Career of Hernando de Soto,* vols. 1, 2. New York: AMS Press, 1973.

BOWERS, ALFRED W. *Mandan Social and Ceremonial Organization.* Chicago: University of Chicago Press, 1950.

BUNZEL, RUTH. *The Pueblo Potter.* New York: Dover Publications, 1972.

CALLENDER, CHARLES. "Social Organization of the Central Algonkian Indians." Milwaukee Public Museum Publications in Anthropology no. 7. Milwaukee, Wisc.: Milwaukee Public Museum, 1962.

CATLIN, GEORGE. *Illustrations of the Manners, Customs, and Condition of the North American Indians,* vol. 1. London: Henry G. Bohn, 1866.

CLINE, WALTER B.; COMMONS, RACHEL S.; MANDELBAUM, MAY; POST, RICHARD H.;

Bibliography

and WALTERS, L. V. W. *The Sinkaietk or Southern Okanagon of Washington.* Menasha, Wisc.: George Banta, 1938.

CODERE, HELEN. *Franz Boas.* Chicago: University of Chicago Press,1966.

CULIN, STEWART. "Games of the North American Indians." *Twenty-Fourth Annual Report of the Bureau of American Ethnology,* 1902–1903. Washington, D.C.: Smithsonian Institution, 1907.

CUSHING, FRANK HAMILTON. *Zuni Breadstuff.* Indian Notes and Monographs, vol. 8. New York: Heye Foundation, 1920.

DANE, CHRISTOPHER. *The American Indian and the Occult.* New York: Popular Library, 1973.

DEBO, ANGIE. *The Rise and Fall of the Choctaw Republic.* Norman, Okla.: University of Oklahoma Press, 1934.

DEVEREUX, GEORGE. "Institutionalized Homosexuality of the Mohave Indians." *Human Biology,* 9:498–527, 1937.

DORSEY, JAMES OWEN. "Omaha Sociology." *United States Bureau of Ethnology Annual Report,* 3:205–370, 1881.

ERIKSON, ERIK HOMBURGER. "Observations on the Yurok: Childhood and World Image." University of California Publications in American Archaeology and Ethnology 35:10. Berkeley, Calif.: University of California Press, 1943.

FLANNERY, REGINA. *The Gros Ventres of Montana: Part 1, Social Life.* The Catholic University of America Anthropological Series no. 15. Washington, D.C.: Catholic University of America Press, 1953.

———. "Position of Women among the Mescalero Apache." *Primitive Man* 5:26–32. 1932.

———. "Position of Women among the Eastern Cree." *Primitive Man* 8:81–86, 1935.

FLETCHER, ALICE C., and LA FLESCHE, FRANCIS. "The Omaha Tribe." *Twenty-Seventh Annual Report of the Bureau of American Ethnology,* 1905–1906. Washington, D.C.: Smithsonian Institution, 1910.

FORDE, C. DARYLL. "Ethnography of the Yuma Indians." University of California Publications in American Archeology and Ethnology 28:4. Berkeley, Calif.: University of California Press, 1931.

FOREMAN, CAROLYN THOMAS. *Indian Women Chiefs.* Muskogee, Okla.: Hoffman Printing Co., 1954.

FORTUNE, REO F. *Omaha Secret Societies.* New York: Columbia University Press, 1932.

FRANCISCAN FATHERS. *An Ethnologic Dictionary of the Navajo Language.* Saint Michaels, Ariz., 1910.

GARTH, THOMAS R. "Atsugewi Ethnography." *Anthropological Records* 14:2. Berkeley, Calif.: University of California Press, 1953.

GEARING, FRED. "Priests and Warriors." *American Anthropological Association Memoir* 93, 1962.

GIFFORD, E. W. "The Cocopa." University of California Publications in American Archeology and Ethnology 31:5. Berkeley, Calif.: University of California Press, 1933.

———. "The Northfork Mono." University of California Publications in American Archeology and Ethnology 31:15–65. Berkeley, Calif.: University of California Press, 1932a.

———. "The Southeastern Yavapai." University of California Publications in American

Archeology and Ethnology 29:177–252. Berkeley, Calif.: University of California Press, 1932b.

GILBERT, WILLIAM HARLEN. "The Eastern Cherokees." Bureau of American Ethnology Bulletin no. 133. Washington, D.C.: Smithsonian Institution, 1943.

GODDARD, PLINY EARLE. "Hupa Texts." University of California Publications in American Archeology and Ethnology 1:2. Berkeley, Calif.: University of California Press, 1903a.

———. "Life and Culture of Hupa." University of California Publications in American Archeology and Ethnology 1:1. Berkeley, Calif.: University of California Press, 1903b.

GOODWIN, GRENVILLE. *The Social Organization of the Western Apache*. Chicago: University of Chicago Press. 1942.

———. *Western Apache Raiding and Warfare*. Edited by Keith H. Basso. Tucson, Ariz.: University of Arizona Press, 1971.

GRAVES, WILLIAM M. *The First Protestant Osage Missions 1820–1837*. Oswego, Kans.: Carpenter Press, 1949.

GRINNELL, GEORGE BIRD. *The Cheyenne Indians*, vols. 1, 2. Lincoln, Neb.: University of Nebraska Press, 1972.

———. *The Fighting Cheyennes*. Norman, Okla.: University of Oklahoma Press, 1956.

HAMMOND, DOROTHY, and JABLOW, ALTA. *Women: Their Economic Role in Traditional Societies*. A Cummings Module in Anthropology no. 35. Menlo Park, Calif.: Cummings Publishing Co., 1973.

HARDACRE, EMMA. "The Lost Woman of San Nicolas." *Scribner's Monthly* (September), 20: 651–664, 1880.

HASSRICK, ROYAL B. *The Sioux, Life and Customs of a Warrior Society*. Norman, Okla.: University of Oklahoma Press, 1964.

HEARNE, SAMUEL. *A Journey from Prince of Wales Fort in Hudson's Bay to the Northern Ocean*. London: Cadell and Davies, 1795.

HEBARD, GRACE RAYMOND. *Sacajawea, Guide of the Lewis and Clark Expedition*. Glendale, Calif.: The Arthur H. Clark Company, 1933.

HECKEWELDER, JOHN. *History, Manners, and Customs of the Indian Nations Who Once Inhabited Pennsylvania and the Neighboring States*. Philadelphia: Historical Society of Pennsylvania, 1876.

HENRY, ALEXANDER. *New Light on the Early History of the Greater Northwest*. Edited by Elliott Coues. New York: F. P. Harper, 1897.

HILL, W. W. "Note on the Pima Berdache." *American Anthropologist* 40:338–340, 1938.

———. "The Status of the Hermaphrodite and Transvestite in Navajo Culture." *American Anthropologist* n.s. 37:373–379, 1935.

HODGE, FREDERICK WEBB, ed. Handbook of American Indians North of Mexico. Bureau of American Ethnology Bulletin no. 30, Washington, D.C.: Smithsonian Institution, 1911.

HOEBEL, E. ADAMSON. *The Cheyennes, Indians of the Great Plains*. New York: Holt, Rinehart and Winston, 1960.

———. "The Political Organization and Law-Ways of the Comanche Indians." *American Anthropologcal Association Memoir* 54, 1940.

Bibliography

HONIGMANN, JOHN J. "The Kaska Indians: An Ethnographic Reconstruction." Yale University Publications in Anthropology no. 51. New Haven, Conn.: Yale University Press, 1954.

HOOPER, LUCILE. "The Cahuilla Indians." University of California Publications in American Archaeology and Ethnology 16:6. Berkeley, Calif.: University of California Press, 1920.

HORNADAY, WILLIAM T. "The Extermination of the American Bison." In *Report of the U.S. National Museum, Smithsonian Institution for 1887.* Washington, D.C.: Washington Government Printing Office, 1889.

JEFFERSON, ROBERT. "Fifty Years on the Saskatchewan." Canadian North-west Historical Society Publications 1:5. Battleford, Sask.: Canadian North-west Historical Society, 1929.

JENNESS, D. *The Copper Eskimos.* Report of the Canadian Arctic Expedition 1913–1918, vol. 12. Ottawa, Ont.: F. A. Acland, 1923.

JOHNSTON, BERNICE EASTMAN. *California's Gabrielino Indians.* Los Angeles, Calif.: The Southwest Museum, 1962.

JOSEPH, ALICE, M.D.; SPICER, ROSAMUND B.; and CHESKY, JANE. *"The Desert People."* Chicago, Ill.: University of Chicago Press. Midway Reprints, 1974.

KELLY, ISABEL T. "Ethnography of the Surprise Valley Paiute." University of California Publications in American Archeology and Ethnology 31:67–210. Berkeley, Calif.: University of California Press, 1932.

KENNEDY, MICHAEL STEPHEN, ed. *The Assiniboines.* Norman, Okla.: University of Oklahoma Press, 1961.

KLUCKHOLN, CLYDE. "Navajo Witchcraft." Papers of the Peabody Museum of American Archeology and Ethnology 22:2. Cambridge, Mass.: Harvard University Press, 1944.

KLUCKHOLN, CLYDE, and LEIGHTON, DOROTHEA. *The Navajo.* Cambridge, Mass.: Harvard University Press, 1946.

KRAUSE, AUREL, and GUNTHER, ERNA, trans. *The Tlingit Indians.* American Ethnological Society. Seattle, Wash.: University of Washington Press, 1956.

LA FARGE, OLIVER. *A Pictorial History of the American Indian.* New York: Crown Publishers, 1956.

LA FLESCHE, FRANCIS. "Osage Marriage Customs." *American Anthropologist* n.s. 14: 127–130, 1912.

———. "The Osage Tribe: Two Versions of the Child Naming Rite." Forty-third Annual Report of the Bureau of American Ethnology 1925–1926. Washington, D.C.: Smithsonian Institution, 1928.

———. "Researches among the Osage." Smithsonian Miscellaneous Collection 70:110–113. Washington, D.C.: Smithsonian Institution, 1919.

LANDES, RUTH. *The Mystic Lake Sioux.* Madison, Wisc.: University of Wisconsin Press, 1968.

———. *The Ojibwa Woman.* New York: Columbia University Press, 1938.

LANGE, CHARLES H. *Cochiti, a New Mexico Pueblo, Past and Present.* Austin, Tex.: University of Texas Press, 1959.

LASKI, VERA. "Seeking Life." *Memoirs of the American Folklore Society,* 50:1959.

LEIGHTON, DOROTHEA C., and ADAIR, JOHN. *People of the Middle Place.* Behavior Science Monographs. New Haven, Conn.: Human Relations Area Files Press, 1966.

LE MOYNE, JACQUES. *Narrative of Le Moyne, an Artist who Accompanied the French Expedition to Florida under Laudonniere, 1564.* Translated from the Latin of De Bry by Fred B. Pukins. Boston: J. R. Osgood, 1875.

LEWIS, OSCAR. "Manly-Hearted Women among The North Piegan." *American Anthropologist* 43:173–187, 1941.

LINDERMAN, FRANK. *Red Mother.* New York: John Day Company, 1932.

LINTON, RALPH, ed. *Acculturation in Seven American Indian Tribes.* New York: Appleton-Century-Crofts, 1940.

LOEB, EDWIN M. "Pomo Folkways." University of California Publications in American Archeology and Ethnology 19:2. Berkeley, Calif.: University of California Press, 1928.

LOWIE, ROBERT H. "The Assiniboine." Anthropological Papers of the American Museum of Natural History 4. New York: American Museum of Natural History, 1909.

————. *The Crow Indians.* New York: Farrar and Rinehart Inc., 1935.

————. "Societies of the Hidatsa and Mandan Indians." Anthropological Papers of the American Museum of Natural History 11:3. New York: American Museum of Natural History, 1913.

LURIE, NANCY OESTREICH, ed. "Indian Women: A Legacy of Freedom." In *Look To the Mountain Top.* San Jose, Calif.: Gousha Publications, 1972.

————. *Mountain Wolf Woman, Sister of Crashing Thunder: The Autobiography of a Winnebago Indian.* Ann Arbor, Mich.: University of Michigan Press, 1961.

LYFORD, CARRIE A. *Iroquois Crafts.* Lawrence, Kans.: Haskell Institute, 1945.

MALONE, HENRY THOMPSON. *Cherokees of the Old South.* Athens, Ga.: University of Georgia Press, 1956.

MANDELBAUM, DAVID C. "The Plains Cree." Anthropological Papers of the American Museum of Natural History 37:2. New York: American Museum of Natural History, 1940.

MARRIOTT, ALICE. *The Ten Grandmothers.* Norman, Okla.: University of Oklahoma Press, 1945.

MASON, OTIS T. *Woman's Share in Primitive Culture.* London: Macmillan & Co., 1895.

MEAD, MARGARET. *Changing Culture of an Indian Tribe.* New York: Columbia University Press, 1932.

MICHELSON, TRUMAN. "Autobiography of a Fox Indian Woman." Fortieth Annual Report of the Bureau of American Ethnology, 1918–1919. Washington, D.C.: Smithsonian Institution, 1925.

————. "Narrative of an Arapaho Woman." *American Anthropologist* n.s. 35:595–610, 1933.

MOONEY, JAMES. "Myths of the Cherokee." Nineteenth Annual Report of the Bureau of American Ethnology, 1897–1898. Washington, D.C.: Smithsonian Institution, 1900.

MORGAN, LEWIS H. *League of the Ho-De-No Sau-Nee or Iroquois.* Behavior Science Reprints. New Haven, Conn. Reprinted by Human Relations Area Files, 1954.

NOON, JOHN A. *Law and Government of the Grand River Iroquois.* New York: Viking Fund, 1949.

O'KANE, WALTER COLLINS. *Sun in The Sky.* Norman, Okla.: University of Oklahoma Press, 1950.

Bibliography

OLSON, RONALD L. "The Quinault Indians." *University of Washington Publications in Anthropology* 6:1. Seattle, Wash.: University of Washington Press, 1936.

———. "Social Structure and Social Life of the Tlingit of Alaska." *Anthropological Records* 26. Berkeley, Calif.: University of California Press, 1967.

O'NEALE, LILA M. "Yurok-Karok Basket Weavers." *University of California Publications in American Archeology and Ethnology* 32:1–84. Berkeley, Calif.: University of California Press, 1932.

OPLER, MORRIS. *An Apache Lifeway: The Economic, Social, and Religious Institutions of the Chiricahua Indians.* Chicago: University of Chicago Press, 1941.

———. *Childhood and Youth in Jicarilla Apache Society.* Los Angeles, Calif.: The Southwest Museum, 1946.

———. "Myths and Tales of the Jicarilla Apache Indians." *Memoirs of the American Folklore Society* 31, 1938.

———. "Pots, Apache, and the Dismal River Culture Aspect" in *Apachean Culture History and Ethnology,* by Keith Basso and Morris E. Opler, Anthropological Papers of the University of Arizona no. 21. Tucson, Ariz.: University of Arizona Press, 1971.

ORTNER, SHERRY B. "Is Female to Male as Nature Is to Culture?" In *Women, Culture and Society,* edited by Michelle Zimbalist Rosaldo and Louise Lamphere. Stanford, Calif.: Stanford University Press, 1974.

OSWALT, WENDELL H. *This Land Was Theirs—A Study of the North American Indian.* New York: John Wiley and Sons, 1966.

PARSONS, ELSIE CLEWS. "Notes on the Caddo." *American Anthropological Association Memoir* 57, 1941.

———. "The Social Organization of the Tewa of New Mexico." *Memoirs of the American Folklore Society* 36:1929.

———. "Tewa Tales." *Memoirs of the American Folklore Society* 19:1926.

PEITHMANN, IRVING M. *Red Men of Fire: A History of the Cherokee Indians.* Springfield, Ill.: Charles C. Thomas, 1964.

PRICE, JOHN ANDREW. *Washo Economy.* Carson City, Nev.: Nevada State Museum, 1962.

QOYAWAYMA, POLINGAYSI. *No Turning Back.* As told to Vada F. Carlson. Albuquerque, N. Mex.: University of New Mexico Press, 1964.

RADIN, PAUL. "The Autobiography of a Winnebago Indian." *University of California Publications in American Archeology and Ethnology* 16:7. Berkeley, Calf.: University of California Press, 1920.

RANDLE, MARTHA CHAMPION. "Iroquois Women, Then and Now." In *Symposium on Local Diversity in Iroquois Culture,* edited by William N. Fenton. Washington, D.C.: Smithsonian Institution, 1951.

RAY, VERNE F. "Lower Chinook Ethnographic Notes." *University of Washington Publications in Anthropology* 7:2. Seattle, Wash.: University of Washington Press, 1938.

———. *The Sanpoli and Nespelem: Salishan Peoples of Northeastern Washington.* Seattle, Wash.: University of Washington Press, 1933.

REICHARD, GLADYS A. *Dezba, Woman of the Desert.* Glorieta, N. Mex.: Rio Grande Press, 1971.

————. *Social Life of the Navajo Indians.* New York: Columbia University Press, 1928.

————. *Spider Woman.* New York: Macmillan Co., 1934.

ROLANDSON, MARY. *Narrative of Captivity by the Indians at the Destruction of Lancaster in 1676.* 6th ed. Lancaster, Mass.: Carter, Andrews, & Co., 1828.

ROSALDO, MICHELLE ZIMBALIST, and LAMPHERE, LOUISE, eds., *Women, Culture and Society.* Stanford, Calif.: Stanford University Press, 1974.

RUSSELL, FRANK. "The Pima Indians." Twenty-Sixth Annual Report of the Bureau of American Ethnology, 1904–1905. Washington, D.C.: Smithsonian Institution, 1908.

SANDAY, PEGGY R. "Toward a Theory of the Status of Women." *American Anthropologist* 75:5, 1973.

SAXTON, DEAN, and SAXTON, LUCILLE. *Legends and Lore of the Papago and Pima Indians.* Tucson, Ariz.: University of Arizona Press, 1973.

SETON, JULIA M. *American Indian Arts: A Way of Life.* New York: The Ronald Press Co., 1962.

SHAW, ANNA MORE. *A Pima Past.* Tucson, Ariz.: University of Arizona Press, 1974.

SHEA, J. D. G. *First Establishment of the Faith in New France,* N. Y. Vol. 1. New York: J. D. Shea, 1881.

SHIPEK, FLORENCE. *The Autobiography of Delfina Cuero.* Morongo Indian Reservation: Malki Museum Press, 1970.

SIMMONS, LEO W. *Sun Chief: The Autobiography of a Hopi Indian.* New Haven, Conn.: Yale University Press, 1942.

SKINNER, ALANSON. "Kansa Organizations." Anthropological Papers of the American Museum of Natural History 11. New York: American Museum of Natural History, 1915a.

————. "Ponca Societies and Dances." Anthropological Papers of the American Museum of Natural History 11. New York: American Museum of Natural History, 1915b.

————. "Social Life and Ceremonial Bundles of the Menomini Indians." Anthropological Papers of the American Museum of Natural History 13, part 1. New York: American Museum of Natural History, 1913.

SMITH, DANA MARGARET. *Hopi Girl.* Palo Alto, Calif.: Stanford University Press, 1931.

SMITH, WATSON, and ROBERTS, JOHN M. "Zuni Law, a Field of Values." Papers of the Peabody Museum of American Archeology and Ethnology 43:1. Cambridge, Mass.: Harvard University Press, 1954.

SMITHSON, CARMA LEE. "The Havasupai Woman." University of Utah Department of Anthropology, Anthropological Papers, vol. 38. Salt Lake City: University of Utah Press, 1959.

SPECK, FRANK G. "Ethical Attributes of the Labrador Indians." *American Anthropologist* n.s. 35:559–594, 1933.

SPIER, LESLIE. "Havasupai Ethnography. Anthropological Papers of the American Museum of Natural History 29. New York: American Museum of Natural History, 1927.

————. "Wishram Ethnography." University of Washington Publications in Anthropology 3:3. Seattle, Wash.: University of Washington Press, 1930.

SPINDEN, HERBERT JOSEPH. *Fine Art and The First Americans. Introduction to American Indian Art, part 2.* New York: The Exposition of Indian Tribal Arts, 1931.

Bibliography

————. *The Nez Percé Indians*. Lancaster, Pa.: New Era Printing Co., 1908.

STEPHENS, WILLIAM N. "A Cross-Cultural Study of Menstrual Taboos." Genetic Psychology Monographs 64:385–416. Provincetown, Mass.: The Journal Press, 1961.

STERN, BERNARD J. *The Lummi Indians of Northwest Washington*. New York: AMS Press, 1934.

STEVENSON, MATILDA COX. "The Zuni Indians." Twenty-Third Annual Report of the American Bureau of Ethnology, 1901–1902. Washington, D.C.: Smithsonian Institution, 1904.

STEVENSON, TILLY E. "The Religious Life of the Zuni Child." Fifth Annual Report of the Bureau of Ethnology, 1883–1884. Washington, D.C.: Smithsonian Institution, 1887.

STRATTON, R. B. *Life Among The Indians or: The Captivity of the Oatman Girls Among the Apache and Mohave Indians*. San Francisco: Grabhorn Press, 1935.

SWANTON, JOHN R. "Aboriginal Cultures of the Southeast." Forty-Second Annual Report of the American Bureau of Ethnology, 1924–1925. Washington, D. C.: Smithsonian Institution, 1928a.

————. "Early History of the Creek Indians and Their Neighbors." Bureau of American Ethnology Bulletin no. 73. Washington, D.C.: Smithsonian Institution, 1922.

————. "Indian Tribes of the Lower Mississippi Valley and Adjacent Coast of the Gulf of Mexico." Bureau of American Ethnology Bulletin no. 43. Washington, D.C.: Smithsonian Institution, 1911.

————. "Social and Religious Beliefs and Usages of the Chickasaw Indians." Forty-Fourth Annual Report of the Bureau of American Ethnology, 1926–1927. Washington, D.C.: Smithsonian Institution, 1928b.

————. "Social Organization and Socal Usages of the Indians of the Creek Confederacy." Forty-Second Annual Report of the Bureau of American Ethnology, 1924–1925. Washington, D.C.: Smithsonian Institution, 1928c.

————. "Source Material on the History and Ethnology of the Caddo Indians." Bureau of American Ethnology Bulletin no. 132. Washington, D.C.: Smithsonian Institution, 1942.

TEIT, JAMES A. "The Middle Columbia Salish." University of Washington Publications in Anthropology. Seattle, Wash.: The University of Washington Press, 1928.

————. "The Salishan Tribes of the Western Plateau: The Okanagon." Edited by Franz Boas. Forty-Fifth Annual Report of the Bureau of American Ethnology, 1927–1928. Washington, D.C.: Smithsonian Institution, 1929.

TITIEV, MISCHA. "Old Oraibi: A Study of the Hopi Indians of Third Mesa." Papers of the Peabody Museum of American Archeology and Ethnology 22:1. Cambridge, Mass.: Harvard University Press, 1944.

TIXIER, VICTOR. *Tixier's Travels on the Osage Prairies*. Translated by Albert J. Salvan. Edited by John Francis McDermott. Norman, Okla.: University of Oklahoma Press, 1940.

TOOKER, ELISABETH. "An Ethnography of the Huron Indians, 1615–1649." Bureau of American Ethnology Bulletin no. 190. Washington, D.C.: Smithsonian Institution, 1964.

TRIGGER, BRUCE G. *The Huron, Farmers of the North*. New York: Holt, Rinehart and Winston, 1969.

TURNEY-HIGH, HARRY HOLBERT. "Ethnography of the Kutenai." *American Anthropological Association Memoir* 56, 1941.

⸻. "The Flathead Indians of Montana." *American Anthropological Association Memoir* 48, 1937.

UDALL, LOUISE. *Me and Mine, the Life Story of Helen Sekaquaptewa.* Tucson, Ariz.: University of Arizona Press, 1969.

UNDERHILL, RUTH. "The Autobiography of a Papago Woman." *American Anthropological Association Memoir* 46, 1936.

⸻. *The First Penthouse Dwellers of America.* 2nd Ed. Santa Fe, N. Mex.: Laboratory of Anthropology, 1946a.

⸻. *The Navajo.* Norman, Okla.: University of Oklahoma Press, 1956.

⸻. *People of the Crimson Evening.* Lawrence, Kans.: Haskell Institute, 1951.

⸻. *Singing for Power—The Song Magic of the Papago Indians of Southern Arizona.* Los Angeles, Calif.: University of California Press, 1968.

⸻. "Social Organization of the Papago Indians." Columbia University Contributions of Anthropology 30. New York: Columbia University Press, 1939.

⸻. *Work a Day Life of the Pueblos.* Phoenix: Phoenix Indian School, United States Indian Service, 1946b.

UNITED STATES SENATE. *Senate Executive Document No. 6.* 44th Congress, first session, 1875–1876. Letter from the Secretary of the Interior; Investigation of Osage Affairs. December 20, p. 48. 1875.

VOEGELIN, C. F. "The Shawnee Female Deity." Yale University Publications in Anthropology no. 10. New Haven, Conn.: Yale University Press, 1936.

VOEGELIN, ERMINE WHEELER. *Mortuary Customs of Shawnee and Other Eastern Tribes.* Prehistory Research Series, 2: vol. 2, pp. 227–444. Indianapolis, Ind.: Indiana Historical Society, 1944.

VOTH, H. R. "Oraibi Natal Customs." Field Columbian Museum Anthropological Series 6:2. Chicago: Field Columbian Museum, 1905.

WALLACE, ERNEST, and HOEBEL, EL ADAMSON. *The Comanches, Lords of the South Plains.* Norman, Okla.: University of Oklahoma Press, 1952.

WATERMAN, T. T., and KROEBER, A. L. "Yurok Marriages." University of California Publications in American Archeology and Ethnology 35:1. Berkeley, Calif.: University of California Press, 1934.

WATERS, FRANK. *Masked Gods, Navajo and Pueblo Ceremonialism.* New York: Ballantine Books, 1950.

WELTFISH, GENE. *The Lost Universe, The Way of Life of the Pawnee.* New York: Ballantine Books, 1965.

WILSON, MAGGIE. 'One With The Clay." *Arizona Highways* (March) 50:48, 1974.

WISSLER, CLARK. "Social Life of the Blackfoot Indians." Anthropological Papers of the American Museum of Natural History 7:1. New York: American Museum of Natural History, 1911.

WOODWARD, GRACE STEELE. *The Cherokees.* Norman, Okla.: University of Oklahoma Press, 1963.

WRIGHT, BARTON. *Kachinas—A Hopi Artist's Documentary.* Flagstaff, Ariz.: Northland Press, 1973.

Bibliography

WYMAN, LELAND C. *Blessingway*. Recorded and translated by Father Bernard Haile. Tucson, Ariz.: University of Arizona Press, 1970.

YOUNG, FRANK W., and BACADAYAN, ALBERT A. "Menstrual Taboos and Social Rigidity." *Ethnology* 4:2, 1965.

ZEISBERGER, DAVID. *David Zeisberger's History of the Northern American Indians*. Edited by Archer Butler Hulbert and William Nathaniel Schwarze. Columbus, Ohio.: Fred J. Heer, 1910.

ZUNI PEOPLE. *The Zunis—Self Portrayals*. Translated by Alvina Quam. Albuquerque, N. Mex.: University of New Mexico Press, 1972.

Index